SIVANANDA
BURIED
YOGA

First published by O Books, 2008
O Books is an imprint of John Hunt Publishing Ltd., The Bothy, Deershot Lodge, Park Lane, Ropley,
Hants, SO24 0BE, UK
office1@o-books.net
www.o-books.net

Distribution in:	South Africa
	Alternative Books
UK and Europe	altbook@peterhyde.co.za
Orca Book Services	Tel: 021 555 4027 Fax: 021 447 1430
orders@orcabookservices.co.uk	
Tel: 01202 665432 Fax: 01202 666219	Text copyright yogi manmoyanand 2008
Int. code (44)	manmoyanand@yahoo.co.in
USA and Canada	Design: Stuart Davies
NBN	
custserv@nbnbooks.com	ISBN: 978 1 84694 151 1
Tel: 1 800 462 6420 Fax: 1 800 338 4550	

Australia and New Zealand
Brumby Books
sales@brumbybooks.com.au
Tel: 61 3 9761 5535 Fax: 61 3 9761 7095

Far East (offices in Singapore, Thailand, Hong Kong, Taiwan)
Pansing Distribution Pte Ltd
kemal@pansing.com
Tel: 65 6319 9939 Fax: 65 6462 5761

A CIP catalogue record for this book is available from the British Library.

Printed and Bound by CPI Antony Rowe, Chippenham, Wiltshire

O Books operates a distinctive and ethical publishing philosophy in all areas of its business, from its global network of authors to production and worldwide distribution.
This book is produced on FSC certified stock, within ISO14001 standards. The printer plants sufficient trees each year through the Woodland Trust to absorb the level of emitted carbon in its production.

SIVANANDA
BURIED
YOGA

yogi manmoyanand

BOOKS

Winchester, UK
Washington, USA

CONTENTS

DEDICATION

It was all your teachings

It was all your trainings

It was all your inspiration

and it is you who is writing this book today.

Thank you for choosing my hands

to write it.

PREFACE TO FIRST EDITION

Why another book on Yoga? There are already too many, and most of them are crying for attention. The addition of one more book to this frenzy held me back for nearly five years. After much contemplation and even more persuasion, I ultimately felt moved to write this book.

Each time before writing, we would discuss the format or synopsis of what was to be written. However, the more we concentrated on its structure or overview, the harder it became to start with even the first sentence. The discussions and struggle to begin continued for days until I was ready to drop the whole idea. Before giving up, I asked my teacher if this book would serve any useful purpose. If so, he should come forward to help. Therefore what had ultimately persuaded me to continue was the assurance of my teacher.

From the next day onwards, I kept my teacher constantly engaged in a conversation. Whatever he said, I then repeated in English. And so it happened. It took us exactly thirty-six days to pen this book. Neither English was my first language, nor had I ever dreamt of writing a book. This book is a reproduction of my conversations with my teacher, who had taken *Samadhi* ten years earlier. Since it is only a conversation, it does not reflect an academic excellence or literary pretense, or even the standard norms of book writing. Behind the writing of Sivananda Buried Yoga, there is but one intention – to find at least one person who is prepared to understand Yoga.

Although we have explained the dynamics of the yogic *kriyas* and practices in as much detail as possible, we intentionally withheld the process and practical application of the *kriyas*. The honest intention behind this measure is only to prevent and safeguard their incorrect use. There is no secrecy or conspiracy behind the withholding of this knowledge. We only emphasize its correct practice under a competent teacher.

Gangotri   manmoyanand

May 2006

PREFACE TO SECOND EDITION

It is barely four months since the release of the first edition of Sivananda Buried Yoga. While writing the preface to the second edition, we experienced an overwhelming sense of gratitude, as well as responsibility. Our readers have accepted the first edition and have chosen to engage us in a constant dialogue about the effect the book has had on them. We take each of their compliments and suggestions with the utmost respect and humility. As the first edition slowly began to disappear from the shelves, we increasingly felt the need to address the expectations that were placed upon us by so many seekers. Thus it became inevitable to present our readers with a corrected, revised and slightly enlarged second edition of Sivananda Buried Yoga.

Needless to say, the second edition contains fewer errors in spelling and grammar. We have also taken care to improve the typesetting for a better print quality. But this is not the primary reason why the second edition is presented. In this edition we have incorporated certain changes that add clarity and higher understanding to the subject. No part or vital point of the book has been deleted; rather we have added substance to the existing explanations to provide a clearer picture of the practices of yoga. For example, the second to seventh paragraphs of chapter three have been added to promote the vital understanding of the structure of yogic practice. We regret our inability to explain more of the Yoga Sutras within the scope of this book. We sincerely wish that our readers will overlook this limitation, and at the same time will pursue their own investigation into the lesser known, mystical, yet scientific practices of yoga.

The last thirteen pages of the first edition have been restructured and certain paragraphs have been re-written to change its tone. The primary intention of that part of the book has not been changed. The second edition has only made it a little more palatable. We sincerely hope the second edition of Sivananda Buried Yoga will meet the expectations of our readers.

Gangotri   manmoyanand
Feb 2007

PREFACE TO THIRD EDITION

With immense pleasure and gratitude we are presenting the third edition of Sivananda Buried Yoga in paperback. It is barely over a year since the first edition was launched, and our readers continue to reveal the effect and intentions of the book. With increased enthusiasm they have kept us engaged in dialogue and have been pressing for more. Many of them recognized the true seeker within and have come forward to begin the practice of Yoga all over again. The acceptance of a new book in the contemporary world of spirituality is the ultimate reward an author can think of. Hence, we have been busy adding finer details to the book.

In the third edition we have included a few little things, here and there, that would help a seeker further examine the notions of modern spiritual belief. We have provided the transliteration and meaning of some of the scriptures and authorities in regards to the new-age controversies of meat eating. Yet another sutra from Maharshi Patanjali has been added to highlight the objective of Yoga practice. In order to give distinction between a state and a process within the meaning of Yoga, we have used capital letters to denote the state, and a lower case letter to denote the process. For example, Asana with a capital 'A' denotes Asana as a state within the meanings of the Yoga Sutra and asana with a small 'a' denotes asana as a process, referring to yogasanas.

The second most important reason of the third edition is to make it available to a larger audience. With extremely limited manpower it had not been possible to expose the book to far-away readers. With our new publishing partner we are hoping to reach out, not only to a larger audience, but also to make the book still more affordable.

We are now convinced that our readers are not going to sit quiet after reading the book and are pleased to witness the re-emergence of the questioning minds of genuine seekers. With our readers' higher degree of participation we feel responsible to continue to provide more details of the finer aspects of Yoga. By presenting this edition we sincerely hope to encourage and further enhance the dialogue with our readers.

Gangotri   manmoyanand
Jan 2008

CHAPTER ONE

A Journey from Consciousness to Super-Consciousness

It took me a little over five years to conclude that the biggest-ever lie that has been repeatedly told to mankind is that man has a spiritual identity. In my belief, there was nothing more vague and misleading than any spiritual 'ism'. Numerous religions with their philosophies and promises have taken mankind on a journey to nowhere. Numerous 'gurus' with their powers and charismas only created a powerful economic empire around themselves. Spirituality as fashion, spirituality as fitness, spirituality as a business and spirituality as a crime are all reasons for which it existed. All of which I never knew when I began to feel 'spiritual'.

I was born into a family who had habitually worshipped Lord Shiva for generations. Our bread and butter arrived from incessant Shiva worshipping. I can't say that we continued worshipping Shiva because of our spiritual destiny or present-life karma. However one thing was clear to me, we continued this mindless worship purely because it was our conditioning and our hereditary profession. It was not because the family was spiritually evolving, but as it appeared to me, the worshippers of my family were self-appointed collectors of 'spiritual tax'.

One day this suddenly ended for me, as I pointed at a Shiva lingam and asked my uncle, who was a much-revered spiritual connection for all the village people, "Why is that stone so funnily shaped?"

I could see a few moments of hesitation and embarrassment in his face, but quickly he regained his composure and answered, "This is the shape of God."

My next question was, "Why is God so funnily shaped? And since no one has seen God, is it his face, his body or only a symbolic representation?"

A middle-aged neighbor, who was standing nearby, obviously enjoying the embarrassment of my uncle, lifted me into his arms and gently whispered in my ear, "It is not God's face or his body. It is his pee-pee."

The answer definitely shocked me, as I jumped out of his arms. I took a good look at the phallic symbol of Shiva and exclaimed, "Yes, you are right. It does look like one!"

What had perplexed me even more was the amount of attention Shiva's penis had received. All the flowers, water and milk and the vast reverence and respect that his penis received were too much for me to comprehend. Incredulously, I asked the little group of people who had gathered around, amused by my childish enquiries, "If I am expected to wash my hands every time I touch my pee-pee, how can you expect me to worship someone else's? Don't you feel shameful or embarrassed touching and pampering someone else's pee-pee?"

I cannot quite describe what happened to all their expressions, but I immediately knew that I had committed an unpardonable mistake. Breaking the silence in a stern voice, my uncle declared that this was no way to talk about God and asked a colleague to immediately take me out of the temple.

It was not until later that evening that I saw my uncle again. But some elders at home had informed me that he had been prostrating before God in the temple, seeking forgiveness for the insult that I had inflicted upon him. This doubled my suspicions; why was my uncle seeking forgiveness for something that was not directly committed by him? It was not until later that I learnt my uncle held a kind of contract with the whole village to seek forgiveness on behalf of whomever commits a sin against God. It was then I thought I had come to understand the basis of our hereditary profession.

At that moment I made a promise to myself never to worship that penis until I knew exactly what lay behind its whole scandal. As far as I can remember, this was to be the first time I was ever branded a 'rebel against God'.

One day I asked my mother, "What am I supposed to be doing in my life?"

At first my mother could not understand what I was talking about. As I began to explain, she concluded that it could be one of my childhood curiosities. She lovingly revealed to me, "Now you are just a little boy. You have to finish your food, do your homework and always listen to me. When you grow up, you will go to study in a college or a university. Then if you are very good boy, you will be able to get a really good job, and then one day you will marry. Then I will have a few grandchildren from you. Then you will grow old."

I asked, "And then what happens?"

She dismissed me by saying, "I don't know what happens after that."

I looked into her eyes and said, "Mum, you know that I will die after that."

She tried to object to my idea of death and tried to brush aside all my thoughts as childish and irrelevant. After getting back her attention, I again bothered her. "As you know, I don't like to go to school, I hate my homework, and I don't like to eat all that food you pile on my plate. I know that people don't like to go to college because I always see them fooling around near the movies. I know that people don't like to work. Not everybody is happy to be married, and a lot of people are very unhappy about their children. I don't think old age is a pleasant idea, and I am sure nobody likes to die. Don't you think life is just a series of unpleasant events that everybody is forced to go through? Why do I have to live through this chain of unpleasant events? Can you please give me at least one good reason why I should continue to live?"

My mother was aghast. As she was beginning to cry out under the impact of my volley of questions, I conclusively declared, "Mum, I don't want to live a life that does not have any better purpose than yours."

These were the set of questions that persistently agitated my mind. Whoever I met in my life and believed to be wise, I asked them the same set of questions. As far as I could remember, these questions had played the central role in determining the course of my life.

Soon my over-religious mother started to take me along with her whenever she went to listen to a religious discourse, most likely with the hope that some exposure to religious people in a sacred environment would change my attitude towards God. I gladly accompanied her to all discourses. For me these occasions were a welcome relief to escape the burden of school homework. The times that I enjoyed the most were the prayer recitals that preceded the discourses. I would sit closer to the speaker, who was usually some kind of guru, and would wait for him to place his garland on the table beside me. I had a strong feeling that these were no ordinary people. If they could keep so many people spellbound with their beautiful narrations and magnetic personalities for such a long period of time, then surely they must have some extraordinary magical power or superhuman qualities.

My mum used to explain to me that these 'Babas' were very close to God: they have all seen God, they know God and they were doing us a great favor by telling us about God. I was, in a way, becoming motivated by the ways of the Babas, and my favorite one became Mouni Baba. Seeing my growing interest in the holy men, my mum asked me if I would like to become someone's disciple. She would warmly explain to me that it would take a few lifetimes of arduous work and penance to come any closer to God, and indisputably these Babas were much closer to understanding God than we were.

These childhood experiences reflect only a few examples that created my notions of God, all of which had a deep impact on my psyche and would play a vital role in shaping my life. Through my childhood observations, God was a man very difficult to meet; he had no worries and was definitely more powerful than any of my comic book heroes. On one occasion a school teacher had asked me, "What would you like to become when you grow up?"

I had replied, "Sir, I want to become God."

Innocently I began enquiring about the process of becoming a god. As I questioned one of the local Babas about the process, he said that I would need to continuously worship God and do everything that I could do to please God. More objectively, I was prompted to incessantly chant the name 'Ram'. The next few weeks went by with the non-stop chanting of Ram in my mind, but as nothing obvious or positive seemed to materialize, I soon became bored of the chanting and eventually lost faith in the whole process.

Whoever came to know of my obsessions with the divine either brushed my thoughts and questions aside as irrelevant, or deemed I was too young to be in pursuit of God. Whilst growing up, I had read mythological stories about how a few small children had realized God; deep down I held a secret belief that someday my quest would also become fruitful.

At the age of twelve, I did a very outrageous thing for one so young. One morning I ran away from home to follow a Baba. Four days and a few thousand kilometers later, I returned home without much insight into either his or my own quest. Upon my return home, I thought it best that I wait a few more years until I could stand on my own two feet and feel safe in the outside world.

While the God-searching project was still fermenting inside me, I had collected bits and pieces of information about how to know or meet God. On one occasion, my brother told me there was something called Yoga, by the practice of which I could come to know the unknowables of the universe. Its practitioners were known to have supernatural capacities and almost God-like qualities. I began to cook up my own image of what a yogi would look or behave like. Then unexpectedly, one day as I was browsing through my new school text books, I came across a chapter entitled 'Yogi Aurobindo'. Immediately I read away the whole chapter and felt inspired by what I had understood. However, what broke my heart was the fact that he was no longer alive to teach me how to be a real yogi. A few months later, I came to know that Yogi Aurobindo had established an ashram in Pondicherry where his students were available to teach yoga.

It was not until a few years later that my first stop in search of super-consciousness was Pondicherry. This is where I started my first practice of what I then called 'yoga'. Every morning at 7am, about twenty aspiring yogis assembled in a large hall and gaped in awe at the instructor as he twisted, turned and gyrated himself into fantastic shapes which he called 'yogasanas'. It appeared as though he had worked in a circus in his early life, as he presented a spectacular exhibition of movements which we were all painstakingly requested to follow. Every now and then he would come closer to me and express his displeasure at my ways of twisting and turning. He would grab and twist my limbs and explain how important it was to bend in the exact manner in which he demonstrated. After weeks of such an ordeal, I asked him, "In what way are these asanas of benefit to me?"

He answered, "The asanas, if done correctly, can give relief from so many different diseases and ailments."

He went on to give me what he called a brief list of some high-sounding diseases and how I could get rid of them by doing these asanas. I became thoroughly confused, as I had the notion that yoga would take me closer to God. Surely anything as serious as finding God should have a process far more respectable than performing mere physical exercises? Besides, I had not come all the way to Pondicherry just to do some exercises to get rid of diseases.

With such notions in mind, I began to dislike the exercise class and was mounting a growing resistance towards the whole yoga system. When I declared my intention to quit, the instructor advised me to meet a certain yogi to help clear my misconceptions about the exercises.

A kind, elderly man began to explain that good health was the path to God since our body is the home of God. He declared that I should continue with the exercises so that someday I would come to realize some divine truth. He further explained that the exercises were also an integral part of the yoga system, and without practising them I would never come closer to God. He advised me to attend his own lectures. I took his advice and started to attend his lectures and discourses, at the same time continuing with the yoga exercise classes.

It wasn't long before I again started to question the integrity of the practice. My confusion and consequent query was, which one of these two teachers would come to know God? One of the teachers performed a lot of exercises and obviously knew very little about the philosophy of Yoga. The other appeared to know a lot about the philosophy, but never seemed to do any exercises. If the knowledge of Yoga and yoga exercises are both indispensable for its success, then both teachers were surely disqualified. How could I rely on these teachers to get me any closer to God if they were both incomplete in themselves?'

My questions led to further confrontations. Everybody in the ashram circle started to look at me in a strange way as I obviously began to annoy them. No matter how genuine and sincere my enquiry, it was always received as a challenge or with defiance.

Under this constant resistance, I chose to withdraw myself from the ashram with only a copy of Sri Aurobindo's biography in hand.

It became my enquiry to find out if Aurobindo himself had in fact become a yogi by doing some gymnastics. I could not exactly decipher from the book what he had done to become a yogi, but his intentions of why he chose to do yoga were definitely clear. In his own words, on 30th December 1907, he told his guru, Yogi Vishnubhaskar Lele, that he wanted to do yoga for work and for action and not for *sannyasa* (renouncing the world) and nirvana. Since no further explanations were available on the subject, I naturally concluded the practice to be futile. I continued to wonder about the relationship between a spiritual quest and these painful physical exercises.

A few months later, still in pursuit of a true yogi, I came to hear of a very famous South Indian yoga teacher who was highly revered by his followers. He even had a whole yoga system named after him, yet he never called himself a yogi in public. His reputation naturally attracted me to approach his school to enquire of his teachings. It was here that for the first time I was exposed to the economics of yoga. A substantial seven hundred rupees was required to participate in a thirty-day yoga program. With the enthusiasm and desire to experience the correct practice of Yoga, I enrolled on the course, promising to find the money from somewhere. I went out in search of a job, eventually working some eighteen hours a day in order to fund my yogic purpose.

With high expectations in mind, I was conducted into a huge yoga class. The introductory speech of the teacher was highly inspiring, and my excitement was increasingly mounting. He further illuminated the divinity of his yogic process and how one could achieve a super-conscious state by following the scientific processes of yoga.

After listening to two different teachers about the spiritual purposes of yoga, I was pretty much convinced that this practice could be my final choice to nirvana. When the much-hyped class began, we were again taught gymnastic fitness with an even longer list of diseases attached to them. The asanas were yet more rigorous, more painful, and many more in number and taught by instructors who were less kind and more impatient than those in Pondicherry. In some respect the instructors forced us students to do the asanas without paying any attention to our levels of receptivity or tolerance. The proud teacher declared that he would get us into 'shape' within a certain period of time. Weeks after enduring these grueling training sessions, I began to revolt against their manner of teaching and the way they treated the students.

One day after hearing a forceful discourse, I again began to wonder about the relationship of the asanas and their expected outcomes. It took quite a few days to gather enough courage to seek audience with the charismatic yoga teacher. When I finally approached him, I asked, "How exactly is an asana related to its benefits?"

I didn't receive a clear-cut answer, so I simplified my question by asking, "In what way is an asana related to its name? To be more exact, what is the relationship between the sun and the sun salutation?"

What was given as an answer did not at all satisfy me. He said that by performing the sun salutation we would acquire tremendous cosmic energy from the sun and that we would, through constant practice, establish a kind of energy relationship with the sun. He did not choose to expound upon this point in any more detail.

I then felt quite silly to ask, "Don't you think that everything under the sun automatically receives cosmic energy? And, is it not true that everything under the sun has a definite energetic bond with the sun and its movements? Why then do I have to do these pseudo-ritualistic exercises to acquire energy from the sun to which I am entitled by birth?"

Until this day I don't quite understand what suddenly turned him against me, as he responded in a sharp and stern manner, "It is beyond human capacity to understand and comprehend the complex process of energy transmission of the sun and its relationship with a yogasana."

He further stated that probably no one on this earth would be able to give me an answer to my question. As he appeared oblivious to my frustration and determination, I got to my feet, and as I was about to leave I told him in a very meek voice that I was not convinced and that I would keep on asking these questions to whomever I may meet in this field. Without waiting to see his response, I hurried away from his presence, highly confused about his apparent failure to answer my questions. I then packed my bag and left the premises. Apart from my bag, I was carrying yet another burden of frustration and had absolutely no idea of what I was to do next.

I went back to my relatively well-paid job and started to discuss my frustrations with my employer. He was one of the few kind men I had met in my life, always treating me like his son and appearing to understand all my confusions and dilemmas. One evening during our usual discussions on spirituality in his house, one of his friends unexpectedly arrived. Upon hearing my state of confusion, he was within no time ready to help me. The friend turned out to be a member of the 'Art of Living' society, and his guru was residing in the city. It soon became routine; after work I would spend most of my free time going to his society, participating in the discourses and attending the different gatherings. What appealed to me most was the apparent happiness that radiated from the face of each member. They were obviously a much happier lot than those I had previously experienced. The guru was clearly the axis of their communal happiness as he had a beautiful and pleasant way about him and never ceased to smile.

His presence and appearance always carried a sense of reassurance and willingness to help.

As the guru began to learn of my personal quest, he agreed to speak to me more frequently. He thus explained the secrets of the happiness of life. The members of the society clearly enjoyed worshipping their guru. However, my way of looking at their cult was definitely not pleasing for the rest of the members as I was perceived as overly analytical about their philosophy and persistently debated for the truth. I was clearly not at all interested in the mutual interactions and general social life of the members, and neither did I look up to their guru in the same way as they did. This situation started to worry me. Therefore I decided to place my dilemma before the guru. This immediately caused a wave of disapproval amongst the society members, and I was warned not to speak out in such an arrogant manner. But as I could not find anything intrusive or disrespectful about my request, I advanced to speak to the guru.

"Do you feel the need to be worshipped?"

After a moment of silence he answered, "I don't necessarily need to be worshipped, but if someone likes to worship me then there is not much I can do about it. Besides, why should I stop anybody from worshipping me?"

After that day I never got my usual appointments with him.

One evening, a couple of weeks later, I stood up at the end of the prayer assembly and requested his permission to ask a question. The request was promptly brushed aside. The question that had been constantly nagging me over the past few weeks concerned whether this art of living was applicable to my definition of life, as my own happiness depended upon something far beyond absolute material fulfillment. I considered happiness only as the pretence of a perpetually unhappy being. My happiness didn't lie in life; it lay beyond it. Whilst navigating through the discussions of the past few weeks, I was obviously widening the dis-comfort zone between myself and the teacher. This, in a way, forced me to arrive at these conclusions, for I was never given the opportunity to clarify my notion that happiness is not eternal.

As my persistence grew, one day I faced the inevitable. I was branded the society nag and was told that the guru no longer had time for my nonsense. The guru of happiness was obviously unhappy with me.

I continued my visits to the society until one day the teacher told me that he had too many other disciples to take care of, therefore he would have very little time for me. After so many weeks of persistent following, I ended up facing yet another blank wall. I became totally disheartened and confused. It was only after a few futile attempts to control my frustration that I burst out saying, "I would not invite any more people to lunch than my capacity to feed them."

I felt shaken and insulted, but that didn't stop me from continuing my quest.

As a result of these experiences I grew to be more humble, for I began to realize the essence of devotion. Whether this was because of my pious mother or the guru-worshipping population, I had a realization that one has to follow their inner belief. I began to contemplate becoming an ardent devotee of some worthy god-head. But which of the many was I to choose? For some reason or another, I was definitely not ready to go back to penis worshipping. One thing was certain; I was more than ready for a complete change of scenario. After returning home, I started to collect a range of religious literature from all kinds of faiths.

I had very few friends at this time of my life. People of my age who knew me didn't carry a high opinion of me. I was always seen as some kind of freak because on the one hand I was very mysterious in nature, and on the other I was always talking about some incomprehensible subject. For a boy of my age, a subject matter relating to Life, Karma, *Brahman* or *Paramatma* was definitely seen as boring. Many people within my circle even claimed that they had seen me talking to myself. They were probably right, as I was aware that I was constantly engaged in some kind of spiritual debate within myself. Hence, I would not have been at all surprised to know that my face may have reflected the thoughts and emotions of that internal struggle.

A few friends seemed to be sympathetic, but most avoided any form of intellectual exchange with me. From my own biased viewpoint, I was a likable but highly misunderstood boy. However, there was one particular classmate who recently converted to christianity, and who after the conversion, to some extent, reflected similar symptoms. He would spend long hours in silence with himself and became gradually withdrawn from the movie-going friendship circle. We soon became friends, and I found myself listening at length to his excitable accounts and revelations of his new found feelings and perceptions towards spirituality. In due course, he introduced me to his pastor and his own church circle.

On a regular basis, I began to receive the church bulletins and literature. On the back pages of one of the booklets I discovered an advertisement for a free bible course offered by a church in a different city. I further enquired of its details and found out that it also included free accommodation. My friend and his pastor were more than happy to make all the arrangements and sent me packing with a letter of recommendation in hand to my new spiritual school. During the ten-hour bus journey to the church, I was full of apprehension and excitement, whilst at the same time questioning my decision to study christian philosophy. I knew for certain that no one in my family or within my limited friendship circle would approve of me studying, let alone supporting, the christian principles. In the eyes of my family, it was possibly the most outrageous thing that I could have ever chosen to do.

During the journey, I can't say whether it was boredom or

curiosity that prompted me to secretly open the letter of recommendation. Upon opening the letter, the content revealed some peculiarities: the first was that I possessed the ripest state of confusion in my mind and that with a little persuasion I could be converted, and the second included a somewhat brief, but highly exaggerated account of my religious background.

Father William Behera was a large jovial man who had spent the better part of his life as a primary school teacher and only became a priest in the latter part of his life. He became my spiritual guardian for the next six months. There were also two visiting priests taking the classes who taught us with unlimited patience and perseverance. In the morning session we studied the Holy Bible, and in the evening sessions the virtues of a believer were drilled into our heads. The morning class was definitely interesting, as the life and greatness of Jesus held my full attention.

As an inquisitive seeker, it was my natural tendency to always pop questions. But having little scope to do this within the stream of preaching I began to maintain a record of all my questions, which I intended to ask later. My first suspicions of the teaching were based upon certain convenient aspects of Jesus and the religion. These aspects were carefully extracted and taught to us with special emphasis, whereas other parts of the bible, in my opinion, were meticulously ignored. I felt extremely silly and unworthy as I began to suspect the truth behind the teachings. Nevertheless I continued the studies whilst keeping the central and fundamental aspects of christianity in my mind. In my comprehension, the teachings were a curious blend of some nice philosophical ideals with a strong measure of blind beliefs.

I was encouraged by the church community to contemplate the life and sacrifice of Jesus, as opposed to reading between the lines and developing an analytical viewpoint. It was quite difficult for me to accept that the rest of the world and I were a product of sin. I didn't like the idea of being a sinner by birth and came to detest this notion as utter pessimism. I had held a strong belief that man is divine and has an inherent attraction towards the absolute divinity. It is this attraction that governs the relationship between man and God. However, what I was currently being taught was the exact opposite of this perception. The church was forcing me to accept the notion that one man is divine and the rest are sinners. It is definitely an easier task to create a religion centered upon this principle if everyone could be made to accept that they are born as sinners. The central idea of my quest was to discover the connections to God, and the bible course was definitely not following my course of personal aspirations to divinity.

Father William was doing his utmost to persuade me to follow the prayers and to chant the mantra 'Jesus I love you, Jesus I believe in you'. He seemed absolutely convinced that by chanting these lines one could obtain the blessings of Jesus. The entire time I spent at this church I had literally turned these lines over and over in my head, but this did not stop the sprouting of questions in my mind. I was never able to get any clarification from Father William or the priests about my growing confusion. However, amidst the increasing doubt and speculation in my mind, I managed to finish the entire bible course.

I had already packed my bags, ready to leave even before the certification ceremony. I went to say goodbye and thank the church officials and the Father. Before I could say goodbye, Father William asked me, "When will you choose to embrace the family of the church?"

At first I didn't understand the question, so he then made it more clear by saying, "When would you like to be converted to christianity?"

He went on to inform me that he had made all the necessary arrangements for what would be the 'most glorious day of my life'. I thanked him for all his efforts and politely declined the offer.

All of a sudden his tone changed as he glared at me and

demanded to know, "Why have you wasted so much of the church's time?"

What followed next is not appropriate to reveal to you as a reader. Leaving behind a group of obviously frustrated, enraged and incredulous believers, I had no hesitation in slinging my bag across my shoulder and leaving the premises. I concluded that my last sixth months learning was more about the limitations of religious faith and belief and nothing about the expansion of knowledge. It became my understanding that knowledge begins where belief ends.

As I strolled aimlessly around the local town for the rest of the day, I wondered what could be wrong with me, and why it was that everywhere I searched, I always faced such unpleasant outcomes. Still brooding and recollecting my past experiences, I dropped my bag on a bench on the railway platform and fell asleep. I must have slept for an hour or so when suddenly I awoke with a shudder and realized that my bag had disappeared from under my head. Instinctively I muttered, "Oh, Jesus!"

The frustration born from the incomplete understanding of the divine, coupled with the fact that I no longer had any personal belongings, resulted in a strange state of mind. It appeared as if the whole world was doing its best to dissuade me from my spiritual quest. Standing in the midst of an over-crowded platform, I started to feel very lonely and somewhat stupid. By this time at least one thing was certain in my mind: I must be some kind of crazy person. On the other hand, I was pleased that at least my ways didn't hurt anyone. I did my utmost to bottle all my craziness and remained absolutely secretive in what I was doing. The only thing that seemed to give me pleasure was that I had formed a notion of myself as being very special. Is it not the case that all saints and sages in their early days of seeking were perceived as being mad or crazy?

Often I had felt the urge to discard all my obscure spiritual notions and live life in the 'normal' way, like everyone else seemed to, but somehow I couldn't throw away all these notions. I wasn't ready to accept that education, occupation, marriage, children and death are all that there is to life. All these material dimensions can make someone rich but not wise, successful but not divine. All those people who we worship today as saints could have led a life of material pleasure and fulfillment, but they chose not to. And I don't think it could have been through the activities of their jobs and romances that brought them to the eminence of sainthood.

The example of a saint's life was telling me that quality of determination, compulsive learning and renunciation from the material desires of life had brought them to such a noble state. Thus whenever I felt silly and stupid about my way of life, I tried to console myself with the pure and rigorous life of saints and sages. Sitting there alone at the railway station, I felt like a neglected saint. This was until my stomach started rumbling. An empty stomach definitely did not support my notions of sainthood. Then again, didn't Buddha give up asceticism because of an empty stomach?

For me it was always a matter of fascination to see how people of different faiths and religions attempted to advertise their cults. Whenever I saw a religious procession, it would intrigue me as to its deeper meaning. The external appearance of these processions was very colorful and often accompanied by music, chanting, dancing, and firecrackers and in some extreme cases, people dancing and swirling in a trance-like state. I always wondered what could be wrong with these people. Since my mind was gradually entering into a void of inconclusive spiritual ideas, I spent a lot of my time practically thinking of nothing. By this time I had grown beyond using my free time stealing mangoes and berries. Instead, I decided to contemplate upon the deeper meanings of these strange trance-like phenomena.

One day I followed a procession of these people, all of whom shaved their heads leaving only a pigtail. They were dressed in pink robes with two vertical lines drawn on their forehead. Four people were carrying a seat on their shoulders, upon which sat a man in a meditative position. Some of them were playing music and chanting, whilst others were dancing in the same trance-like state. They reached a white towering temple. The outside board read 'International Society for Krishna Consciousness'. The procession came to an end at the temple, and the seat was lowered to the ground. They lifted the man out of the seat, and to my surprise, it was not a man - it was a statue.

After depositing my shoes in a rack, I casually took a walk around the temple. It was, indeed, a beautiful piece of architecture. It was very well maintained and pristinely clean, reflecting the sense of care, affection and wealth of those involved in the society. It gave me a beautiful sense of peace and tranquility to just sit in one corner and attempt to absorb the surroundings. There was also a little bookstore filled with books that were written by the founder of the society, whose name seemed somehow familiar, but at the time, I could not recall exactly where from. I collected a few copies of the free books that were handed to me. It was not until I had read the books a few days later that I was to return with an intention to further enquire about their spiritual ideas.

It took some time to frame the questions in my mind. I went to the office on the first floor and asked if anyone was available to talk to me about the society and its teachings. I was referred to a well-built man who was sitting on the floor behind a writing desk. He introduced himself as Atmaram. He began to tell me that I would need to be a member of the society to join its spiritual guidelines. The membership was beyond my paying capacity, so I diverted and restricted the conversation to their beliefs and practices. At the beginning, he explained the efficacy of *bhakti* as a mode of divine transformation. He stated that Krishna, the ultimate expression of God, had personally advocated that *bhakti* was the only effective path for self-realization. He seemed absolutely convinced about the meaning behind his every word. I could detect a tone of corporate salesmanship behind his explanations, to which I did not take a liking.

Since I had no means to purchase anything, I accepted the tone of his explication. At the end of the conversation, he suggested I go to Mathura, said to be the birthplace of Krishna, where I could get further help about studying the principles and path of *bhakti*. Keen to explore the path of devotion, I joined the Mathura centre of ISKCON as a non-paying *sannyasi*. The most important activities at this centre were service, chanting, rich food and trance dance. Irrespective of my limited participation in the regular temple activities, my inclination towards the deeper values of *bhakti* was soon noticed by the temple seniors, and I was granted access to the library.

Broadly speaking, the total membership of the society consisted of two types of people. One type appeared to retain a genuine interest in the spiritual quest and spent most of their time reading or discussing spiritual matters. These were predominantly westerners. The other set of people were mostly of Indian origin that seldom participated in any intellectual exchange and spent most of their time running the business of the temple. Interestingly, it was the Indians who danced more energetically.

Soon I developed a friendship with a western devotee who was doing research on Krishna's teachings. His birth name was Stephen. During my stay and study at ISKCON, Stephen was of great help as he was, until now, the first person to understand my spiritual hunger. It was here that I learnt a very important lesson on how the teaching is more important than the teacher. This was ironically opposite to the central idea of the society.

The principles held in very high esteem by the society were by no means any different than those sublime features of any other religion. A good catholic devotee may be in no way different than a devoted Krishna follower. Both share a certain degree of pessimism and both worship what they claim to be the supreme manifestation of God. Additionally, the 'Praise the Lord' slogan is also evident from the *kirtans* of the Krishna followers. One day, even my close friend Stephen said that a certain section of chris-tianity identified Jesus with Krishna.

The study at Mathura was both a matter of interest and intrigue. Here I was turning from being a spiritual seeker into a Sherlock Holmes of religion. This is not to say that I was losing track of my inherent quest, but I developed an entirely new way of looking at religions. My study area did not remain confined to the ISKCON circle, as I visited Delhi, Allahabad and Varanasi on frequent occasions to emphasize and explore the origins and developments of all religious thought. Although it was hard work, the findings proved insightful, yet painful, as I discovered that no religion actually developed in a positive way after its inception. The great minds that had once created the pure structure of a religion were not available to see their ideas go through the turbulence of civilization. The inceptions of all religions actually deteriorated over the passage of time. The reasons and forces that twist and distort a fine religious stream are an entirely different subject matter than the framework of this book. Yet, from the study of religious thought I reaped some benefit. I found that the pure and original ideas of a religion are entirely dependable in a spiritual quest, but not in a religion under its present conditions.

The process of Krishna investigation led me through all those scriptures and mythologies that are manifestations of the original hindu ideology. It is amazing how vividly the ancient religious forefathers portrayed the notions of God, as every scripture reveals and glorifies a definitive set of the divine dimensions of Godhood. The scriptures undeniably contain a high degree of inspiration for their readers. In a way, these books are now revered as the religious textbooks of hinduism. In the words of my friend Stephen, "These are the books that ultimately turned India into a land of fairytales."

Evidently not many people have understood the true messages behind these scriptures, but at least everybody has derived some inspiration from them. As a result, an entire civilization became identified with their myths and legends.

It took me a significant amount of time and struggle to extricate myself from the jumbles of religious complexities and shift my attention to the true depths of the Bhagavad Gita. The more I immersed myself in the nectars of its philosophy, the more I came to realize that a lifetime is not quite enough to comprehend its profundity of meaning. As one of the prominent commentators of the Gita had rightly stated, 'It takes one no less than Krishna to explain what the Gita means and it takes one no less than an Arjuna to understand what it could mean.'

Hence all those trying to explain and understand the full meaning of the Gita are merely amusing themselves. The task becomes even more difficult when one attempts to comprehend the ultimate path to realization, independent of the emotional or devotional obligation to a godhood. For instance, 'If love can be comprehended independent of the lover, why can divinity not be comprehended independent of a manifested godhood?'

Having spent just over another week in the society, I departed with a profound and deep insight of the Bhagavad Gita in my mind, leaving their Krishna behind for them to keep on worshipping.

Over the next few months, I developed a strange, detached and indifferent state of mind. I became completely overwhelmed by the wisdom contained within the teachings of the Bhagavad Gita. In a way, it was very clear that Vyasa, the author of the Gita, was not telling a story about a prince on a battlefield. The character of Arjuna represents a spiritually ripe seeker who identified himself with the hundreds of material human traits and emotions. At the most decisive point of his life, he was required to kill all his personal inhibitions to crossover into a state of equanimity. The only thing that could make him go beyond his material identity was the presence of absolute knowledge. The hundred brothers and the hundreds of other relatives were nothing but the multiple manifestations of a single mind, and a human mind makes the mistake of identifying himself with these manifestations. In order to go beyond this illusion, the support and direction of true and pure knowledge is absolutely necessary. It is essential to treat this knowledge as a friend and guide rather than a god, as the vision of God is already inherent in the pure state of knowledge.

The Bhagavad Gita explicitly revealed three distinct pathways to self-realization. The paths of knowledge, action and devotion all made absolute sense to me, but I concluded the path of knowledge as the most suitable for my quest. Now the practical problem – how does one find a teacher who believes in the pursuit of absolute knowledge without any undesirable attachments?

The only other kind of people who seemed to be more sincere and humble in their practices was the buddhists. I was told they had the least number of 'arm-chair' teachers, and as a reader of Indian religious history, I was aware of the simple, yet profound tenants of buddhism. The two aspects of buddhism that appealed to me most were the emphasis on knowledge and the concept of renunciation. In the past I had also read some literature on the buddhist understanding of past-life karma and present-day spirituality.

My ideas of rebirth were derived from whatever I had been told by different ascetics, *brahmins* and *pundits*. I thought a good past-life therapy would help me decipher the mysteries, behavior and development of a spiritual freak, such as myself. Naturally, I had a certain degree of reluctance to jump into yet another pseudo-spiritual community. But I must admit, I had an insatiable drive for knowledge and would have done anything, no matter how outrageous it may have been perceived by others. Hence it did not take long for my spiritual thirst to prevail over my mundane constrictions. I had chosen a buddhist monastery near Darjeeling. It was located in a quiet and serene setting.

Once I reached the monastery, I asked if it was possible for me to stay for a few days. An old lama with an 'I know it all smile' on his face replied, "What would be the purpose of your stay?"

On hearing about the purpose of my quest and my existing state of confusion, he kindly invited me to not only stay, but also to participate in an exchange of buddhist wisdom. The next day I found myself nosing around every nook and cranny of the monastery whilst contemplating if I felt any different here.

There was a huge and magnificent statue of Buddha in the altar and underneath were hundreds of smaller statues. I decided to sit in front of the statue with closed eyes to pray in silence to Buddha to help me discover the truths of life; the prayer filled me with a peaceful and pleasant sensation. Once I opened my eyes, I remained seated in contemplation, gazing in a state of wonder at the calm and benign face of Buddha. It seemed as though he were talking to me through a mischievous smile, almost like he was saying, 'Have I not already done that bit of discovery? You don't have to bother about discovering the truths again. It will be more useful if you follow my teachings by the letter and spirit.'

This beautiful and subtle exchange between the Lord and myself sent me back into another prayer and an even deeper contemplation.

I spent the rest of the day inspired, making a list of the four noble truths, the noble eight-fold path and all the teachings and refor-mations of Buddha. From the memories of my history classes, I double-checked its accuracy with the old lama, who was growing more enthusiastic by the hour. Three days later, he called me into the prayer hall where he asked me to sit in front of him and said, "Do you know who you are?"

I replied, "No."

He again asked, "Do you think you are prepared to know who you are?"

"I think so, as that is the reason I have being running around the country in the search to discover myself'."

He flashed his 'I know it all smile' once more and said in a conclusive tone, "Let me reveal something to you. I can tell you who you are."

My heart skipped a few beats as I waited in anticipation. With an edge of satisfaction in his voice, he continued, "You have been a member of the *sangha* (buddhist community) for a very long time. In your last life, you were a follower of Buddha, and you always carried the blessing of Buddha wherever you traveled. You have also lived in this monastery. This monastery, in a way, looked up to you as a strong pillar of the faith. No one knew exactly what happened to you after you left on a pilgrimage to Tibet. Many years later a group of traveling lamas arrived from Tibet with a little information about you. The chief lama had sent a message that you might turn up at this monastery sometime after the next twenty years."

He opened an old book and pointing to a particular line, read something to me in Tibetan. "What is written in here confirms your arrival to this monastery."

I had never before experienced a sensation as compelling as that which pervaded through my whole system in that moment. I do not know exactly what was said after the initial few lines, for I only came back to some kind of reality when I felt the gentle touch of his palm on my shoulder. He then offered his hand to help me to my feet, and said softly, "Go to your room and sleep for a while."

Later that evening, I decided to stay and participate in the prayer and proceedings without taking my usual stroll into the countryside. I was sitting in the kitchen and helping a young lama in the preparation of the evening meal when suddenly I heard sounds of a huge commotion accompanied by what appeared like the sounds of slaps and kicks. I jumped to my feet and peeped out of the window.

With no one in sight I turned to ask the young lama, "Do fights often break out amongst the monks?"

He replied calmly, "There is no fight."

Confused I asked, "So why are people out there hitting each other?"

He replied, "Why don't you go out and see for yourself?"

I immediately dropped my knife and half-peeled potato and rushed outside. The lama was right; there was no fight. Instead it was the monks in the process of some kind of exchange as a select few were sitting, talking to a standing counterpart. The standing monk rapidly spoke a few lines and then would slap his right palm on his awaiting left palm, simultaneously stamping his left foot on the ground. Collectively, the congregation of monks made a huge racket and appeared in a state of frenzy, which seemed peculiar as it took place almost immediately after their prayers. I enquired about the meaning behind the behavior and was informed that it was the process of a debate. I was intrigued to know the significance of the slapping and stamping.

From what I could decipher from the variety of explanations, the sitting monk was demanding a proof, and the standing monk was submitting an argument and sealing it with a clap and a stamp. The overall energy and tone of the exchange appeared somewhat macho, akin to the manner in which a person would bang on a table to emphasize his point. I was both amused and intrigued by the eccentric combination of knowledge and strength.

I found it difficult to sleep that night as the evening's spectacle had created waves of questions in my mind. Out of respect towards their religion and the kindness they had shown to me, I chose to contain all my thoughts and speculations. Instead, I began to spend more time listening to the wisdom of the old lama. In a way, he appeared absolutely sure of what he was talking about, and I agreed with many of his philosophies. But I was never completely happy, as still nothing had presented me with the opportunity to reveal my questions that had been tormenting me for the past few days. I knew that it was fruitless to proceed with the teachings if my mind remained stagnant, so I decided to ask the old lama my first question.

The concern itself was related to the relationship between buddhist philosophy and martial arts: 'How could the absolute non-violent principles of buddhism have given rise to some of the most deadly forms of martial arts in the world?'

Historically, the Chinese and Tibetan buddhist monks had developed various forms of hand-to-hand combat techniques to save themselves from bandits who they encountered over the remote Himalayan passes. Since the beginning of this trend, numerous Oriental buddhist communities developed various modes of deadly techniques, and thus martial arts became synonymous with the buddhist nations. What is common amongst all these martial arts is a deep understanding of a cosmo-human energy system which is the basis of their fighting technology. These fighting skills have their roots in the buddhist form of meditation and religious discipline. Every deadly martial artist is foremost a disciplined buddhist, and the Shaolin temple transforms from a place of spiritual pilgrimage into a university of martial arts.

A second question and ambiguity surfaced in my mind as I was reading a booklet on the religious activities of the monastery. It proudly declared that this monastery was one of the few who held the resources to accomplish the most complex buddhist rituals. As far as I have studied, Buddha had launched a crusade against the *vedic* rituals and endeavored to simplify the religious beliefs of 6th century BC India. It was this simplicity that facilitated buddhism to prevail over the existing complexity of religious conditioning. The present emphasis on complex religious rituals was far removed from my notions of buddhism.

My third, but by no means last, question to the lama was, 'Why do the buddhists worship the statues of Buddha when Buddha himself condemned and renounced image worshipping?'

The good old lama then explained to me a twelve hundred year-old history and development of Tibetan buddhism. He was very patient in his explanations, and there was no change in the rise of his smile. His explanation was impressive, but not quite convincing. We both agreed that the buddhism introduced in Tibet thirteen hundred years after the death of Buddha lacked the purity and originality of 6th century BC buddhism. We also agreed that the present state of Tibetan buddhism is a blend of the buddhist monastic structure and the shamanistic practices of ancient Tibet; hence it is known as Tibetan buddhism. I enquired if I could find the traces of the original buddhism anywhere. The old lama, who will forever remain respectful in my eyes for his honesty and open-mindedness, said with a rather deep and depleted sigh, "Wherever buddhism has traveled in this world, it has blended with the local beliefs and rituals. If it is Tibetan buddhism here, it is Zen or Theravada buddhism elsewhere."

After a moment of silence, he concluded in a very steady and mindful tone, "We will all miss Buddha forever."

I looked at his wise and graceful face and wondered to myself for a moment, 'Isn't this the face of Buddha himself?'

My quest and investigation into buddhism did not end in Darjeeling, as I continued to collect information and study the meanings of their rituals in much finer detail. A sad conclusion began to take shape: the more I observed the original texts, the more it became apparent that Buddha's 'ism' might be extinct from the face of this planet. Whatever I found in the name of buddhism offered many nice things. But one thing was for sure, they were unable to give me my much sought-after path to self-realization. If the supreme spiritual head of Tibetan buddhism does not attain nirvana, then what chance do other followers have in achieving the state of nirvana? And if the Dalai Lama is a reincarnation of Avalokiteswara (Buddha), then Buddha's claim of nirvana is surely nullified.

I spent a couple of weeks studying the history of Tibetan buddhism. This gave me a deeper insight into the ancient Tibetan beliefs. I was always fascinated to study the origin, format and rituals of folk religions. I was enthralled to learn about the colorful descriptions of the Tibetan past. Neither Buddha, nor buddhism figured much in the Tibetan history, but their ancient religion had definitely become streamlined with the introduction of the monastic order of Buddha.

After leaving the monastery, I wandered aimlessly through the eastern coast of India. As the monsoon clouds were gathering, I headed to Puri in the state of Orissa. Puri is a small, crowded and chaotic town. At the beginning of the rainy season this little town receives as many as half a million tourists and pilgrims who gather to witness a ten-day festival of Lord Jagannath. It is one of many yearly activities where you can find sages, seers and holy men from different parts of India. This eight hundred year-old festival has remained well known in history, as it always attracted great spiritually-revered people. Most people turn to this town to have a glimpse of the images of the Lord carried in huge gigantic wooden chariots, pulled by thousands of people. But the purpose of my visit was very different. I had a deep yearning to meet some of these great people who may have chosen to visit the town at the same time.

Without much difficulty I spotted a few of them, but none of them showed any interest in engaging with me in discussion or debate. At least one of them suggested that I should meet Jagadguru Shankaracharya at his *muth* (monastery).

The history of Shankaracharya goes back to the eighth century. At a tender young age, Adi Shankaracharya had explained the profound meaning of the Bhagavad Gita, *Brahmasutra* and *Vedanta*. He is one of the greatest exponents of the *vedantic* philosophy. After sage Yajnvalkya, a great spiritual philosophy had developed. It became famous by the name *Advaita Vedanta*. Shankaracharya is one of the greatest exponents of this school of thought. Before his demise at the age of thirty-two, he was said to have established four spiritual centers in the east, west, north and southern regions of India. The center in Eastern India is in the town of Puri. These centers are headed by some holy men who belong to the lineage of Shankaracharya. These people even today are known as Shankaracharyas.

Soon I was on my way to meet the Shankaracharya of Puri. I managed to get an appointment to meet him, but not before the end of the ten-day festival. The meeting didn't last long. Without even bothering to listen to my questions, the old Shankaracharya gave one single conclusive statement and dismissed me. "The world you live in is *maya* (illusion) and nothing else. Go and wake up to reality. The knowledge of the 'real' is supreme, because the 'real' is the only one that has neither a beginning nor an end. The realization of this truth is all that you will need to achieve humanly."

I asked, "What do I have to do to come face-to-face with this reality? How do I find the 'real' one?"

He gave one curt reply. "Stop dreaming! It is impossible to comprehend the 'real' in your dreams. Go, think and use your head to what I have just said, instead of asking me questions. Come and attend the *pravachans* (discourses) in the evenings. There you may learn a little bit more."

He dismissed me without any further ado.

I walked out wondering why this stupid old man was so arrogant. He seemed to have much less time at his disposal than anybody else in the world. He carried the manner and air of a god. I didn't like the old man at all, but my greed for knowledge drove me to his discourses every evening. He spoke on the Bhagavad Gita, the *Upanishads* and the life and teachings of Adi Shankaracharya in his usual god-like manner. Every now and then he repeated what seemed to be his most favorite line - 'Stop dreaming!'

After a few dozen of these orders, I could not help but question, 'What makes this fellow think that everyone else is dreaming and he is not?' It appeared as if it was he who badly needed to wake up in the first place. Throughout the discourses of his high-tech philosophy, I was barely listening to what he was saying, as most of it I had heard or read somewhere before. There was nothing more to be learnt from him. According to him, the only answer to every problem was 'Stop dreaming and wake up to reality!' Yet he never actually revealed how to stop dreaming or how to wake up.

After about two weeks of listening to his 'all fart, no shit' philosophy, I decided to meet him once more before going on my way. Again I had to be content with a few more days of waiting. I couldn't understand why so many people came to meet him, as in my understanding, he didn't seem to have much to say. As I was patiently waiting for an audience, I began to take some interest in the people who visited him. I noticed that most of the people were politicians, bureaucrats, local mafia and the like. I could not quite understand why this holy man had connections that no one else would like to have?

One day a local newspaper answered my queries about the integrity of this holy man. The paper declared that there were two Sankaracharyas in Puri. Both of them were claiming to be the true descendants of Sankaracharya. This feud had taken both of these holy men to new heights of spiritual showdown. They were constantly engaged in abusing, rebuking and challenging each other. As an outcome of this conflict, the whole religious circle of the town was divided into two warring groups. A couple of people were injured, and there was news about threats to the lives of the Shankaracharyas.

During my audience with the Shankaracharya, I persistently stuck to my one and only question, "Is there a practical method to practise or realize the claims of the philosophy of *Advaita Vedanta*, or is it merely just another bunch of ideas?"

No matter from whom these ideas started, they are nothing more than mere impractical notions. I refused to accept *Advaita Vedanta* as a valid subject, as long as I wasn't shown a definite process of practising and realizing it. The old man gave me a mantra and advised that this was the most effective and shortcut path to the realization of the Reality. The feuding nature of the Shankaracharya was very apparent in his speech. I could not understand why time and again he compared the philosophy of Adi Shankara with other spiritual paths that he argued were useless and worthless. He even had the audacity to state that the philosophy of *Advaita Vedanta* is far more superior to that of Yoga. This poor fellow had definitely no knowledge of how Shankara had advocated and glorified the practice and philosophy of Yoga. The more he spoke, the more his ignorance became apparent. This time it was not he who dismissed me - rather it happened the other way round. Nothing came as a surprise when only last year I learnt of the news that the Shankaracharya of South India had been arrested and tried for murder.

Until now, my journey appeared to be nothing more than a ridiculous and perpetual pillar-to-post run. It was hard, painful, amusing, insightful and desperate in nature. I had a strong urge to let go of this hopeless search and resign myself to fate, but for one particular reason I could not abort this search. The reason being everybody else other than myself appeared to be happy with whatever faith, belief or guru they entertained. Many people prompted me to stop what they described as beating around the bush and follow a single religion or guru until the end, asserting that only with a lifetime of sacrifice and dedication to one path would I be able to find some of the meanings of life. As a friend once said, "A lifetime is not quite enough to understand what life is all about."

On the contrary, I made a promise to myself that I would never again follow an organized religion. I identified myself as a good and simple boy who had embarked upon the truest journey of life. With knowledge as my path and self-realization as my destination, I confined myself to reading only. Every now and then I would find myself in an intellectual wrestle with some scholar or teacher, and most of the time I emerged as the victor. As I found myself winning these battles, it adversely boosted my pride sky-high.

I had very few friends who did not mind my over-enthusiastic spiritual indulgences. One evening a friend arrived to invite me to the cinema. I was not particularly in the mood to go and watch a film. It felt like every minute of that day had been spent reading and contemplating the Bhagavad Gita, and as a result, I was completely immersed in a highly spiritually charged state of mind. After much persuasion, I agreed to go for a walk, although I remained relatively silent and detached as the lines of the Gita filled me with their beautiful rhythms, meanings and vibrations. To this day, these *slokas* still resonate in my mind:

'Vasamsi jirnani yatha vihaya, Navani grhnati naro 'parani, Tatha sarirani vihaya jirna, nyanyani samyati navani dehi.'
('As a man shedding worn out garments, takes other new ones, likewise the embodied soul shedding its worn out bodies, enters into new ones.'- 2:22)

'Nainam chhindanti sastrani, Nainam dahati pavakah, Na chainam kledayanyapo, Na shosayati marutah.'

('Weapons cannot cut it, nor can fire burn it; water cannot wet it, nor can wind dry it.'- 2:23)

'Achhedyo yam adahyo 'yam, Akledyo 'sosya eva ca, Nityah sarva-gatah sthanur, Acalo 'yam sanatanah.'

('For this soul is incapable of being cut; it is proof against fire, impervious to water & undriable as well. This soul is eternal, omnipresent, immovable, constant & everlasting.' - 2:24)

As we continued to walk, we met a group of friends sitting and chatting in a lonely place. We decided to join them. A few minutes later, one of them produced a packet of homemade biscuits and offered them around. I think I had eaten about three of them when I began to notice the sweet poetic rhythms of the Gita in my mind transform into powerful waves of energy.

Within a few minutes, I was experiencing a very high voltage of sensations traversing through my body, and the world before me transformed into a gigantic colorful screen. I then saw a vivid image of Krishna standing and talking to me. Involuntarily I brought both my palms together with reverence and felt the gentle touch of a hand on my back. My surroundings were transformed into an unbelievably beautiful and pleasant illumination. I looked around to try and see my friends' reactions, but I could not find them around me as they seemed to have disappeared. I asked myself if I was dreaming. I even pinched myself to be sure I was not dreaming. This was happening for real. Unbelievable, but real.

My attention shifted back to what Krishna was saying, as he started to elucidate on the profound meanings of the lines which were ringing in my head. With a sweet smile on his face, he went on to speak of the hopeless and illusory nature of this mundane life. Expounding further, he explained that my existence was no more than a human manifestation of a deathless and timeless soul and that I am already divine and an integral part of his supreme self. It appeared that ages had passed before the image of Krishna slowly began to fade into the background. I continued to sense his divine presence all around me.

This experience gave me a huge sense of fulfillment, and my level of desperation eased. I confidently eradicated my inhibitions of meeting any guru or god-men, since I now considered myself no less than one. According to me, this experience was no less than that of Enlightenment. It was many years later that the reality of this experience was explained to me. My visions of Krishna and the subsequent revelations were a neuro-psychic reaction which was triggered by some kind of hallucinogenic substance that was in the biscuits I had eaten.

However, with my new-found enthusiasm, I decided to continue my quest. I went to Puttapartti to see the afro-headed god-man Sai Baba. I was not at all impressed by his popularity or his magic tricks. I then went onto Kerala and received a hug from Amma everyday, for two weeks. I not only failed to perceive any divinity within her, but was disgusted by the complete commercialization of human worshipping that was being promoted directly or indirectly by her organization. I then went onto some Yoga Vedanta ashram in Kerala that supposedly had a 'classical approach to hatha yoga'. After performing one month of classical gymnastics with every bone of my body screaming with pain, I was in no way closer to good health, let alone spiritual growth. After dumping their idiosyncratic philosophies, I proceeded to Kanya Kumari. I spent a few weeks studying raja yoga at the Vivekananda Trust. Here I was introduced to the Yoga Sutras of Patanjali.

My wandering continued for a few more months, but my seeking had come to an end. Whether this was due to the economics of the Tirumala Temple, the immoral practices of Puri, the meaningless devotion at Nadiya, the terrible cult of *aghoras* or the blind fury of the *naga sannyasis*, all in some form or another had collectively sealed my path for further seeking. My journey from consciousness had ended nowhere. The collective under-standing of life until now, in particular the desperate search over the last five years, had convinced me that the subject of spiritu-ality was no more than a lie. I slowly began to withdraw from all possible spiritual encounters. The only thing that seemed to keep me alive was my deeper sense of soul identity. I was prepared to wait until eternity for truth to manifest itself, resigned to allow the forces of evolution to carry me forward to my evolutionary end; every step I walked, every breath I took, was a move closer to my spiritual destiny.

∞∞∞∞

I was lost in a deep thought, comparing the speed of the train in which I was traveling at that moment with the speed of evolution. I was in the process of weaving a fantasy about getting down at the station of Enlightenment. The faster the train moved, the more elated I became. My anxiety levels rocketed, and I knew by the minute I was getting closer to the last stop of self-realization.

After a short while, above the rumble of the train I became exposed to some irritable noise in the background. The noise made me furious, as it interfered with my tranquil, dreamy stupor. I looked around and spotted a group of ascetics huddled near the carriage doorway. It was their collective chanting, chiming and chattering that broke my delightful fantasy. I went up to them and barked, "Stop this noise at once!"

They stopped and gaped at me in disbelief. I then threatened to throw them out of the carriage if they caused any more annoyance to the peace-loving people in the carriage. This effectively silenced them, so I went back to my seat to regain my train of thought.

A short while later, one of the men approached me and politely asked if he could take the vacant seat opposite to mine. I quickly moved my feet from the vacant seat to gesture a positive response. He had a pleasant and friendly face that made me question why I was so rude to them in the first place. I struggled with myself to justify my uncouth and abrupt behavior. He started a conversation with a polite question, "What does a civilized young man have against a group of harmless ascetics, who have nothing other than thinking about God?"

Pointing with a stern finger, I corrected him by saying, "Your god! I don't care a damn about your god - who is so deaf that you have to make noise to express your thoughts and feelings."

He again politely asked, "Are you against God or his followers?"

I replied, "Both." Then I delivered a quote from a book that I had only recently read. "The creator of god was a fool, the believer of god was a scoundrel, and the follower of god was a barbarian."

From the expression on his face, he was evidently shocked.

"What makes you think so?" he blurted out. "What kind of faith do you come from? Have you not read a single religious scripture?"

I thought in my mind, this poor guy is asking for it! All the failures, frustrations, confusions, insults and conclusions of my whole life triggered by his recent interference and audacity of challenging my spiritual status unleashed a tremendous fury, and in a controlled rage, I shot back. "Who the hell are you? And what bloody god are you talking about?!"

I continued my avalanche of disparages, "Have you ever seen a god or know him or are you just carried away by the superhuman characters from the mythological epics and plays? The holy scriptures you were talking about are only full of mythological and legendary figures, and the personality and qualities of each of them are barely anything above human."

I continued to blast my way through his so-called gods and scriptures without giving him a single moment to defend himself. My opinions were furious and insane, but the strength of my arguments achieved their purpose.

I then described the pretence of his supposed ideals: how unfair and treacherous it is to murder someone who is engaged in a fight with someone else; how immoral it is to put one's wife into a fire after having failed to protect her; what an injustice it is to banish a woman into a jungle in her advanced stages of pregnancy without giving her a chance to be heard - a tale that reveals the murder of a very wise scholarly king who ruled a kingdom made of gold by an inhumane prince who had neither wisdom nor prosperity mentioned in the whole epic!

"So, you worship such an un-real mythical character as a god?"

I downsized every mythological character that he thought was divine in nature. The images and ideas of all the gods and goddesses began to crumble with the furious onslaught of my arguments.

I took this shocked, surprised and devastated god-man on a journey of historical truth, religious fantasy, blind imagery and the ignorance of the common gullible religious man.

I reminded him, "If you cannot read between the lines and form an unbiased, analytical judgment without only following the gross apparent characteristics, then at least do not preach it, as the god-fearing common man blindly accepts anything about his god without any form of questioning. It is because of this shortcoming that the spiritual values of our ancient civilization are lost."

I went on to say, "If Krishna rejected the worship of *vedic* gods, to what religion did he belong? Why don't you worship Buddha if you have accepted him as the ninth incarnation of Vishnu?

More importantly, why should I follow a religion if God doesn't have one?"

I then paused for a brief moment as I noticed the approach of my station. Before my arrival, I was eager to tell him of my opinion of ascetics or sadhus. I then said in a well-balanced and measured tone, "Do you know how you people are such a burden on the state's economic structure? This economy sustains you. We, the taxpayers, are paying for your food and fantasies, and you people have zero productivity and contribute absolutely nothing for the growth of the state or society. Instead, you people are escapists who have run away from human and social respon-sibilities and are hiding in jungles and mountains. Whatever you are doing in your god-damn hiding places, it is completely for your own selfish interests. Once in a while, you crawl out of your burrows and exploit the religious emotions of innocent and gullible people."

As I was walking towards the carriage door, I hurled, "To hell with you!" Then I walked off the train.

∞∞∞∞

Exactly three months later, there was a knock on my door. Upon opening it, I was confronted with an ascetic. Lifting his folded hands, he politely said, "Namaste."

I instantly recognized this man to be the one I had encountered on the train three months earlier.

Trying to be friendly, the man asked, "Do you recognize me?"

I replied, "Of course I do. You are the same guy I met on the train. What brings you here? Was the blasting on the train not enough for you?"

For the first time, I saw him smiling. "That was quite a lot. I am not here to take any more of that," he said. "I have something more important to tell you."

I replied, "I'm sorry. I don't have time for you people."

Then just as I was going to close the door on him, he stopped me with an impatient gesture and said, "Listen, my guru has sent me to fetch you."

It was my turn to smile. "Oh, so you also have a guru! What does he have to do with me?"

"I don't know, but he wants you to come to our ashram at once. He thinks it is time you came."

"I am not at all interested in your guru and his reasons." I finally told him to get lost and leave me alone.

Later that day, I found the man sitting under a tree a short distance from where I was staying. Even though he was looking in my direction, I ignored him and went my own way. The next day I needed to go out of town. Returning after two days, I found the man sitting in the same position, under the same tree.

He stood up as I approached him and asked me politely, "Have you changed your mind about going with me to the ashram?"

I replied, "No! Why are you still here?"

His answer irritated me. "I am waiting for you."

I told him in a matter-of-fact way, "You can wait here until you die. I am still not coming with you. Secondly, waiting for me in this way is beginning to make me feel very uncomfortable, so kindly go away somewhere else and die peacefully."

He got up and started to walk towards the end of the street.

I spoke loudly from behind, "If you ever appear by my house again, I will hand you over to the police."

He carried on walking without looking back. A few days later, I spotted him near a bus stop further down the street. I went up to him and asked, "Why are you still here? How long can you afford to stay here like this? How much longer do you think your money will last?"

He replied softly, "I don't need money to wait for you, and I didn't come here with any money."

"In that case," I said, "how are you surviving? What are you eating?"

Without a quiver in his voice he answered, "I have not eaten since I have been here." After a moment's pause, he continued, "I had decided not to eat until I get you to my ashram."

I thought this was some kind of emotional blackmail so I hurried away from him.

I could not concentrate for the rest of the day, as dozens of questions bounced inside my head. It was too much to believe that this man was so determined to take me. Had he really not eaten in the last seven days? What if this fellow dies of starvation whilst waiting for me?

The thought that he was suffering for my sake made me feel very uncomfortable. Apprehension began to give way to anticipation. Maybe his invitation held the key to a real opportunity of a lifetime. I did not sleep a wink that night, as my perception about the real meaning of his presence suddenly changed. I became restless as I wondered what a loss it would be if he actually decided to go away. I also began to feel guilty and rotten about myself causing him to suffer starvation for seven days. I took a strong resolve to give him food first thing in the morning and discuss his invitation in a more rational and realistic manner.

After tossing and turning in bed for the rest of the night, I ran to meet him at the first sight of daylight.

"I am so sorry to have kept you hungry for all these days," I said in a miserable tone. "Please come with me and have some food, and let's discuss about going to your ashram."

He looked skywards with a sense of relief and gratitude in his eyes and brought his palms together as a mark of respect to some invisible presence. He then said in a gentle voice, "Never mind about my hunger. Just let me know how soon you can be ready to go."

He politely declined all my attempts to give him food, and as I had no other apparent reasons not to go with him, a few hours later we were in a train to Delhi. From there this old ascetic was to take me somewhere into the deep remoteness of the Himalayas where his ashram was located.

During the journey I was feeling truly grateful and entirely attracted towards him. It was not at all difficult to strike up a conversation about himself or his ashram. His name was Kripanand Saraswati, a naga sadhu by initiation, and he belonged to the Saraswati sect of the *Dasanami Sastradhari Naga* community.

The guru he was taking about was Yogi Angadanand Saraswati. He revealed that his lineage of teaching could be as old as the 4th century. They are a sect of yogis who are highly analytical and disciplined in the practice of the science of Yoga. Unlike various other religious cults, they do not observe any meaningless rituals which, in their belief, take away the true substance of knowledge. They consider the science of Yoga to be truly sacred and divine. Apart from practising the purest and time-tested equations of Yoga, they also strive to preserve the purity and sanctity of the science as a divine responsibility.

Four days later, I found myself walking along a path across meadows and glaciers. In spite of my high level of fitness, I was quite tired and breathless, but Kripanand showed no sign of fatigue or distress as we ascended higher and higher into the mountains. After almost two days and twenty hours of trekking, we entered into a small horseshoe-shaped nook that housed the ashram.

Pointing to a small waterfall, Kripanand stated, "This is the origin of the river Saraswati. Saraswati is the goddess of knowledge and learning in hindu mythology. This sect of sadhus is named after goddess Saraswati because they practise no other religion but knowledge."

As we came into clear view of the ashram, Kripanand paused and asked me to go directly ahead and enter a cave.

I asked him, "Are you not coming?"

He smiled and replied, "No, maybe I will take some food after all these days of waiting."

I took a quick glance around to get a feel for the place. I found many ascetics at various stages of activity that all paused to gape at me. As our eyes met they all raised their folded hands as a mark of respect. I continued my walk and entered the cave that Kripanand had pointed out.

Entering the cave, I found a lean, athletically built old man standing with his back towards me. He was holding a book in his hand, and without even turning or looking in my direction, he said in a pleasant voice, "Yogi Manmoyanand, you made us wait for such a long time."

He turned towards me as I took a step forward. As soon as I met his gaze I asked, "What is the meaning of getting me here in this way?"

With a smiling and graceful manner he told me, "You must be very tired. Please have your food and then rest for a while. Don't worry. I will still be here to answer all your questions."

The night in the mountains was cold and breezy. In spite of my tiredness, I still found it difficult to sleep. I was very uncomfortable rolled in a coarse blanket lying on the hard stone floor of the cave. A throbbing headache due to the high altitude worsened my situation. Towards the end of the night, I somehow fell asleep. When I woke up it was already late morning, and my eyes opened to glimpse the dazzling sunshine.

I came out of the cave and had a good look around. I noticed a fairly large-sized crowd of ascetics sitting in a congregation and listening to the guru. I walked around the ashram area enjoying the fabulous views. Snow-peaked mountains were in all directions. This part of the Himalayas primarily contained three

**The birthplace of Saraswati river that
lends its name to the lineage.**

distinct colors, all bright, vibrant and warm: the white of the snow, the blue of the sky and the orange robes of the ascetics.

Around midday the teaching ended, and I followed the guru to his cave. He made me sit in front of him and started to talk to me in a grandfatherly-like manner. Seeing so much love and affection from a face that highly radiated knowledge and wisdom softened my stance.

"My dear young yogi, if I had not arranged to get you here, how do you think you would have embarked upon the journey towards consciousness? For you never knew who you are or where your destiny lies in wait for you."

I felt the heavy impact of each word, but managed to reply,

"Do you mean to say that you know where my destiny awaits? And, who gave you the authority to grab control of my life?"

He began to explain at length how every yogi of his lineage owes a responsibility to his teacher to find spiritually ripe seekers and give them proper guidance and knowledge. He further stated how he was simply delivering his responsibility by extending his guidance and knowledge to me, absolutely free from any personal expectation.

This definitely surprised me, so I asked him, "What made you think that I could be the one you are looking for?"

He replied that he was not looking for anyone in particular, but had perceived my existence and conditions the moment he felt my exchange with Kripanand in the train. He had asked Kripanand to go back and fetch me as soon as Kripanand had returned to the ashram. He asked me not to bother my head about how he knew of my whereabouts, as he concluded by saying, "Yogis simply know everything."

This was to be the first time I would reel under the weight of a spiritual adversary. In my opinion, he was either a truly enlightened one or a highly crafty pretender. Many years of so-called spiritual searching with its futilities and reflections made me think that he could only be a pretender. Even though each of his words made perfect sense, due to my heavy preconditioning I still could not accept the fact that they could all be genuine. I braced myself for the ultimate intellectual wrestling match with this guru.

What followed for the next six months was a clash between enlightened wisdom and, what I would call today, 'university-educated pride'. This man had unlimited patience, tolerance, information and wisdom, unlike any other specimen I had encountered in my life. Nothing affected him, no matter what kind of question or insult I projected onto him. Despite all my efforts, I could not dent his ego because he simply didn't have one. He was forever ready to answer any of my questions, at any time of the day or night. I was beginning to feel that he could not be human, as I had never seen him eat or sleep.

I rarely attended any of the guru's discourses, but whenever I did, I popped in numerous questions in the midst of an explanation or flow. My undisciplined brat behavior was never desisted. The more I grappled with the unsurpassed knowledge of the guru, the more I realized the substance of his teaching, and subsequently my stupidity. Every encounter with him gave rise to deep contemplation, and I would always conclude that he was right in his proof. But the brat in me always found some insult or another to hurl at him. I was becoming aware that I was gradually losing the intellectual battle. I felt like a fool who always tried to swim against the current. In the past I was able to swim against the current because my ego was too powerful. What I was experiencing here was the complete opposite. The prevailing flow not only defeated me by crushing my ego, it also sustained me. Drifting in the bliss of surrender, I finally decided to let go.

The next day I was quietly and obediently participating in the ashram activities, surprising everyone as I attended the classes and discourses without being a nuisance. At the end of the discourse, the guru asked me to follow him to his cave. When seated in front of him, he said, "Why did you not ask any questions today?"

"I have no questions."

"Do you not have at least one argument or insult to throw at me?"

"No."

"Do you have absolutely nothing to ask?"

"No."

After a few moments of silence, he asked, "Do you want to go home?"

I replied, "No."

Without looking at him, tears began rolling down my face. The guru then looked out of the cave to call Kripanand.

As he arrived, he introduced me to him and said, "Kripanand, here is your student."

The old ascetic, who I had crushed with my ego and arrogance several months earlier, led me away by holding my hand into the world of absolute knowledge and enlightenment.

CHAPTER TWO

The Last Line of Truth

It was a beautiful evening, and a cold but soothing breeze was blowing in from Tibet. Sitting on a piece of rock I was completely immersed in my surroundings. Looking skywards I noticed that the stars appeared to be much closer here than anywhere else I had seen before. It gave the impression that I was right amongst them, and the closeness bestowed a pleasant sensation. I naturally began to wonder about the possible reasons for this phenomenon. My mind darted back to academic physics to find some kind of explanation. Then, as if appearing out of nowhere, Kripanand was sitting next to me.

"What are you wondering about?" he asked. I related my query and its rationalization by the law of physics. I explained that at such an altitude, because of the low density of air and absence of dust, smoke and other air pollutants, we were able to see the stars without much obstruction. He acknowledged my answer and offered his interpretation. I was obviously intrigued to know if there could be an alternative explanation beyond that of physics.

With a rising smile he said, "People elsewhere rarely perceive the stars, planets or the entire cosmos as a part of themselves. While you are here, you will naturally begin to look at the cosmos from an entirely different viewpoint. Here you perceive the cosmos only as an extension of your own physical self. Hence the stars do not appear so far to us."

This insightful and profound explanation jolted me thoroughly, but I still demanded to be prescribed a more scientific explanation than a philosophical one. He burst out laughing, and whilst putting his hand on my back, he affectionately uttered, "*Prakriti naiva muchyate*," (one's inherent character never changes). This can also be commonly translated as 'Once an idiot, always an idiot'.

He then asked me, "Do you know what a DNA is?"

"Yes. I know."

"Can you tell me what the length of one DNA code is?"

"About eight meters."

He further explained, "If you stitch the DNAs of one human body together, it can actually reach all the way up to the sun and back eight hundred times. And do you know why it is so long? Because it contains the complete data of your entire evolutionary history, which proves the whole process of evolution was but one continuous chain of consciousness."

Incredulously I said, "But I was not present through these millions of years of evolution."

He replied with an insightful recital from the Bhagavad Gita,

" 'Na tvevaham jatu nasam, Na tvam neme janadhipah, Na caiva na bhavisyamah, Sarve vayam atah param'. "

(It is a fact that there never was a time when you or these kings did not exist, nor is it a fact that hereafter we shall all cease to exist. – 2:12)

He continued by saying, "If you were not present, then how do you think your DNA contains so much information about your evolutionary process?"

I was not only speechless, but also perplexed by the phenomenal blend of spiritual philosophy and scientific fact that was being expounded. The secrets of evolution were being revealed before me in an irrefutable flow of fact and logic.

The whole evolutionary story started at a very precise moment thirteen thousand million years ago. In its first billionth of a second, the hot expanding universe was a primordial soup of scores of types of particles that varied enormously in their properties. The quarks started combining to form protons and neutrons. One down, two up movements created a proton, and one up, two down formed a neutron. Within one hundred eighty seconds, the proton and neutron collisions formed the atomic nuclei of some of the most original elements. In the next three thousand years, protons and helium nuclei created hydrogen and helium atoms by capturing more and more electrons. After such a precise elucidation from Kripanand, understanding the rest of the evolutionary process was a comparatively easy task.

Planet Earth was formed four thousand, five hundred million years ago. After another five hundred million years, life forms were created. Beginning from a unicellular organism, nature managed to create gigantic dinosaurs. This exact and precise scientific fact of evolution was not sufficient for my ever-questioning mind. I was forever intrigued about an unknown something which was behind everything.

Kripanand then asked, "Prior to the Big Bang, what do you think existed?" Seeing my bewilderment, he offered, "Something cannot be created out of nothing."

I agreed to this because I was aware that matter could not be created and could not be destroyed. This is a scientific truth. Hence, it is irrefutable logic that prior to the creation of every-thing, everything existed in a non-physical and un-manifested form. Kripanand described that state as 'the purest and un-manifested state of consciousness'.

He further explicated its characteristics. "An all-pervading state of nothing and everything, without a beginning or an end, the start and end points of infinite cycles of evolution and an absolute state of knowledge and energy."

In complete awe of his illumination, I enquired, "Can I call it God?"

Kripanand smiled and reminded me of my previous comments on God, when I had once said, 'God, the bastard, does not exist!'

He suggested, "Let us start our journey without the bias of any religious notion."

I immediately interrupted, "Do you mean to say that God is merely a religious notion?"

In an assuring manner he replied, "Have patience my boy. Soon you will realize it."

I asked him to wait for a moment so I could run and collect my notepad and pen. I was eager to take necessary notes of what I considered to be 'knowledge that defies all reasoning'.

This pure state of consciousness has two characteristics: one is the cause of the entire physical manifestation, and the other part is the intelligence that lies behind it. These two characteristics are regarded as the masculine and feminine aspects of the divine. The union or interplay between these two elements is in fact the process of evolution. They are called *purusha*, the masculine and *prakriti*, the feminine. The first and foremost creation in this divine intervention is *buddhi* (cognitive awareness). It is this cognitive awareness that is the same cause behind the creation of the ego, and the three manifestations of this ego are the *gunas* (qualities) known as *rajas*, *tamas* and *sattva*. The interplay of the natural forces accordingly unfolds.

The fusion of *raja* and *sattva gunas* manifested the five senses and their corresponding organs. The fusion of *tama* and *sattva gunas* formed the five *tanmatras* (cognitive faculties), which in turn created the *panchamahabhutas* or the five great elements – earth, water, fire, air and space. Modern science explains these five great elements in an array of one hundred seventeen elements. Hence, the gross or physical body was created for the sole purpose of interaction between the gross and subtle elements of the universe.

Cognitive awareness, ego and the five cognitive faculties are all causes in nature and effects in behavior. After the manifestation of the species, the absolute divine consciousness did not become lost, but continues to live within the dimensions of the twenty-four entities: that of the mind, ten sense organs, five sense objects and the *prakriti* consisting of eight other faculties (*avyakta, mahat, ahankara* and the five *tanmatras*).

The divine consciousness that is present within the twenty-four entities is described in a variety of terms by different philosophical schools. It is often termed as *jiva, atma, jivatma,* or the individual soul. The use of these different terms merely refers to the supreme consciousness, which is present in the gross body and does not refer to an entirely new entity or form. It is this divine presence of consciousness in the species that regulates and determines its relationship with the entire universe and causes the further unfoldment of consciousness in the species known as evolution. In other words, the process of evolution is the gradual unfoldment of consciousness. After the creation of the first living organism, consciousness further evolved and created many more species with a wider range of characteristics.

A close observation of the evolution of the species reveals a significant trend, witnessing the gigantic species with limited intelligence at one extreme and human beings with extremely high intelligence at the other extreme. The evolutionary process of down-sizing the physical elements is accompanied with a corresponding development of intellectual substance. This peculiar trend gives us a clear indication of the ultimate purpose of evolution. This conclusion is not derived merely out of logic; it is also scientifically proven. The whole trend of evolution is available in our subtle memory, as the entire data is recorded in every minute cell of our body. Secondly, we relive the entire process of evolution every time we undergo gestation inside the mother's womb.

As Kripanand continued explaining the evolutionary process, I thought back to when I was a child and suddenly realized the true reason behind all the penis worshipping. I wanted to confirm my understanding of this, so I interrupted and asked him in a much simpler way, "Does the whole creation and evolutionary process get re-enacted every time a man and woman have sexual intercourse and give birth to a baby?"

"Yes, you could say that, as it always takes the masculine *purusha* and the feminine *prakriti* to interplay and cause the Big Bang. Do you understand what I mean?"

I nodded and said, "Yes."

He then went on to say, "After the Big Bang, the feminine *prakriti*, being impregnated by the seed of creation, goes on manifesting itself into a baby. In the mother's womb the ova, a unicellular organism, gradually transforms into an aquatic form of life. This then continues to develop into an amphibian, a reptile, a quadruped mammal and finally emerges as a fully developed human baby."

During the last four thousand million years, nature has brought us from the unicellular organism to our present state. As we have seen, the intention of nature is to arrive at a point where species are characterized by their evolved consciousness rather than by their limited physical dimensions and characteristics. Merely by birth, human beings do not become the ultimate species of evolution, as they are still required to undergo further unfoldment of consciousness. Hence, a true human being is one who is aware of his evolutionary status and strives to move forward in the same direction as the evolution of supreme consciousness. The one who is born as a human being, but is not aware of his evolutionary position nor recognizes the evolutionary direction, and identifies himself with the gross and physical characteristics, is merely a lesser species in a human body; it is not the body but the awareness that determines the species.

The last few lines of Kripanand's explanation were too much for me to comprehend, let alone digest. I was not ready to believe how the physical characteristics of a human being were not enough to be defined as a human. Was there no other difference between a human being and an animal?

He answered, "No! I will try and explain to you the differences between a body-centric existence from one that is characterized by awareness."

Pausing to gather his thoughts, he then elucidated, "Anyone who has a body and identifies himself as the body spends his lifetime for the preservation, glorification and gratification of the body. One's mode of life is constantly determined and limited to food, sleep, fear and sex. When one is born as a human being and yet is perpetually concerned with these four considerations, he is only an animal.

To make this clear, let's look at the activities of an animal. What are the most important concerns of an animal? Firstly, it constantly wanders for food. Secondly, it sleeps wherever and whenever it feels tired since it has no other use of its time. Thirdly, it lives a life full of perpetual fear and does everything from a viewpoint of insecurity. Lastly, it does not have any control over its own sexual behavior as it knows no decency or purpose of pro-creation. If a man lives life in this way, is he any different from an animal?"

Perplexed by his explanation I asked, "How then does a human being come to know that he is a human being? And who teaches him about human behavior?"

"Every time one is born as a human being, one undergoes certain physical, mental and spiritual changes during a lifetime. After a person lives a conscious life without the animalistic considerations, he moves forward in the evolutionary direction. At the end of the lifespan, all those changes which are physical in nature finish with the death of the body. But there is a certain part of us which is death-less. All the unfoldments of consciousness move forward and manifest again in a new body; this is what we call rebirth. At every rebirth, one is born with the collective spiritual unfoldment of all their previous lives. Their 'spiritual account' becomes bigger and bigger, and one naturally develops the insight and quest of a spiritually conscious being. The forces of consciousness are so strong that no one can resist its consequences."

Looking up at me Kripanand asked, "Take a look at your own life. Did someone teach you your spiritual behavior? Why do you think you are so desperate for self-realization? The only explanation is that you have spent many a lifetime acquiring and accumulating spiritual growth, and no one in your condition can rest in peace until they achieve the final stage of evolution."

Each of his words contained so much truth and relevance. I began to feel so fortunate and privileged, as the biggest mystery that I could never quite understand about myself suddenly was no more.

Reflecting upon my own journey prior to entering the ashram, I recalled the intense restlessness from trying to discover the mysteries of myself. I slowly began to wonder about the fate of other desperate seekers like me. I was sure there were many more people struggling with the force of their spiritual hunger. What about them? How would they ever find an explanation or guidance? I was eager to be in Kripanand's presence again, so that I could pile all my accumulating questions before him. As I started to describe my concern, he seemed pleased that my spiritual hunger extended beyond myself.

After I voiced my apprehensions, he smiled and said, "A symptom of a true yogi is the concern he has for others."

He went on to reveal, "The spiritual account of a person, which is called the *prabajya*, becomes bigger and bigger and generates a resonance at a very high psychic level. Accomplished gurus can perceive this resonance and are able to identify the person behind it. Every time a guru finds such a seeker, he extends his support and guidance as part of his divine responsibility. In the tradition of yogis, it is always the guru who finds his disciple, not the other way round. In order to choose his teacher, a student has to be more competent and accomplished than the teacher himself, which is by no means possible. Hence, all that an aspiring student can do is to allow the teacher to choose him, instead of wasting time judging a teacher."

Whenever such an aspirant faces an 'ism', religion or practice that does not match his own flow, there develops a clash of forces. After a brief struggle, the aspirant naturally rides over these obstacles and once again moves in the correct direction. Such times are essential for the transformation of a seeker. Many aspirants delve into the wrong company and become susceptible to the exploits of false gurus, or alternatively pursue temporary bliss by the experiments of unhealthy drugs or other damaging hallucinogenic substances.

∞∞∞

I was by far the youngest disciple of the ashram when I started my practices. My guru and other senior teachers turned out to be absolute geniuses, as they possessed the answers and explanations to every question that I could think of. In the ashram there were many ascetics practising various subjects and disciplines, focusing mainly on *Sankhya*, *Vedanta* and Yoga, with Yoga being the primary thrust of practice. Along with our main subjects, we were given teachings and discourses on a variety of other relevant subjects; it was astounding to receive teachings ranging from astrology to microbiology from the same man.

Before the initiation of my practice, my guru had called me to his cave to explain the intricate details of my *prabajya*. He provided me with a surprising account of my past-life activities which accurately reflected the course of my present life and behavior. As my guru continued to expound upon my spiritual compatibilities with the intended practice, I suddenly interrupted him by exclaiming, "I want to do Yoga!"

He paused for a brief moment, before asking in a mischievous manner, "Why do you want to do Yoga?"

Until this moment, I had never attempted to define my exact purpose of spiritual practice, but I managed to somehow intuit an answer. "I want to read all the books that have ever been written or are going to be written, I want to listen to all the teachers, those who have spoken or are going to speak, and I want all that knowledge in this lifetime!"

My guru's face illuminated, as he seemed more than satisfied with my answer. In a very loving voice he declared, "We are going to teach you Yoga, and I would like to see you develop into a fine yogi."

I felt like a little child that had suddenly received the biggest chocolate bar in the world!

There were seven of us in total sitting in a semi-circle around Yogi Nirupanand, another one of the masters of the ashram. There were so many stories that I had heard about this guru, and the other ashram-ites treated him with great respect and fear. However I never found anything ferocious about him, as he was as friendly and fluid as Guru Angadanand. He was originally a tantrist who had mastered numerous *vidyas* and *sadhanas*, and he was said to have the power to invoke various kinds of divine or lesser spirits. Someone told me that he had once turned a man into a dog. Nirupanand was also said to be the human embodiment of all the tantric and yogic *siddhis*, or super-human capacities.

This was my first experience listening to Nirupanand who was also regarded as a great scientific exponent. He was about to explain the development of spiritual science and the birth of Yoga.

"Spiritual science is the study and realization of the natural process of the evolution of consciousness. After the complete understanding of this process, whenever we use our psycho-physical resources as tools to invoke and accelerate the process of unfoldment of consciousness within our own body, we describe this as the 'practice of spirituality'. The beginning of this practice is voluntary in nature as the gross elements of the body are at play. Gradually the practitioner learns to go into the more subtle elements deep within and accordingly enters into an involuntary or spontaneous state. This spontaneous state can be expressed as the state of Meditation. At this stage the practitioner experiences the finer and subtler elements which are free from the afflictions of the gross or physical body."

The physical or voluntary practice of the *sadhana* is called *kriya*, which literally means 'to act upon'. The exact dynamics of the *kriya* can be explained in terms of modern science. The human body is a miniature form of the universe and is built with the same matter of which the universe is made. It is also operated with the help of the same energy that operates the universe. Its direction and evolution are determined by the same intelligence as that of the universe, and it lives by the means of the same consciousness as the universe.

The physical arrangement of the cosmos and the astronomical arrangement of the body are identical in nature. Different civilizations have demonstrated clear understanding of these facts. From the earliest of times, the spiritual temperament of people has been observed and identified. Great minds created particular practices or rituals in order to perform this *kriya*. The nature of the practice was dependent upon the dimensions of their knowledge. In India, people have worshipped the union of the *purusha* and *prakriti* through the symbolism of the *lingam* and *yoni*. Other early civilizations showed great appreciation regarding the process of creation.

The spinal cord of the body was identified as the primary energy axis of the universe. At the north of the axis in the body lies the masculine *purusha* called the *ojas*, and on the southern extreme lies the feminine *prakriti* called the *kundalini*. Under the most correct conditions, the union of these forces completes the primordial energy circuit, the result of which causes a Big Bang-like reaction to be experienced in the body. This reaction primarily was used as a launch pad to enter into the pure state of consciousness.

This demonstrates the dynamics of the early tantric rituals. The practitioners of Tantra had to choose their partners with extreme care on the basis of their sexual, spiritual and evolutionary characteristics. The male-dominated and female-dominated tantric rituals gradually evolved into two distinct sects. The male-dominated sect came to be known as the *shaivites*, and the female-dominated sect developed into the *saktas*. In spite of their differences in practice, the central idea of tantric philosophy remained the same. However, undergoing developmental changes for thousands of years, the true essence of the practice has become noticeably dissolute.

Apart from the tantric ritualism, the ancient civilizations gifted us with the powerful philosophy that would explain the mysteries of the universe and its relationship with the human psyche. Lord Kapil, the father of *Sankhya* philosophy, had already explicated the oneness of the universal and individual consciousness. *Sankhya* philosophy had prevailed over most of the ancient explanations of the universe, not only illuminating the presence of universal consciousness within man, but also formulating ways and means to invoke the supreme soul within oneself.

Certain contemplative and meditative practices were devised to invoke and integrate the cosmic consciousness within oneself. The practice which aimed to achieve the union (*Yog*) between the individual self and the cosmic consciousness came to be known as 'Yoga'. Meanwhile, the tantric practice of uniting the two ends of the primordial energy axis also came to be termed as 'Yoga'. *Sankhya*, in its own way, was explaining the cosmic nature of the individual and sought complete awareness within oneself, while

Tantra prescribed the experimental details to accomplish the same. By means of a beautiful synthesis of the *Sankhya* philosophy and the tantric practices, a new system of practice was born, complete both in the provisions of philosophical explanation and practical application. The authenticity of this new practice was soon categorized and taught by various ancient philosophical scholars. The *Upanishads* described this practice as *Shadanga Yog*, which literally means 'Yoga of six limbs'.

The two thousand year *vedantic* period witnessed further implementation of these yogic practices and went on to form the basis of all spiritual and religious systems. No matter what spiritual or religious thought and practice we see in the world today, it is only the modern and often distorted adaptation of that fine and original *Shadanga Yog*. During the third century BC, Maharshi Patanjali formulated the first comprehensive practice manual by integrating all the available and absolute substances of Yoga. This text was compiled in the mode of sutras, or aphorisms. A microscopic examination of the Yoga Sutras reveals, not merely the anatomy, but also the genetics of all the religious and spiritual practices of the world.

After coming face-to-face with the stark reality of the all-pervading equation of Yoga, I was thrown into a state of confusion, and something began to revolt in me again. How dare somebody claim Yoga to be the last line of truth! Until now I had experienced several different kinds of practices and to some degree, had experienced their relative validity. Therefore I was certainly not ready to accept an apparent silly practice of gymnastics and gyrations to be the absolute process to self-realization. Nevertheless I decided to keep my questions and reservations in my mind. There were two reasons for my silence: firstly, I had an inclination and a strong feeling that the answer would somehow manifest itself at a later period of my practice, and secondly, due to my deep growing respect towards the teachers. Needless to say, I did not quite have the courage to challenge the so-called ferocious Nirupanand.

The next day I was not allowed to attend the discourse of Nirupanand. Instead my guru wanted to have a word with me. I went to my guru's cave as requested, but admittedly I was in a hurry to get away from him to attend the discourse. My guru perceived my eagerness and immediately told me to relax, and as if reading my mind, he avowed, "There is no purpose in listening to the discourse if one is not mentally prepared for it. And besides, why don't you, without fear, tell me your difficulties."

Seeing my hesitation, he said with affection, "My dear young yogi, never fear to ask when your mind is in doubt. Do not be afraid if it is your guru or God that is before you. Without asking, you get nowhere. As you know, we all are here for the same objective, the realization of the supreme knowledge. How do you expect to move forward on this path if you fear to ask? Do not think that your questions will embarrass the teacher. Do you know why? No true teacher identifies himself with his teaching. No one owns knowledge, and no one can possibly own knowledge.

Knowledge is a manifestation of supreme consciousness, and wherever there is a manifestation of the divine, you will have knowledge. A teacher is only a channel who guides you to become another channel of knowledge. My job is to introduce you to your true inner self, and there cannot be a better teacher than one whose objective is simply that. To be a teacher, all you need to do is to connect to the higher realms of consciousness. If you think your questions will embarrass your teacher, you are, in a way, insulting the teacher. Remember that the human mind is not only the final product of evolution, but also in itself a manifestation of the Divine. It is the answers that can be silly, but never the questions."

Guru Angadanand continued, "The second most important

lesson is to not allow yourself to be restricted within your precon-ceived notions while you are approaching the vast ocean of knowledge. I respect and recognize your years of struggle and efforts, but please do not permit your preconditioning to be an impediment to the way of your learning. I can perceive your mental turbulences, and I can recognize your doubts regarding the efficacy of Yoga. My dear yogi, so far you have not seen anything more than a few physical and breathing exercises. What makes you possibly think that Yoga is all about doing exercises and breath manipulations?"

By then I had already realized the futility of hiding any questions from my guru, as he seemed to know every complexity and instability in my mind. Since I had already made myself completely open to his teachings, I decided to ask anything and everything that would surface in my mind.

"The asanas and *pranayamas* in my experience were useless. Are they the absolute path to self-realization?"

My guru answered patiently, "Asanas and *pranayamas* form only a small part of the complete Yoga system. Practices of these alone do not contain the capacity to take you to a state of pure consciousness. Besides, at what point in your life do you think that you have done any asanas or *pranayamas*?"

I gave him a long list of my experiences of doing a multitude of asanas and *pranayamas*. My guru laughed innocently and said, "Never mind about your previous practices. Instead pay attention to your present training, and soon you will realize the differences between asanas and exercises."

I knew from that moment I was in for a big surprise.

∞∞∞∞

As the years passed by, my questions gradually disappeared. I came to realize that Yoga is a path more profound than any form of gymnastic fitness. Before coming to the ashram, I had some funny notions about Yoga symptomatic of what I had already been exposed to and taught. All my previous teachers placed great emphasis on the therapeutic values of yogasanas. The asanas were identified on the basis of the disease they supposedly cured and no other. My former teachers had also held the belief that asana in some way or another develops spiritual awareness. But all of them failed to describe in what way the spiritual element was available inside an asana.

The whole of yoga practice, as per my previous notions, was broadly divided into three distinct divisions. The major and most practised part was 'asana', in conjunction with some 'bandhas' and 'mudras'; its aim and objective was to attain physical fitness, relaxation and freedom from common diseases. The persons practising these asanas were generally obese and stressed individuals, and doing some yoga was very much limited to part of their weekend activities, akin to a hobby like weekend fishing, etc. For such a clientele, going to a yoga class once in a while earned them social respect and provided a worthy subject of discussion in pubs and bars. These image-conscious consumers had a natural tendency to opt for any yoga or guru who was the fastest, latest or richest on the scene. It is such people who have sustained the yoga products industry. Their yoga practice is not identified by spiritual growth, but instead by the brand of their yoga mat, yoga bag and all the new and latest yoga fashions. It had always intrigued me, 'Does the successful practice of asanas require a glittering air-conditioned studio or being clothed in next-to-nothing?'

The second division of yoga practice consisted of a slightly smaller group of individuals practising 'pranayamas'. In my notion, it was supposed to be the most powerful yogic ritual. Pranayama, as I had seen, was the tampering of one's own breathing process in a variety of fashionable ways. Some teachers taught the importance of providing more oxygen to the body by an increased and complete breathing activity, while some others emphasized the method of the reduction in breathing to prolong one's life span. With these contradictory opinions, who was I to believe? To some extent, it made sense that the higher and more appropriate supply of oxygen to the body was for decarbonizing the blood; indeed, an increased supply of oxygen, the foremost requirement of every blood cell, is a welcome practice. On the other hand, what is the use, if increasing the number of breaths reduces one's life span?

On countless occasions I had asked about the true nature of *Pranayama*. What I commonly received as an answer was that oxygen is *prana* (life-force), and the most rational control (*yama*) of it is *pranayama*. But no one had been able to clarify in what way less number of breaths can promise a longer life.

All justifications received on this topic were highly conflicting and ambiguous. Nevertheless, a fairly large quantity of people practised this breath-tampering exercise, and the chief reason for many to continue was to gain relief from stress. Many 'gurus' have explained the miraculous health effects of the '*pranayamas*'. On one occasion a famous 'guru' in India, whilst appearing in a television show, had promised cure from ailments like diabetes, hypertension, insomnia, etc. Even some of the younger generation practise '*pranayama*' in the belief that its effects will give them better concentration and focus in study, work and even sex.

The third type of training, which an even smaller number of people practise, is 'meditation'. My understanding of meditation had previously been accumulated from some of the most famous yoga teachers of India. One of the professed masters of yoga, while throwing some light on *pranayama*, explains the importance of sitting correctly. In dozens of different ways he explains and illustrates how to sit in the lotus pose to practise the 'art of meditation'. While under his training, I could never understand how to replicate his sitting posture, with buttocks and thighs firmly and evenly placed on the ground, but without having both knees touching the ground. After elucidating this impossible sitting posture in geometric detail and giving all its prior formalities, he then offers no suggestion as to what the student should do thereafter. Meditation is then said to be successful, and the state of awareness is achieved when one sits in this 'great' posture and struggles for half an hour against the physical discomforts and mental conflicts.

Once a friend explained to me how practising meditation had benefited him. "Meditation is amazing. Initially, I always thought about the pretty girl next door whenever I sat in meditation. But after persistent practice I had successfully driven the thought of her out of my mind."

I asked him what he now thought of during meditation. He replied, "I think about the burden of my loans and taxes."

After numerous examples of similar eccentric meditation practices, I decided to create my own illustration. The whole hoax about meditation can be compared to a beautiful children's story.

Once upon a time, two cheats came to a king posing as dressmakers. They told the king that they had invented a fabric which only the wise were able to see. Since there are not many wise people around, they decided that the king would be the most worthy person, and if the king accepts, they would happily make a dress for him. The king took it as an opportunity to distinguish the wise from the fools in his kingdom. He ordered the cheats to make a dress for him and paid a huge amount towards the cost of the material.

After a week, the cheats returned with the magical dress. They said it would be appropriate if they dressed the king themselves. As the king agreed, they stripped him of his last thread, and then in an elaborate manner began to 'dress' the king with nothing in their hands. While doing so they described and praised the grace and delicacy of the dress. The king was confused as he saw that there was no dress, but he did not dare to ask a question since the material was visible only to the wise, and he was in no way ready to accept himself as a fool. The cheats completed dressing the king with the magic dress, and the king expressed his satisfaction about the quality of the dress.

The king walked into his court, and everyone was shocked to see the king completely naked. The king smiled to himself about his little trick and declared, "Fools cannot see my dress. Only the wise can appreciate it."

He instantly received a standing ovation, accepting hundreds of compliments about the regal beauty of the dress. No one in the court wanted to be singled out as a fool. Before the cheats left, they received a huge sum of money as remuneration and reward.

Satisfied with his proven wisdom, the king decided to appear in public with his magical dress. A grand parade was arranged. Sitting on a glittering and fantastically decorated elephant, the king roamed the streets of his kingdom. Everybody saw that the king was stark naked, but no one wanted to be branded a fool, so they all praised the dress and derived happiness and satisfaction from being wise. The king was immensely happy for being wise and being the ruler of a wise kingdom. That was until a small boy started to laugh from the crowd. This made the king furious, and he ordered the boy to be brought to him at once. The boy told the king that he was completely naked, and he did not mind being called a fool when he could not actually see any dress on the king. The king immediately realized his own folly. It takes only one small sincere and honest statement to disillusion a whole kingdom of fools, including the king himself.

Analogous to the story, no one in the world of meditation is prepared to accept and be labeled 'unspiritual' or a 'fool'. Hence everybody is found glorifying the 'magical' effects of meditation, which in most people's reality is no more than half an hour of struggle, discomfort, confusion and anticipation in waiting for the ordeal to come to an end.

For so many years in my life I had imitated only the apparent aspects of Yoga. On no occasion had anyone adequately explained the true nature of the practice of Yoga, which was now beginning to unfold. The biggest mistake that is being committed is directing the practice of yoga for the development of the body and its physical attributes. If the practices are aimed at the body, the practitioner acquires only physical effects, and in the process, the practice gets reduced to a mere form of exercise. It is only when a student aims towards the spiritual benefits that he attempts to derive the spiritual elements from the practice. These spiritual elements hold the key to spiritual transformation and growth.

A physical practice for a physical benefit is something that everyone knows, but a physical practice for a spiritual outcome is the unknown secret of Yoga. Since the body is only a material manifestation of the supreme consciousness and the supreme consciousness itself is very much present in the body, there has to be a way to bridge the gap between the physical body and the spiritual self. After years of struggle within the limitations of the body-centric practices, I was beginning to see this hidden bridge.

This bridge lies across five great barriers. In order to be united with the supreme consciousness, every individual has to battle their way through these barriers. Let us take the example of an impregnable fort, using the fort as a metaphor for the body.

The fort has five barriers of security. Each of these security barriers are unique in nature and need a specific skill or weapon to break through. Our objective lies beyond these five barriers. There are three extremely necessary elements to acquire before a successful breakthrough: the first is the correct tool or weaponry; the second is the correct training and skill; the third is the correct trainer or guide. In the absence of any of these three, the mission will be futile. The first and foremost requirement in order to even attempt this is the absolute knowledge and understanding about the nature of the forthcoming barrier and the strength of its resistance.

In the language of Yoga, this bridge is explained as the transition between the body-centric experiences to the realization of the innermost self. Every other spiritual philosophy of India has explained the position of the soul as the supreme consciousness that is living within a five-layered cocoon, something like that of an onion. The outer layer of the onion peel is the gross layer, which is the physical body that we have all generally felt and perceived of as ourselves. This is known as the *annamaya kosha*. It is this body that eats, gets diseased, decays and eventually dies. Every change that may occur to this body is only transitory in nature, since the body is impermanent itself.

The second layer is made of 'life-force' or energy, known as 'Chi' in China and 'Qi' in Japan, and termed as the *pranamaya kosha* in Yoga. Energy is the subtle dimension of physical matter. Physical matter is created out of energy, and energy itself can be created out of physical matter. Matter and energy are two aspects of the same thing: energy is liberated matter, and matter is energy waiting to happen.

The third layer is termed as *manomaya kosha* and contains the mind-stuff. Mind is more subtle than energy. This is the sheath of intelligence and all rational judgments take place from within this layer.

The next layer is of intuition and awareness, wherein the ultimate source of knowledge lies. All that is to be known is stored within this layer. It is known as the *vijnanamaya kosha*.

The fifth and final layer is the *anandamaya kosha*, the realm of ultimate bliss and beatitude; this bliss encapsulates the purest consciousness.

This elucidation of the individual bodies proves two specific theories. In one respect, it confirms the theory of the evolutionary process. As one looks from the state of consciousness to the outermost physical body, it illustrates the process of evolution, revealing how the supreme soul manifested itself through various stages and evolved into the physical embodiment known as the species. On the other hand, looking from the gross physical body into the inner depths of the self, one comes to understand the barriers that one must penetrate and transcend to arrive at the supreme state.

Until this point, all my disease-curing asanas and practices had been nothing more than an illusory merry-go-round within the confines of the outer physical layer. All so-called mystical and spiritual experiences were mere amusements of the ego. I finally came to realize that my journey had not been in a spiral descending into the core of my self, rather a course restricted to the barrier of the gross body. How I was taken for a ride by all my previous teachers, giving me physical experiences in the name of spiritual development! As soon as these thoughts became transparent in my mind, I ran to my guru to ask if my practice would take me beyond the physical limits.

Listening to my question, my guru reassured me that my practices would definitely go beyond the body. Perceiving my insistence, he then explained how the transition from the body to the self would be practically accomplished.

"Out of the five layers of our existence, we are generally only aware of the first and outermost layer. Within this outer sphere we have control over no more than thirty percent of the body. A predominant seventy percent of the body functions are involuntary. Accordingly, our physical resources are thirty percent of the body and less than five percent of the mind. As long as we do not gain higher control over the body and our senses, it is difficult to go beyond this layer. Hence most of the spiritual practices are comprised of some physical and voluntary action. What is most important is that the minimal physical activities should be directed inwards to invoke experiences of the more subtle layers, rather than further hardening the body. The sequences of practices in yoga are meticulously designed to gradually take the individual beyond the gross limits of the body and into the subtler layers, until one realizes and becomes established in their innermost self."

My guru then asked if Kripanand had explained to me the eight limbs of Yoga. I responded with a very immature and silly answer, as I told him that I had once asked Kripanand, "What kind of yoga is taught at this ashram?"

He replied, "We all learn and teach *Ashtanga Yoga*."

I carelessly explained to my guru about my previous experiences of *ashtanga yoga*. In one single breath, I uttered all the eight limbs, all the *yamas* and *niyamas* together with all the theoretical aspects of this type of yoga. According to my previous experience, '*ashtanga*' was only another brand of yoga that consisted of asanas, *pranayamas*, etc. that were for the purpose of gymnastic fitness or as a means to cure all diseases, whilst the rest of the limbs were merely for spiritual information.

My guru smiled and replied, "I am aware of your so-called *ashtanga* practice, but let us now discuss the eight limbs of Yoga instead of the *ashtanga* brand of yoga."

My guru emphasized that the first two limbs are not simply for one's spiritual information. "The *yamas* and *niyamas* are practised consciously with the help of some voluntary *kriyas*. It is not possible to integrate the restraints of *Yama* and the principles of *Niyama* without practising appropriate *tapah* or mortification. *Yamas* and *niyamas* provide the correct psychological conditioning which is necessary for the success of any spiritual practice. No matter how much one knows about the virtues of honesty or truthfulness, it does not help one's spiritual practice. What is more important is being honest and truthful, not just for a day, but for an entire lifetime. Every single activity of a yogi must reflect the virtues of the *yamas* and *niyamas*, and the first two limbs of *Ashtanga* are not simply accomplished by reading a few books or listening to a few discourses on the restraints and observations of one's self. Nirupanand will teach you the correct and exact practices of this *tapah*."

Before commencing my physical practice, I was informed of the importance of learning and mastering the skill of directing its effects inwards and preventing the results to manifest in external activities. For example, Asana has to be practised with an aim to invoke the subtle elements rather than for the purpose of fitness or cure. The technique of the physical practices can be compared to the process of cooking.

'How does one cook food?' You take a cooking pot, put some food inside, and place the pot on a fire.

'Why are you heating the pot whilst your aim is to cook the food?' To cook food you need a pot, as putting the food directly on a fire will only burn it.

For proper cooking, the food requires an indirect heating method rather than a direct flame. In the process of cooking, it is the pot that takes the heat first, and then the food begins to cook. As soon as the food begins to change, we no longer pay full attention to the heating of the pot. As the food approaches its final stages of preparation, our attention shifts to the finer aspects of the food until eventually we switch off the heat. After the food is cooked, the pot cools off and is discarded, but consequently the food does not become uncooked. Even though a pot is necessary to cook food, we must remember our purpose is to cook the food and not the pot. The changes affected in the food are permanent and irreversible in nature.

Our body is like a pot that contains our subtle self. The practices are intended for the subtle self and should not be limited to the body. Even though we need this body for the performance of spiritual practice, it should never be the objective of the practice. Always remember, we are cooking the food and not the pot. I immediately realized I had cooked, heated and overheated my pot for the last five years and had received no food in return. I addressed my guru as a master chef and requested him to teach me the finer skills of cooking.

Whether it is a spiritual practice or cooking, one needs to

develop the finer skills of perception, as most of us have not seen
or felt the inner self and do not know what it looks or feels like.

In order to be able to direct the effects of our practice towards the
inner self, let us first know and understand the channels of the
subtle elements. Our tantrist forefathers have provided us with a
clear anatomical picture of the subtle self and the nature of the
movement of energy within its subtler layer. Before the beginning
of the practice, we must purify all our subtle nervous channels
which will play a vital role in the process. The purification of
these nervous channels (*nadis*) involves a specific practice; this
entire process takes a definite period of time dependent upon the
individual's capacity. The effects of purification have to be clearly
seen, felt and demonstrated before it is considered complete. As a
result of purification and the simultaneous *tapahs* of *Yama* and
Niyama, the practitioner begins to feel the presence and functions
of all the subtle elements in the body.

The next stage is Asana. It is important at this point of the
practice to keep in mind that the successful accomplishment of
these preliminary practices brings out the correct spiritual effect
of an asana. Without such accomplishments, an asana is nothing
more than a physical exercise. Without having the ability to
control and focus on the subtle elements, the effects of an asana
cannot be directed for spiritual development. The practice of an
asana depends upon the individual's physical and spiritual
qualities. Asana is a specific tool that helps the practitioner go
beyond the outer physical layer of the body. After the successful
penetration of this outer shell, there still awaits four formidable
barriers to breakthrough before the completion of our journey.

The tool required for the successful penetration of the
pranamaya kosha is Pranayama. The practice of *pranayama* is only
possible after the successful breakthrough of the first shell. The
correct practice of *pranayama* takes the practitioner beyond the
body of energy and into the realm of the mind. The functions of

the mind are merely a means to an end. As long as the supreme end is not achieved, intelligence must be treated as an obstacle.

The next tool in hand to take us beyond the illusions of the mind is *Pratyahara*. Similar to the other tools and practices, *pratyahara* is a set of definite voluntary actions or *kriyas*. This limb of practice helps the practitioner to withdraw deeper into the core of the inner self and transcend the limitation of the *manomaya kosha*.

Its success then takes the practitioner to face the second innermost layer, the *vijnanamaya kosha*. This is the stage of intuitive awareness. An experience of this stage is very important and a prerequisite for the comprehension of the inner self. This stage reveals the ultimate knowledge and clears the way to contain the forthcoming supreme bliss. This supreme knowledge is experienced in the form of various *siddhis* or accomplishments. However, the *siddhis* and all other accomplishments are by no means the purpose of the practice. Instead of being carried away by the overwhelming powers, the practitioner has to maintain his focus to further penetrate and transcend this layer. The necessary tool for the penetration of this barrier is Concentration or *Dharana*. It is again a very specific practice that helps one break away from the final bind of the ego.

The next stage is the realm of supreme bliss. This overwhelming phase contains the ultimate sense of fulfillment, and a practitioner can easily forget the objective of his journey. Only within this stage can one have a glimpse of the supreme consciousness, and here it remains essential to hold onto the ultimate objective of self-realization. The tool or methodology to go beyond the *anandamaya kosha* is Meditation. The practice of meditation exists only within the realms of supreme bliss, which is far beyond the afflictions of the body, senses, awareness and ego. Meditation is the last tool or methodology that helps the practitioner transcend into the union or Yoga with the supreme self. Yoga is the final point in the whole journey from all physical notions to self-realization.

I began doing a mental calculation about the process of yoga practice. The two foundation practices of *Yama* and *Niyama*, the five main practices of *Asana*, *Pranayama*, *Pratyahara*, *Dharana*, *Dhyana* and the last phase of *Samadhi* constitute the eight component parts of *Ashtanga Yoga*. *Ashtanga Yoga* is not a brand of yoga; rather it is the ultimate structure of Yoga. The term Yoga in itself does not denote a series of practices, but rather its objective.

I thought to myself, 'This all appears so straightforward, but surely Yoga cannot be so simple in its practice and understanding?' Initially, it was not difficult for me to comprehend the validity of the evolutionary and involutionary processes, but it was truly amazing to see how Yoga has accurately formulated a step-by-step process to accelerate one's own involutionary journey. Is this process a creation of these sadhus, or had it existed for an even longer time?

My guru continued explaining to me, "The knowledge of Yoga has been known to mankind for many a century. But only recently it came to be presented in such a concise and systematic manner. Sometime during the third century BC, there lived a great sage and yogi called Maharshi Patanjali who compiled and presented the practices of Yoga in the form of a practice manual. This great work is known as the Yoga Sutras of Patanjali. Prior to Maharshi Patanjali, the knowledge about the practice of Yoga was only available in bits and pieces scattered across hundreds of different spiritual literature. The Yoga Sutras of Patanjali has undoubtedly been tested by time and proven by experience for over thousands of years. The Yoga Sutras is famous for its accuracy and efficacy."

Keen to learn more, I asked my guru if it is possible to acquire a book and practise on one's own. After a moment's thought, my guru replied, "The answer can be both yes and no. Acquiring the book is one thing, but reading, understanding and practising is a whole different matter. The book was written in the third century BC, when the human conditions of practice were definitely very different from that of modern times. The level of sincerity, honesty and socio-physical conditioning of that time is no longer present today. The sutras of Patanjali have explained the finest factors of practice, but the sutra format of the book provides limited scope to expound upon the detailed descriptions of the practices. However, minute examination of the sutras reveals the exact nature of the practices."

Nirupanand had already explained that yogic practices were a derivation of early tantric practices, and one needs a good understanding of Tantra for the successful application of the Yoga Sutras. It is Tantra that provides us with the knowledge about the human body, its subtle channels, its energy dynamics and above all the subtle relationships between the gross, subtle and causal bodies and the seat of ultimate energy. For these reasons it is essential one attracts the help of an experienced guru in the field of Yoga. The practice of yoga without the help of such an experienced guru can be harmful and very much counterproductive.

This was already an overwhelming amount of information to be absorbed in one day. It was approaching evening, and I was waiting to go to my favorite point in the mountains to enjoy the breathtaking sunset. However, before getting up I was keen to ask two last questions.

"Am I going to study Tantra here?"

"Yes, you will study Tantra, along with many other ancient scriptures. As it is important for a yogi to study Tantra, it is equally important to study dozens of other subjects to enhance our understanding of Yoga."

My second question was, "May I borrow a copy of the Yoga Sutras of Patanjali from someone in the ashram?"

My guru smiled and answered, "Everyone here has a copy of the Yoga Sutras of Patanjali, but I don't think it will be easy for you to borrow one since each of them carries their copy inside their head."

Many years have passed since then. Every single day, every single teaching and every single mystical experience of those years is clearly imprinted in my memory. These days, I too carry the Yoga Sutras in my mind, along with many other insightful scriptures. During these years my teachers had supported me in refining my approach to learning. The whole lineage of gurus upheld the notions of pure knowledge by demystifying the age-old beliefs. They always encouraged me to debate the validity of a statement from any teacher, as when one is on the path of knowledge, one cannot allow doubts to survive and breed in the mind. There is no place for confusion and ambiguity in the light of absolute knowledge. Time and again each of my masters proved themselves to be as true as their words. They were always amused with the manner and nature of my debates and helped me to remove any unreasonable notions from my mind.

For every aspiring yoga student, it is necessary to develop the habit of a healthy debate. In order to challenge the age-old beliefs of practice, one may have to sacrifice the notions of 'spiritual correctness' of the modern times. A code of appropriate behavior does not create a yogi; rather a yogi sets the course of appropriate behavior. In the years of my study and practice without the bias or obligation towards any notion of spiritual correctness, I had been branded a rebel. But at least Yoga did not remain yet another vague and mystical belief for me. I can wholeheartedly say that whatever will be delivered and narrated in the forthcoming pages will be devoid of any myth and mysticism.

CHAPTER THREE

The Kriya of Macrocosmic Velocity

The successful practice of Yoga rests upon three pillars. In the language of Kripanand, they are purity of body, clarity of mind and divinity of heart. To me, this description sounded very much like the toothless advice of an old villager. However I soon came to realize that these simple words held a vast ocean of meaning as they carried the secrets of the entire substance of yogic practice. The practice of Yoga always begins with the performance and observation of a set of voluntary actions. The collection of these voluntary actions is called the *kriya* or action of yoga. Whenever a young aspirant of Yoga asks, 'When and how do I start the practice of yoga?' The answer is, 'You always begin with this set of *kriyas*.'

The Yoga Sutras of Patanjali provides a clear, compact and succinct structure of the practice of yoga. This structure is applicable to any practice of a spiritual nature. Even though the ingredients of practice differ at times, the structure always remains the same. It is extremely important to understand this structure for the success of a yogic or any other spiritual practice. The sutra 28 of *sadhana pada* (second chapter) of the Yoga Sutras reads, *'Yoganganusthanadasuddhiksaye jnanadiptiravivekakhyateh'*. This sutra needs a very careful and microscopic examination to understand the depth and profundity of its meaning. The closest we can get to the meaning of the sutra in English will read as 'On the destruction of impurities, by the gradual achievement of the component parts of Yoga, the light of knowledge expands to the intellective revelation'. Let us now examine the sutra part by part.

This sutra reveals three parts of the practice process. The first part lays down the conditions of the practice. The second part emphasizes the process of practice, and the third part indicates the effects of the practice.

The conditions of practice are 'the destruction of impurities'. By this, Maharshi Patanjali means that a practitioner must attain a state of purity before the practice of any other *kriyas*. The phrase 'on the destruction of impurities' makes purification a mandatory pre-condition before commencing with the component parts of Yoga.

The second part of the sutra emphasizes the gradual achievement of the component parts of Yoga. The components parts of Yoga are provided in the next sutra, they are *Yama, Niyama, Asana, Pranayama, Pratyahara, Dharana, Dhyana* and *Samadhi* (sutra 2:29). It is important to note that the Yoga Sutras does not speak about the 'practice' of the component parts; it unambiguously emphasizes the 'achievement' of the component parts. According to the sutra, the eight limbs of Yoga are to be achieved one after the other.

There is a widespread misunderstanding about this extremely vital principle of Yoga. Many modern-day teachers and scholars have clearly missed the emphasis on 'gradual achievement'. This emphasis upon the gradual achievement of the limbs of Yoga can further be studied from the subsequent sutras. When we take a close look at the sutras from 2:46 to 3:5, we notice the structure of gradual achievement. These sutras reveal that each of the limbs of Yoga acts as a cause as well as an effect. The achievement of each of these individual practices leads the practitioner into the next. The success of each of these practices is always heralded by a *siddhi* or supernatural psychic achievement. Only upon the attainment of this milestone is the practitioner allowed to move onto the next practice.

The third part of the sutra indicates the effects of the *kriyas*. According to this sutra the gradual achievement of the eight limbs of Yoga, after the successful practice of purification, results in the expansion of knowledge to the intellective revelation (aka enlightenment).

The *kriyas* or the conscious practices have been defined by various writers and scholars in a variety of different ways. Whatever may be the diversity of explanations, *kriya* essentially denotes the strict adherence to the truest equation of Yoga. Let us now examine what can be that truest equation. For the sake of clarity and under-standing, let us recapitulate in brief what has already been discussed about the relationship pertaining to the oneness of the individual and cosmic body, since the practice of Yoga has been derived from the evolutionary cycles of both the microcosm and macrocosm.

The cosmos can be perceived in two forms: its tiny or miniature form and its extended or large form. They are not two different kinds of cosmos, but the same cosmos perceived in two different ways. The tiny or miniature form is called the microcosm (micro+cosmos), and the extended or large form is called the macrocosm (macro+cosmos). Keep in mind that both of them are the same cosmos, the only distinction being the micro or macro form. The prime characteristic that makes the differentiation of these forms is their relative time-space dynamics. The nature of space is dependent upon the mass of the body around which it exists. Gravitation is the product of the bending of space time. The denser the mass, the stronger is its gravitational pull, and the higher the curvature of the space around it. The less dense the mass, the weaker is its gravitational pull, and the lesser the curvature of the space around it. The dynamics of time can in no way be studied or quantified without its relationship with space.

The cosmos is a collection of huge and gigantic bodies of stars and galaxies. Such enormous bodies with their unimaginable mass and force have an entirely different time-space structure than those conditions which exist on earth. The time-space dynamic in which human beings live is dependent upon the basis of the mass and gravity of the physical earth. Hence there exists a difference between the time-space on earth and the time-space in the external cosmos. The evolutionary process of the species is a direct outcome of the time-space dynamics on earth. In other words evolution, which in reality is the unfoldment of consciousness, is subject to the limitations of the time-space conditions on earth. A species that does not ascertain the sufficient level of awareness or intelligence cannot comprehend a superior dimension of existence.

For the sake of simplicity, it can be said that we as humans live in a three dimensional space, whereas there also exists a fourth and higher dimension. The yogi knows that the fourth dimensional dynamics can be applied to his three dimensional existence; when this is invoked, a yogi transcends the entire process of evolution. The human body is the ultimate platform to achieve the acceleration of this evolutionary process and for the interplay of the microcosmic body and macrocosmic principles.

The practical application of the time-space principles in the human body is called *kriya* in the yogic language. Different yogis and yogic scriptures have explained and described the cosmic nature of the human body. The astrophysical nature of the human body reveals both the solar and lunar conditions. The physical cycles of the male species is predominantly regulated by the solar conditions, whereas that of the female is regulated by the lunar conditions. One cycle of the moon contains four *kalas* or stages, which are the two waxing and two waning periods of one lunar month. One cycle of the sun contains twelve *kalas*, which consists of the twelve zodiacs through which the sun transits during its yearly cycle. Life on earth experiences three hundred sixty-five days of spiritual and evolutionary transition in three hundred sixty-five days, whereas a yogi achieves the same within a split second. *Kriya* in Yoga is the process in which the cosmic energy travels through the solar and lunar pathways or channels in the human body at a macrocosmic velocity.

The purity-clarity-divinity equation of the *kriya* is explained by Maharshi Patanjali in his profound and succinct sutras. The first line of the second chapter of the Yoga Sutras states that *tapah* (austerity), *svadhyaya* (self-study) and *Iswara-Pranidhana* (respect for the cosmic will) collectively constitute the voluntary practices of yoga. However simple these three little words may appear, they need a microscopic examination in order to form a clear picture of the *kriyas*.

Tapah, as a *kriya*, acts like a fire that purifies metal. Hence it is regarded as *yoga agni*. The fire of austerities burns and destroys all impurities of the body and mind. Yogis consider *tapah* to be the most important part of spiritual development. The journey from impurity to purity entails a tremendous amount of sacrifice, as a practitioner is required to undergo the rigors of discipline and the discomforts of change. In the practice of *tapah* one has to give up all notions of comfort and compromise for the achievement of a single purpose. Getting up for early morning practice instead of procrastinating with one's pillow and compromising the satisfaction of snuggling in a warm blanket for a longer period of time is *tapah*. Retiring into a jungle or cave instead of living in a luxury apartment for the purpose of practice is *tapah*. Not being fazed by the harsh conditions of the weather and climate for uninterrupted practice is *tapah*.

There can be a million and one examples of *tapah*. No individual can practically devise a list of 'spiritually correct' activities and practise them accordingly. The practices of austerity are closely interrelated. All one has to do is select one of the practices and adhere to it with sincere discipline. As you pick up one flower in a garland of flowers, the whole garland is lifted. Similarly the practice of a single austerity can make all the other good qualities follow. Different yogic scriptures have provided us with various examples of austerities, but let us now source one of the most concise and comprehensive lists of *tapahs*. Maharshi Patanjali in his Yoga Sutras has enumerated a number of restraints and principles that are necessary for the success of yogic practice. The restraints are named *yamas*, and the principles are known as *niyamas*.

Now you must be thinking that you already know so much about *yamas* and *niyamas*. Like most modern-day yoga practitioners, I had also once read them thoroughly and memorized them by heart. However the practice of *yamas* and *niyamas* is by no means complete by merely reading and memorizing them as simple affirmations. They are essential *kriyas* that contain the keys to the powerful secrets of Yoga. Knowing all about truthfulness does not make one truthful. Furthermore it is not the knowledge of truthfulness, but the actual practice and adherence to truthfulness that essentially makes it a *kriya*. For this reason, definite methods have been conceived for the practice of truthfulness.

The first and most important *tapah* is *ahimsa* (harmlessness), substantiated in the language of *Vedanta* by the phrase 'Ahimsa param tapah', meaning harmlessness is the absolute austerity. The study and understanding of *ahimsa* involves a notable propensity for logic, rationality and awareness, as the exact meaning and application is nowhere standardized. There is no minimum or absolute degree of harmlessness. It is not possible, nor by any means practical, to create an appropriate list of do's and don'ts that are applicable to each and every person or circumstance.

Everybody in my ashram was pretty amused with my preconceived notions of *ahimsa*. I had thought that *ahimsa* could not be anything more than hurting somebody in a very physical way. Harm meant something very physical to me, and I definitely failed to see all those non-physical implications that could lead to being harmful. One day my guru explained that every physical action is a manifestation of a thought, speech or merely an attitude. Our thoughts and attitudes always culminate into an exchange or an interaction which can be harmful, and these exchanges or harmful thoughts, when taken to their extremities, result in violence. Violence or harmfulness always includes some element of pride, greed, fear or ignorance. An act that may appear violent and harmful may not necessarily be so if it lacks one of these vital ingredients. On the other hand, an act would be termed violent and harmful if any of these elements were to be found in it, no matter how innocent the act in itself may appear. Let us now solve this paradox.

In my younger days I used to go hunting. I had a few good friends whose company I enjoyed, and there were so many things to learn from them. On one such occasion, I had gone out hunting with a serious hunter who had great knowledge about wildlife behavior. After wandering for some time, we came upon a herd of deer. Both of us hid behind a fallen tree, watching the herd grazing peacefully. The setting was serene and beautiful. The herd comprised of a dozen adult deer and three little fawns.

While the adult deer were grazing, the fawns were running about with sheer joy and excitement. Watching the little fawns in their play, a sense of delight came over me, and I forgot all about hunting. I began enjoying the blissful moment and mentally became a part of their play. All of a sudden, a leopard rushed into the field and grabbed one of the little fawns by its throat. The whole herd immediately scattered in panic. The leopard held the fawn down while it was kicking helplessly. The serene and joyful moment had suddenly transformed into a tragedy. The happy and innocent play of the fawn was still alive in my mind.

Seeing this dastardly act, I immediately sprang into a mood of anger and retribution. I grabbed the gun from my friend's hand and took aim at the leopard. Nothing would have satisfied me more than to see the brute destroyed. Before I could shoot, my elderly companion tried desperately to snatch away the gun from my hand. I was bent upon killing the leopard. However my friend was determined not to allow me to do so.

I knew I would not be able to kill the leopard, but out of sheer frustration, or maybe to vent my anger, I fired a shot into the air. The leopard was as startled as my friend, and it dropped the fawn from its teeth and bounded away. I ran to the rescue of the fawn only to realize on my arrival that it was too late. I sat down next to its little body and gently ran my hands over it. It was so soft and tender and still warm, which surely didn't match its lifeless eyes.

I would have shed tears as if losing someone very dear, but my friend immediately walked over to me, and before I could ask for an explanation, he gave me a long blasting as to what a stupid fool I was. I furiously snapped and shouted, "What the hell do you mean?! How can you possibly expect me to witness and tolerate such a barbaric act and overlook such unjust harm inflicted on an innocent animal? That brute deserved to be shot. Can you not see yourself what he has done?!"

My old, wise companion fell silent for a moment. Then in a soft and gentle voice he reminded me, "Don't forget that it was you who came to hunt in the first place. Tell me why is it that when you hunt it is pleasure, yet if the leopard hunts it is a barbaric act? Don't you know the leopard, like other carnivores, hunts only for its food and survival? There is no hunting in the law of nature which is meant for pleasure or machismo. The deer is its natural food; so by hunting deer, the leopard is remaining honest within its food discipline and is only contributing to the balance of nature.

Your first mistake was hunting for pleasure. Your second mistake was to interfere in another's process of acquiring its livelihood. The third and possibly biggest mistake was that your interference did not save a life, rather it will result in the end of two or more lives."

I was perplexed as to how my attempt to save one life could possibly result in the loss of two lives.

"The leopard killed because it was hungry, and you chased the leopard away from its food. Know that the leopard is still hungry, and to satisfy its hunger will go on to kill another animal. The death of this deer, without your interference, could have saved another animal which is likely to be killed by the leopard in a short while. And yet there is still one more remote possibility of another death. If the leopard was too hungry, weak, sick or old, it might not be left with the strength to kill

*another animal and would itself consequently die of hunger. Now use
your stupid head and try to understand what a serious violation you
have committed."*

*I began to shed tears for a different reason. The old, wise hunter in
his tribal wisdom had given me one of the greatest lessons of natural law
which I will never, ever forget.*

The words of the old tribal were still ringing in my ear whilst I
was listening to Kripanand and his explanations of *ahimsa*.

I asked Kripanand, "Would you consider the food chain of the
species to be the guiding principle of the ecological balance?"

Kripanand had a very straightforward answer, "You are living
in a world of species and not the world of man. It is a mistake to
take this world as a propriety right of man and attempt to apply
human laws and notions to the animal world. What we as humans
think violent or harmful may not be so in the eyes of nature.
Nature has created all the species and has arranged them in such
a way that each and every one is food and sustenance for the
other. The ignorant human being with his limited understanding
of the process of nature only contributes to his own confusion and
misunderstanding about *ahimsa*. It can never be termed harmful
when an animal in pursuit of the law of nature kills and acquires
its natural food."

I once again fell silent to pay my respects to the old tribal who
never hunted for any purpose other than food.

Later that day, I was debating with my guru. "Do animals
constitute the natural food of human beings? If so, what is then
spiritually incorrect about eating meat?"

My guru replied, "As far as human beings are only another
member of this animal world, they can eat other animals."

I asked in my usual childish and mischievous way, "What
about some fried chicken for dinner?"

Without any change of expression he replied, "You can have
some fried chicken for dinner the moment the chicken is seen as

food for survival and not for taste or pleasure. As a yogi, the only purpose of your survival is to achieve the final goal of life. Food for a yogi is only a means for survival. He does not eat for taste or pleasure. It does not matter what you eat. What matters is that the food you choose supports your journey and is not against the balance of nature. We will study what is human food at the appropriate stage of your practice."

Today an act of killing is usually termed as violence per se, which is incorrect. It is not the act but the attitude that constitutes violence and harm. Complete refrain from the act of killing is not sufficient to be termed harmlessness; rather the complete renunciation of all harmful acts, thoughts, speech, ideas and intentions is the austerity of *ahimsa*.

The intention of the ancient yogis was to completely eliminate the genesis of injury. The formulation of spiritual conduct and behavior was not just to provide a list of spiritually correct do's and don'ts. In the modern day we often see the practice and application of these conducts as merely ritualistic. Since there is no exact measure to term a particular act or behavior as harmful, everyone has created their own interpretations and justifications of their own behavior. What is important is the uprooting of the entire family of vices with all their manifestations and implications. Harmlessness towards others is merely one of these manifestations. A vow of non-injury towards others is meaningless if it is not coupled with truthfulness, as untruth can result in more harm than the physical act of harming others.

This was only the beginning of my learning about the relationship between food and *ahimsa*. Even though the explanations from my guru about *ahimsa* and its practices were beyond all doubt and made perfect sense to me, I could not apply them to the notions of modern pseudo-spirituality. My quest towards the unraveling of the vegetarian/non-vegetarian conflict extended beyond the confines of my ashram.

The dictionary meaning of the term vegetarian comes from the Latin term 'vegetate', which means to 'enliven' or 'add life to'. Non-vegetarian, on the other hand, in the same parallel should mean 'food that does not add life'! This is highly confusing. People use these terms for the exact opposite purpose!

Secondly, if it is the element of life which is inherent in the substance or food that determines the distinction between vegetarian and non-vegetarian, then these people surely do not know what they are talking about. In reality, every single particle of this universe contains life. It is absurd and utter nonsense to say that a rock, a vegetable or a leg of lamb of the same weight hold different amounts of matter, or life. In fact, they all carry the same matter and the same life-force in them. The distinction on the basis of the apparent shape or color of an object can never be the discriminating factor between 'live' or 'vegetable' food, as it is life which is the vital ingredient of all matter. Apart from these scientific explanations upon which people can agree and disagree as per convenience, this is only one of the many explanations of vegetarian or non-vegetarian food. Conclusively, no matter can be categorized as 'live' or 'dead' within the meanings of physics. The Yoga Sutras does not provide any dietary guidelines for yogis, most probably due to its scientific nature. The restrictions of meat eating came into existence only in more recent times as spiritual science lost its meaning in the haze of religious dogma.

The term *sattvic* as found in several ancient scriptures means something that contains *sattva* which stands for 'substance'. Hence, in the context of food, *sattva* means 'life substance' or 'the purest essence of life'.

According to Ayurveda, *sattvic* food is described as food of a sweet nature or quality which is easy to digest, nourishing and promotes health and healing of the body. Anyone with elementary knowledge of Ayurveda would know that only meat fits this description.

Caraka Samhita, the oldest written scripture of Ayurveda which is believed to be written by Maharshi Patanjali himself, states*'Sharirabrinhane Nanyat Khadyam Mamsadwishishyate',* which means 'for the promotion and nourishment of the body, no other food item is better than meat'. Another ancient and authentic scripture of Ayurveda, *Bhava Prakash,* states *'Sadyohatasya Mamsam Syadbyadhidhatiyathaamritam',* which translates as 'the meat of freshly killed animals is like *Amrit* (the ultimate life-giving fluid that sustains the Divine)'. Different scriptures of Ayurveda describe the various sweet and nourishing properties of meat, and according to *Bagabhatt (Ashtanga Samgraha),* nothing equals meat for the promotion of health and substance of the body.

The *vedic* text *Satapatha Brahamana* states *'Paramam Annadyam Yan Mamsam',* which means 'meat is the best kind of food'.

These references are not provided in the scriptures with any different context than what is mentioned here.

If these references are not convincing enough for the highly 'spiritually-correct', let us go further and understand the structure and functions of human anatomy.

The structure of the jaw and teeth of every animal is designed for its natural food. Meat-eating animals have cutting teeth, or incisors with a vertical jaw movement, and plant-eating animals have grinding teeth, or molars with a horizontal jaw movement. In the case of man, both these types of teeth and jaw movements are available, which clearly indicates that human food constitutes not only vegetable matter, but also meat.

The second important factor is the length of one's intestine. Vegetable matter is more difficult to digest than meat. That is why pure plant eaters like cows, buffalo or goats, have an extremely long intestine and multiple stomachs to digest their food. This is not required for a meat eater. Pure meat eaters, like tigers and wolves, have much shorter digestive canals. The study of the human intestine apparently shows that it was never created purely for vegetable matter.

Thirdly, meat eaters use digestive acid to assimilate their food, whereas plant eaters need bacteria and protozoa as their primary requirement for food processing. A human digestive system presents both of these digestive agents. In fact, human beings are the most versatile eaters of creation.

The final and irrefutable proof of meat as human food can be derived from the study of the evolution of species. The Homo sapiens is a descendant of a series of meat eaters.

Of course, when someone prefers to abstain from meat eating on the basis of taste, preference, medical incompatibility, or protest against improper treatment of animals, it is an entirely different matter. For such reasons the age-old definition of *sattvic* food cannot be re-written. Food is that ultimate substance which in its simple and universal nature, serves as the ultimate balancing factor of ecology and the interdependency of species. Life depends on life. All other animals subscribe to this unwritten law of nature and any contradiction to this leads to their destruction. Strict adherence to a food pattern that is determined by the principles of creation is the ultimate respect towards nature.

∞∞∞∞

The modern connotation of truth is very much black and white. A statement is spoken on the basis of its correctness without any consideration toward its effect. The speaker is often very much aware that the uttered statement will have a harmful effect even before it is spoken. He seldom cares about the effects that it may have on others. He speaks simply because he doesn't like to be held legally or socially responsible. The modern-day society does not allow for the use of discretion while voicing harmful information. For example, a police officer has barely any discretion in reporting an accident to the victim's parents, or a school teacher may use little discretion in the manner in which he informs his student that he has failed. No matter how correct these statements are, they cause harm and misery to the listener.

Such statements, though they are apparently correct, cannot be taken as truth. No statement can be truthful based only upon its correctness; the correctness of a statement is judged by its actual effects on others. Then you may ask, 'What is truth?' Truth is appropriateness on the basis of its time, place and person.

Let me use an illustration to explain this.

An old man was suffering from a serious heart problem. He was hospitalized because any sudden event or excitement could kill him. While this old man was under such a condition, he won the lottery of ten million dollars. When his son received this news of his father's winnings, he was perplexed as to how to break the news to his father. He knew very well that the old man could not take the news nor contain the excitement. He was sure his father would end up having a heart attack and die upon hearing the news.

Now he had a great dilemma. After much wishful thinking, he decided to consult his father's cardiologist to find out the right way of breaking the news. Upon hearing the situation, the cardiologist decided that the old man should be given the news under the most appropriate and comfortable condition. He was very sure that the unstable and stressful environment of a hospital would not be the right place to give the old man the shock of his life. So the doctor discharged the old man from the hospital and shifted him to the more comfortable environment of his own home.

The next morning, wearing his jogging suit, the doctor dropped in to see the old man at his home. The old man was surprised, but happy to see his doctor in such a casual way. The doctor told the old man that as he was out jogging, and thought it would be a good idea to drop in on his favorite patient to check on his health and enjoy a morning cup of tea with him.

The old man was delighted to hear the doctor's reasons for his visit. The doctor started a conversation with some casual enquiries about his health. A short while after discussing his health, the doctor shifted the conversation to hobbies and pastimes. Soon the doctor got onto the topic of playing the lottery. Being careful to choose the right moment, the doctor said, "I have never won a lottery in my life, but I would definitely like to know how you would react if you were to win a million dollars?"

The old man thought for a while and said, "I'd give it to my wife."

The doctor was happy that one million dollars made no effect on the old man. After going through discussions on many more subjects, he again came back to the subject. He enquired, "What would you do, if you were to win two million dollars?"

The old man was confused by these strange questions from the doctor, but still managed to give an answer.

He said, "I would give the second million to my children."

The doctor was happy and grew more confident. After some more discussion and a few more cups of tea, the doctor cautiously asked, "What would you do if you won five million dollars in a lottery?"

The old man was beginning to get irritated, but the doctor tolerated all the irritations and persisted with his questions. Within moments of mental calculation, the old man replied, "I have already told you what I will do with two million. Out of the other three, I would keep two million to buy a luxury villa in some tropical island and give the last million to charity."

The doctor was very happy as he praised the old man's intentions of charity. A few hours passed by, the old man was getting more and more confused about the doctor's unusual behavior. At the same time, the doctor was mustering up the tact to ask the final question. Ultimately seeing the old man in a very relaxed mood, the doctor presented his question. "What would you do if you won ten million dollars on the lottery?"

The doctor had crossed the limits of the old man's patience. With a note of irritation in his voice, the old man said, "Would you believe me if I told you?"

The doctor replied, "Why not? I have always believed you."

The old man continued, "I have told you what I will do with five million dollars. The remaining five million dollars I would give to you."

The doctor died.

Let us now evaluate the story on the basis of truth and appropriateness. The son's behavior was definitely appropriate because he took every care to see that the winning of the lottery did not kill his father. The doctor was also very appropriate as he was careful to consider the right time and place to prevent any ill effect of the news. He was also truthful as he introduced the news to the old man in a very causal way so that he contained the excitement of it. All the efforts and statements of the doctor could be taken as truthful and appropriate. However the statement of the old man, that he would give the five million dollars to the doctor, was harmful. No matter how honest and innocent the statement may have been, the old man unknowingly committed untruthfulness.

The practice of truthfulness as a *tapah* seemed to be a tricky one. It barely appeared to be any different than tactful diplomacy. A person gifted with the skill of talking could virtually turn everything he speaks into the framework of truth. I later asked Kripanand, "If I tell a man to go to hell in such a way that he actually begins to look forward to the trip, would you consider it to be a truthful statement?"

Kripanand replied, "No matter how nicely you put it, your intention of sending a man to hell is clear, and you surely won't enjoy a trip to heaven for that."

Once Mahatma Gandhi had stated, 'One of the most difficult things to achieve humanly is truthfulness. It is not important to be truthful; it is important to remain truthful.' Being truthful once in a while, or being half-truthful, does not serve any useful purpose. As a friend of mine used to say, "I do not tell a lie; I only say half the truth. It's your luck which half you get." What my stupid friend never realized was that half the truth is no truth. In order for it to be truth, it has to be one hundred percent. It is only absolute truthfulness that is considered as a *tapah*.

While the *kriyas* of *ahimsa* and *satya* (truthfulness) intend to prevent all direct and indirect physical and mental injury to others, *asteya* (non-stealing) aims at preventing all harm to another's property. *Asteya* includes absolute honesty and complete refrain from greed and accumulation. Stealing, as we normally think, is not limited to merely taking away others' belongings, as there are so many ways by which we can harm the entire society even though we did not steal anyone's property in particular. *Asteya* can broadly mean 'no improper gain to self and no improper loss to others'. An act can be deemed as stealing even though one does not gain any material benefit, but indirectly deprives somebody else from a benefit. It is a very difficult *yama* to practise in the modern day. Different countries have different kinds of trade regulations. Most of such regulations do not consider the ill effects of trade practices on others. Trading and business alike have become opportunistic as it is more a means of gambling than an honest trade. At least in gambling both the parties are ready to win or lose, but in modern-day business we gamble with an unintending partner. When it comes to property and possession, we tend to justify absolutely everything in our favor.

Asteya is not only taking away one undeserving rupee from another; it also includes the hoarding of every single rupee. For example, where do we get our income from? It always comes from someone else's spending. What if someone else minimizes their spending? Naturally, our earnings will be diminished. Similarly, every rupee we spend results in someone else's earning, and this spending-earning cycle goes on indefinitely. Within this eternal cycle which we term as an 'economy', if someone happens to break this process by hoarding their money, they become guilty of depriving all those people of their livelihood. Within modern-day ethics we often overlook these misconducts. But in the ethics of Yoga, this amounts to stealing.

"You are going to make people's lives miserable," I complained to Kripanand.

He coldly replied, "I have not done that yet."

I slammed my notebook to the ground and stood up. Kripanand calmly but firmly said, "Please sit down. The lesson is not over yet. And what I am going to say now is better noted in your head than in the notebook."

I sat down and asked in a sarcastic manner, "To cut things short and make things easier, why don't you just give me a list of things that you think modern people are stealing?"

Kripanand continued, "I have no intentions of branding a whole bunch of modern-day people as thieves and liars. All I intend to do is give you the courage to question your own integrity every time you commit a wrong."

Kripanand went on to illustrate his point with a sweet little story. The story to this day resonates in my mind every time I am presented with the opportunity to compromise ethics.

"In the old days, there lived a king. He was known for his wealth, courage and benevolence. His subjects lived happily under his protection. One day, the king decided to surround his capital with a strong wall in order to provide safety and security from any sudden invasion. He employed an old, wise architect to accomplish the job. After all the necessary arrangements were done, the architect, with his team of workers, set out to work.

Soon the capital was surrounded from all sides with a strong, formidable wall. As the work was near completion, the old man decided to take a walk to inspect any possible defects in the construction. He was accompanied by his young son, a budding architect and builder. The father and son were discussing the merits of this particular building style and its appropriateness in regards to the future of the people's safety. Suddenly the old man noticed that two bricks were smaller and misfitting in the wall. He immediately sent someone to fetch the correct fitting bricks to redo that part of the wall. But his son suggested otherwise, as he said to his father, "What difference does it make if only two bricks are not fitting? This will not even be noticed by the invaders. Why don't you just leave it the way it is?"

The old man explained, "It is not about what it looks like. This wall is meant for our future safety. This defect, in spite of how little it looks, could render the entire wall weak. As you know, the total strength of a chain is only that of its weakest link. Furthermore, how can you show your face to anyone who knows about it?"

The son incredously replied, "There is virtually no one who knows about it."

The old man smiled and said, "My dear son, there are at least two people who know about it – you and me! Also, after the fall of the wall, even though the entire slain population may forgive us for what we have done, will we be able to forgive ourselves? For, can we account for the loss of all those innocent lives saying that we corrupted only two bricks?"

Kripanand further explained, "It takes real courage to face your own conscience and question your own integrity. We have been committing innumerable wrongs in everyday life and always try to get away with them. The moment you learn to take responsibility for your own conduct, you will realize what a wrongful life you have so far lived."

The moral of the story had a great impact on me, but I was finding it difficult to fathom how far it was practical.

In one last desperate attempt to save face, I asked Kripanand, "Do you really think all these little insignificant things that we do in life matter? As a child I have on so many occasions broken into my neighbors' orchards to steal mangoes and berries. Do you think all these innocent acts really stand in the way of my present spiritual development? I can honestly tell you, I never intended harm to anyone, and neither do I believe that my innocent little mischiefs were of any significant consequence. Believe me, I don't think we civilized, grown-up people commit anymore of such 'stealing' that you despise so much."

Kripanand stood up and exclaimed, "Oh really? Can you describe to me the life of one of your civilized grown-up people? Randomly select a single day of your working life and give me a true and honest account of how much stealing was committed on that day. I will see you in a while. In the meantime, contemplate and find out how much of a spiritual hypocrite you are."

'Spiritual hypocrite'! This expression hit me squarely on my face as I collected myself to reflect upon an honest account of a day. It was difficult at the beginning, but soon volumes of instances from my memory slowly unfurled. What gave me comfort was that all my thoughts and reflections were happening well inside me, hidden away from others' notice. Slowly, I began to craft the events of a day.

We so-called civilized, modern human beings live in a city, happily squeezed between home, the office and a nine-to-five existence. We get up in the morning and run to catch the bus to work, rarely managing to throw in a wash or an occasional breakfast. We hop on at the back of the bus and take a quick glance as to where the conductor is sitting. We make our way to a double seat which is furthest away from the conductor. We sit in one seat and occupy the other with our belongings. When we succeed in doing so, we have the pleasure of a little more space, not bothering about how many people may be standing in the bus. Unless another demands the seat, we keep it occupied until the end of our journey. The journey finishes with our eyes looking out of the window, secretly keeping in mind the whereabouts of the conductor. If we make it off the bus without paying the fare, we congratulate ourselves for being a few cents richer.

After getting down from the bus, we take a short detour to the coffee house. A little coffee, a little more politics, a lot more drama, and

munching on a half-eaten sandwich, we finally stroll into the office.
Twenty minutes late! We are sometimes pleased to find ourselves as one
of the first few arrivals. A sense of punctuality sweeps over us if the boss
is yet to arrive. Our office desk is usually the breakfast table. The
company or government pays us a good five figure (or more) salary to
engage ourselves in the endless business technically termed as 'gossip'.
The office working hours are well-utilized in discussing anything from
one's never-ending personal problems to the dramas of the previous
night's drunken affairs, followed by the perpetual office circus of 'he said
this, and she said that'. Within this rhapsody, we rarely fail to complain
about the extra workload squeezed into our hours.

After an ultra-stretchable lunch hour, we spend the afternoon
making a list of chores and a shopping list that we need to do before
getting home. As the list of the chores increase, our grumbling increases
proportionately about the Hitler of a boss that we have, who does not
allow us to wind up a few minutes earlier. The last hours of monotony
are dealt away by shuttling from desk to desk, making a few personal
phone calls or surfing the net. At least ten minutes before the end of the
official working time, we pick up anything from a paper clip to a printer
that we choose to 'borrow' indefinitely and rush to the railway station to
catch the earlier train home.

Upon reaching the railway station, we find that the ticket-vending
clerk also 'sincerely' left ten minutes earlier than official working time.
We then compliment ourselves for not having to pay for the train
journey. On our way home, our next stealing is enacted in the super-
market in front of the fruit display, as we invariably 'taste and sample'
a good quantity of grapes and cherries. We then reach home, never
failing to miss our favorite television soap. As we settle down in front of
the television, blissfully thanking God Almighty for having let us invent
this last hope of human happiness, we, of course, never bother to
remember that we quietly abstained from paying the television license.

I was beginning to question, if this more or less reflects the life of
a modern man, then where do we stand at this point? I was

experiencing a sense of shame, guilt and disgust. All these feelings and emotions might have been very apparent from my face. I don't know exactly what I looked like at that moment as Kripanand came over to me and asked, "What is wrong with you? Why do you look like that?"

I hid my face with both my palms and mumbled, "Everybody does it."

As he sat down, he sternly told me, "'Everybody does it' is no justification. If a wrong is committed by everyone, it does not become a right. Besides, you have your own responsibilities and your own character, conscience and integrity to account for. If every single day of our life we steal, in what way can we expect to have pure conduct for spiritual development? When we cause harm to others either physically or by telling inappropriate statements, we continue to inflict the mean acts of stealing. Then what kind of mindset do you think we will cultivate for spiritual growth?"

I looked up at him to see if he was enjoying my state of embarrassment. I found he wasn't. Instead his face reflected a strange mixture of firmness, kindness and sympathy. I delicately asked, "Is it possible to live a modern life without participating as a thief or a liar?"

He replied with a cold firmness, "If not, what is the purpose of living?"

For the next two days, I was left alone with my thoughts. No one bothered me much. They were probably all getting the stink, as I was wallowing in my own shit. Later that evening, I walked gingerly into the cave of Guru Angadanand. My mind was completely troubled and perplexed in regard to all the blind irregularities that we commit in everyday life. I was wondering if there was a way out, and since I had confessed the follies of modern social life, I was hoping for help.

After being in the company of my guru for some time, I felt

that I had regained some strength. Facing this ocean of kindness I was confident that I would be given a chance to wash away all my sins.

I started, "Acharya Kripanand has been teaching me the *yamas* that need to be practised for spiritual growth. But it seems to be an impossible task, to accomplish the perfection of the *yamas*. Is there a way or practice by which I can cultivate these divine qualities within myself without consciously having to follow a list of do's and don'ts? If a *tapah* is a *kriya*, then there should be a process to acquire and live these qualities, instead of just understanding them academically or intellectually. I have realized that the *yamas* are the greatest virtues to be lived. What a blissful and blessed life it would be, when we actually live a life that is absolutely harmless towards others."

My teacher interrupted me. "That is a nice piece of revelation. But my son, never forget about cultivating harmlessness towards yourself."

I continued to gape at him, as I could not quite understand what he was talking about. He read my mind and explained at length that the practices of *brahmacharya* (celibacy) and *aparigraha* (non-receiving) are powerful *tapahs* to protect a yogi in his spiritual pursuit. Before I could jump the gun and blabber my textbook understanding of *brahmacharya*, my guru held his palm up. I understood the sign and sheepishly reverted back to listening mode.

My guru began to explain in detail. "*Brahmacharya*, the term, is derived from the fusion of two words: '*Brahma*', which stands to denote the 'supreme element or substance' and '*acharan*', which denotes 'one's attitude, conduct, behavior or function'.

The human body consists of seven *dhatus* or primal substances: plasma, blood, muscle, fat, bone, bone marrow/nerves and semen or menstrual fluid, also known in Sanskrit as: *rasa, rakta, mamsa, medas, asthi, majja* and *shukra* or *arthva*. Each of the *dhatus* is created from another and in turn, serves as the source of creation of another *dhatu*. The first *dhatu*, *rasa* or plasma, is created from the food and nutrition that is added to the body. Its quality depends upon the amount of live elements that existed in the food. *Rasa* then goes on to create *rakta* (blood) in the body and so on, until the final stage when the *shukra* (the supreme element) is created."

My guru explained the importance of this supreme element. "The food taken in the period of a year, or one complete solar cycle, creates the full amount of *rasa* needed for the body, which in turn creates the amount of blood that is needed for a month. In this process, one year's food ultimately results in the creation of one drop of semen. Hence the *shukra* (semen) is of paramount importance for the body. The availability of semen in the body determines the strength, vigor, productive capacity and energy level of the body. *Brahmacharya* in its common parallel means the appropriate preservation, control and use of this supreme essence of the body. The deposit and behavior of semen in a person can be explained in terms of the energy substance of a battery. The more preserved and controlled *shukra* (semen) a person possesses, the more potency he has for spiritual growth."

I was beginning to realize the absolute unreasonable conduct of the modern man. If only some were taught the virtues of *brahmacharya*, it would have saved them from their present erratic and miserable condition. During my days of seeking, I read umpteen books and listened to an equal number of lectures about the virtues of *brahmacharya*, but never quite understood what exactly had to be done to cultivate and practise *brahmacharya*. Naturally, my next question to my guru was fermenting in my mind. "So what the hell do I actually have to do to practise it? I have already heard enough about it."

As if he had read my mind, my guru smiled and said, "For this purpose, I am going to send you to one of my good friends for a few months. His name is Acharya Sukhabodhanand. He is currently living in Nepal in a small ashram where he teaches about the great science and practices of Tantra. I could not recommend anyone better to teach you the tantric explanations of the yogic *kriyas* and the *kriya* for the practice of *brahmacharya*."

I began to get restless, as in my knowledge the seemingly vast impossibility of the spiritual ocean was getting broader by the day. The more I learned, the more I realized how little I knew. I was desperately trying to imagine what the end of this learning process would look like. I had a bleak smile on my face; I was beginning to imagine the cosmic vastness of super-conscious knowledge. I was feeling like a tiny speck of something confronting an endless void.

My guru's voice suddenly brought me out of my stupor. "Wisdom is not the realization of how much you know; it is the realization of how much you don't know."

He then enquired about the practical difficulties I had been facing during my nerve purification, which I started about a month earlier. I could not give him an instant answer, as my mind was still occupied with the subject of *brahmacharya* and Tantra.

Instead of giving him a straight answer, I said, "I thought we were talking about *brahmacharya*. Why did you suddenly change the subject?"

He immediately replied, "I have not changed the subject. I am talking about the nerve purification, which is the basis and foundation of all other subsequent *kriyas* that you will be doing. How do you think you can move forward to perform advanced *kriyas* and practices if you have not completed your purification yet? I am planning an appropriate time for you to visit Nepal, and therefore it is important for us to know what is happening in your purification practice."

For the n-th time that day, I apologized for my impatience. Until the late hours of the night, we discussed in detail my purification practices and my experiences in the process. At the end of our discussion, my guru nodded his appreciation for all the efforts I had put into my practice and made no bones about how slow an achiever I was.

Over the past few months at the ashram it became absolutely clear to me that these people up here surely know what they are talking about. Every time they would pause to give me explanations about the finest details of my practice and remind me how important it was to be extremely clear and beyond any doubt about my practice, for only then would come the right devotion and commitment. Before I fell asleep that night, with a deep sense of respect for my teacher I resolved to practise with the utmost sincerity until I no more remained a slow achiever.

Two weeks passed by, and in the meantime, I had very little direct contact with anyone in the ashram. I was always up well before sunrise and would take a wash before visiting my teacher for his blessings. I would always place my head at his feet and remind myself of my resolve. This daily practice always gave me the right steam to go beyond my mundane difficulties.

On this particular day, my morning sitting of purification was over, and I was sitting on a rock in the bright sunshine. I slowly closed my eyes and gradually merged into a blissful meditative silence with the surroundings. I could not say how long I remained in that state.

Suddenly it appeared to me as if my teacher was calling out for me. The sound of my name from his mouth was the sweetest music that I had ever heard. I did not move so I could hear my teacher calling my name a few more times. Finally I got up and looked around for him, but he was nowhere to be seen. I hurriedly went to his cave, but he wasn't there either. I went around the ashram asking where I could find him, but no one could give me an answer.

At first I was a little confused. I slowly started walking towards the nearby mountain ridge. There I found my teacher sitting on a piece of rock with his eyes closed and seemingly in a deep meditative state. I felt like running to him the way a small child would do after missing his mother for the whole day, but I did not want to disturb him. I slowly approached him and without opening his eyes, he spoke to me.

"Manmoyanand, this ridge is full of sharp rocks. Don't you think that you should have worn your slippers before coming up here?"

Only then did I realize that I had walked up the ridge of rocks and ice without my slippers. I decided to answer this question only in my mind. "Sharp rocks are not going to hurt me when I am walking towards you, Gurudev."

He opened his eyes and asked me to sit next to him.

With a gentle voice he said, "You will be going to Nepal in a few days, so you need to get prepared."

I was astonished and replied, "But Gurudev, what about my purification? Was I not supposed to complete it before I move anywhere?"

It came as a shock to me when he declared that my purification had been successfully completed. I was thrilled and elated, but very stupidly asked him, "How did you know?"

In a soft voice he said, "I do a little bit of Yoga myself sometimes."

After a short silence, I showered him with questions. He was definitely very amused as he gently placed his hand on my head and ruffled my hair.

After my excitement, he said, "And so much so, mister young yogi, at the moment you have four beautiful little gifts, and in the language of spirituality, we call them *siddhis*. They are like super-human psychic powers."

I immediately wanted to know, "What do I do with these *siddhis*?"

"The *siddhis* are the unintentional but necessary side-effects of every spiritual practice. We never practise solely for the achievement of *siddhis*, and it is not actually possible to achieve these powers in that way. For a practising yogi, the *siddhis* act like a measuring rod to denote the progress of the practice. The entire process of spiritual practice is dotted with a series of *siddhis*. You could say they are like little milestones on a journey. We don't take a journey only to a milestone, but still the milestone has its own role in the journey. It stands at its own point only to be approached and to be left behind. Never, ever be carried away by the power of your *siddhis*, as the one who stops at the milestone seldom completes the journey."

I was curious to know, "Is it possible for me to experience them?"

"Yes, they are yours; you can experience them at any moment and at any time you like. But for the time being, let me withhold their demonstration process from you. Only after you return from Nepal will I let you demonstrate them."

Still intrigued, I asked, "How will I be different after my stay in Nepal?"

He replied, "You will be a little more serious and a little less child-like than you are now."

∞∞∞∞

Nepal is a beautiful country. It didn't take long for me to recover from the fatigue and tiredness of the eighteen-day trek. Guru Sukhabodhanand and Mataji were more than happy to receive me as a reference from my guru. On the evening of my arrival, I took a walk around the ashram. I found a few men and women in clean white clothes meditating in the garden. All of them carried a bright, radiant and serene appearance about them. As darkness gathered, all of these men and women assembled in the ashram courtyard for evening prayer. There was a nice ambience, and a sense of peace prevailed over the whole ashram. After the prayer and the aarti, the men and women separated and went away in opposite directions. Mataji went away with the women, and Guru Sukhabodhanand asked me to follow him to a room.

In that room I was given my tantric initiation. He gave me a new piece of white cloth and asked me to change into it. After the nice and warm relaxing bath, my eyelids became really heavy, and I was almost falling asleep during my walk. Upon reaching the initiation room, the first thing I asked the teacher was if it may be possible to perform the ceremony the next day, as I was too tired and sleepy to participate. The teacher told me that my initiation had to be done there and then.

Very patiently he explained to me that no one, unless initiated, can spend a night in a tantric ashram. It was one of the many rules that the ashram followed to maintain its pure integrity. On hearing his explanation, I had nothing more to say. I tried my best to keep awake during the initiation. After the initiation, the teacher told me I would have to sleep in that very room for the night. He didn't mention anything about dinner. He just walked out and closed the door behind him, leaving me all alone in the room.

Whilst looking around the room and trying to understand my situation, I fell asleep. My sleep was far from peaceful; I was continuously awakened by strange sounds around me and constantly perturbed by many terrible nightmares. However an interesting thing in my dreams or delirium was the sound of the mantras which were being whispered in my ear during the initiation.

In the morning I was awakened by Mataji, who very lovingly took me to the kitchen and gave me some really nice food. After a satisfying breakfast, I took a wash, got into my whites again, and joined everybody in the courtyard. On noticing me, the teacher got up from his seat and took me to a corner of the garden where no one else could see me. He asked me to drop my clothes. He folded them nicely and made me stand on them. Facing the sun he asked me to hold my arms out-stretched to the sides with palms facing up. Reminding me of my initiation mantra, he then gave me complete instructions on how to chant the mantra and concentrate. Finally, he asked me to continue practising until I got at least five complete hard erections. He left me there alone as I tried to apply all my mental energy and imagination to achieve an erection.

During the days in my ashram this was the most neglected part of my anatomy. After a considerable amount of coaxing, I could not even manage to achieve one single erection. I was toying with the idea of touching and pampering to achieve my goal, but then Mataji appeared from nowhere. I hurriedly grabbed my cloth to wrap it around me, but she prevented me from doing so. With waves of embarrassment and shyness sweeping over me, I regained my posture of crucifixion. Mataji's comforting and assuring words helped me to relieve my tension. She then came around, sat directly facing me, and asked me to try the practices again. This time she gently touched my otherwise limp member while I tried my best to get an erection. With a little more effort I was pleased to find that this part of me was still functioning. A few minutes later I repeated the whole exercise again and after four repetitions, I found it was near impossible to get another erection. Mataji kindly asked me to put on my clothes and said it was enough for the day.

For the next two weeks I was to practise this exercise each morning. After the first few days I didn't need any more of Mataji's help to operate my own physical function. The next lesson added to my practice was to maintain the erection for as long as possible, and I was told that I had to maintain my erection for at least twenty minutes every time over the next few days. It took me another three weeks to achieve this feat. The third exercise involved the task of lifting weights with my erection. I began with the lifting of a hand towel, and soon I was a weightlifter of a massive one hundred grams. The lifting of the weight was not all to be achieved, as the weight had to be held as and when I wished, in addition to keeping it lifted for at least twenty minutes.

The stamp of the slow achiever followed me everywhere, as in this ashram I, too, was considered a pigmy among the colossus of sexual power. Most of the men in this ashram were able to lift at least one kilogram of weight, as well as being able to suck up nearly one ounce of milk or honey through their penises. I later learnt that this practice was known as *vajroli*, one of the most powerful *kriyas* to develop the ultimate control over one's sexual desire. It is the practice by which a yogi can have sex with any number of women, for any length of time, yet won't shed a single drop of his supreme essence. Mataji explained to me in detail the virtues of *brahmacharya* and the exact procedure of remaining in control of one's own sexual desire. During the discourses the teacher also made it very clear how the *Bindu* (the drop of supreme element) plays such a profound role in the cosmic play and the process of self-realization.

I lived for nearly six months in this ashram, and the time spent there would prove extremely valuable in my future yogic life. In that ashram I learned the practical processes of achieving and mastering *brahmacharya*. In addition to this vital *sadhana*, I also gained invaluable knowledge about the evolution of yogic practices and *kriyas*. It was amazing to learn about the cosmic and galactic nature of the human body and experience the movement of the divine forces within it, of which I will describe in the subsequent chapters.

Back in my ashram I clearly realized that I had grown up a little in the meantime. Very rightly, as my guru had said, I was not so child-like anymore. From being a very weak and timid boy, I had metamorphosed into a robust and confident yogi with absolute self-control. I was feeling very much like a living specimen of a forceful and virtuous *brahmachari*. Many of the ashram people also had begun to address me as *brahmachari* (a practitioner of *brahmacharya*). I had developed a very different opinion and respect about myself. Taking a good look at me, my guru nodded and said, "The suppression of desire is quite meaningless without the suppression of the ego."

In the presence of my guru, I began to understand the total implications of the *kriya* of *brahmacharya*. I learnt that the loss of semen is the last and extreme act against celibacy. Hence it is not the only act that makes us lose our vital energy. *Brahmacharya*, like other *yamas*, has to be total. It is not only the shedding of semen, but also any act, thought, idea, dream or fantasy that sends a tickle of sensual excitement through the body, resulting in the loss of sexual energy. For example, at the sight of a beautiful or sensuous woman, a certain electro-chemical reaction occurs in the body. This reaction is the first trigger of expectation or desire. This leads to the thought, behavior and consequently, our actions towards fulfilling this desire. The person in pursuit of this desire either gets to know her or fantasizes about her and consequently pleasures himself to tame his desire. Whatever be the action, the ultimate event is the loss of semen. This happens to both sexes. It is not to say that every time you see a person of the opposite sex the entire chain reaction takes place, but the first trigger almost invariably occurs. This varies from person to person depending upon their degrees of self-control.

Brahmacharya is the practice by which a person manages to contain the very first reaction and does not allow it to manifest. The moment the first trigger of sensuality takes place in the body, the vital energy storehouse, which lies at the base of the spine, begins to vibrate. It sends powerful electrical impulses throughout the body; this is experienced as the waves of desire and excitement that traverse the whole body. From this moment onwards one begins to lose energy, and by the time this automatic ongoing process is checked, one has already lost a considerable amount of vital energy. For that reason it is very important to have complete control over the vital energy system and never allow it to manifest in any sensual activity, thought or fantasy. In one's day-to-day life, these sensual expressions can be seen almost everywhere. The love for good food, the desire for a soft and comfortable bed, the obsession with looking good, the desire to be touched or any sensual behavior for that matter: all are, in a subtle way, a means to the loss of vital energy. Thus *brahmacharya*, in broad terms, denotes the absolute control of all the sensual expressions and reactions of and within one's own body.

By this time, I had satisfactorily completed several *kriyas* of purification, and after acquiring the right standard of purity, I had undergone the *kriyas* of *brahmacharya*. These *kriyas* were not exhaustive in themselves; they merely formed the foundation of the yogic or spiritual structure. Many of these practices are to be continued throughout one's life. They are no more the path, but the limits that define the path.

As I was beginning to relish the bliss of yogic life, I was yearning for my next practice. All those years of reading and intellectualizing about the virtues of non-receiving had barely resulted in any understanding. Here in my ashram, I was going through a process of true knowledge and real experience and was eagerly awaiting the unfoldment of the true essence of these highly intellectualized and misunderstood concepts.

One day while talking to Acharya Kripanand, I told him how fortunate and blessed I was to be spiritually guided by someone no less than Guru Angadanand. I did not remember earning this great fortune any time in my life.

I asked him, "Do you think I really deserve this privilege of being your student? Do you ever think of the incident in the train and think of sending me away? Why do you continue to tolerate me here, even though I am sometimes quite nasty and nagging or obstinate towards you?"

The ever-smiling face of Kripanand will remain in my memory forever. Through my eyes he has the most benevolent of faces in the world. He always appears to me as a very loving, kind, compassionate and utterly wise grandfather. I was mesmerized by his grace as he spoke to me.

"Manmoyanand, we always get what we deserve, and we never get anything beyond our worth or before its time."

I replied, "Do you really mean to say that I deserved the privilege to come to this ashram to be guided by you? Sometimes I feel so much indebted for all that I am receiving. Please tell me how I can feel happy and comfortable and not feel like a burden on you?"

Kripanand regarded me in silence for a while and replied, "Can you please ask the same question to Angadanand? I am sure he has a more convincing answer."

After spending a little longer with Kripanand, I ran to my guru and, as usual, bombarded him with my questions.

One thing I didn't like about everybody in the ashram was that they always knew my questions before I could even think them. In addition to this fact, they were always able to provide me with the best answer, almost as if they had been waiting to deliver it for quite some time. My guru patiently listened to all my questions, whilst at the same time busily arranging the pages of an old palm-leaf book. As he began to put the book away, he turned to face me and asked, "Can you guess how long I have known you?"

I replied, "A little more than a year."

He shook his head. "No, I have known you for at least the last five hundred years."

During the last year or so I had learnt not to laugh at such statements. I knew for certain that there would be a higher and greater implication of his statement. In disbelief, I stood gaping at him. So many thoughts were racing through my mind. I had not completely understood how and why these masters had agreed to shower me with an unlimited and unconditional flow of knowledge. Firstly, I always wondered what I had done to deserve this. Secondly, these people definitely knew something about me and my life which was unknown to me. Thirdly, my teacher was now telling me that he has known me for the last five hundred years. These unexplained mysteries were slowly forming a formidable matrix in my mind.

It was a great relief as my guru assured me there was nothing unusual about my thoughts. "What kind of yogi is he whose mind does not span the universe and whose thoughts do not race beyond the limits of the present life? No yogi will ever remain content without having an understanding of the cosmic arrangement of events. As a normal human being, one perceives only that lifetime in which they live. But a yogi's life is not limited to one lifetime; a yogi lives and perceives a much greater part of the whole evolutionary scheme.

As he begins his quest of the cosmic understanding, he stretches his lifespan beyond death. Death is only the end of the body. Life does not end there. The end of breath does not mean that there is an end of air. Yogis are, in fact, individuals constantly racing across the barriers of life and death, and whilst they remain in this process of cosmic movement, they know each other in just the same way you know your neighbor. They might be light-years apart from each other, but as long as they are traveling in the common space, they are definitely aware of each other's existence and progress. There is little to be astonished about the fact that I knew you for five hundred 'human' years."

Things were beginning to make sense to me, but the matrix was still not totally clear. Perceiving this my teacher continued, "The confusion that you are suffering today comes from the ignorance of the fact that we have been giving and taking from each other for a very, very long time. You do not have the account of all these transactions, of which I do. What appears to you as only one-way giving, in truth is not so. As Kripanand has already told you, we always reap the benefits of our past efforts, and without giving at some time in the past, we do not receive anything today. Now you can be very comfortable in knowing that all you are receiving today is solely the rewards of your past efforts."

I suddenly began to relax as I was beginning to relate to his explanation. I further asked, "Do you mean to say this is the law of karma? In truth, I don't quite like that. It makes one fatalistic."

My teacher laughed. "Now look who is talking!" He continued to speak whilst still laughing, "The term fatalistic is such a poor excuse against the law of karma. If you are not ready to accept the effects of your karma, then how do you relate to the law of physics? What happened to your university-educated pride when you nodded in agreement to Newton's law of motion? If the law of karma is wrong, then Newton's third law has to be discarded."

To my bewilderment, he continued to explain, "Newton's third law of motion is only a physicist's explanation of the law of karma. Every reaction has an exact opposite reaction. Every single thing that is happening at this moment is the reaction of an act that has occurred in the past: now it is daytime because there was a night sometime ago; I am teaching you now because I have studied in the past; you were born as a result of your death in the past; you see the great Himalaya around you as it is only a result of a collision in the past. Today you are standing at this point of life precisely because the entire collective forces of your past actions have brought you here."

My mind went back to my studies of the philosophy of *Advaita Vedanta*. Wasn't the old man who was 'playing' Sankaracharya saying something along this line? I was trying to recollect what he had said about the acceptability of the law of karma.

My guru lifted his folded hands to his forehead in reverence and said, "Today we don't have many people who actually understood what the great Sankaracharya had said about *Advaita Vedanta*. Instead, we have at least a couple dozen of *advaita vedantists* who dismiss the karma theory without having any understanding of it. The whole cycle of karma is applicable as long as you are only a physical living entity. The moment you perceive yourself beyond physical existence in the realm of non-duality, you are no more governed by the law of karma. The law of karma merely determines life, but a yogi who has transcended beyond the state of dualities experiences only one law. You can call it 'cosmic law', 'non-duality' or '*Advaita*' - as you like."

I asked for clarification. "Do you mean to say that if anyone dismisses the karmic cycle whilst still living within it and has not reached the non-dualistic state himself, it would be considered utter nonsense?"

"Yes, you can say that."

My teacher didn't allow me to continue fantasizing about how I would go and dismiss that old man and his non-sense.

A yogi cannot stay content without solving these mysteries: 'Who was I?' 'How was I?' 'What is this?' 'How is this?' 'What shall be?' 'How shall be?'

A yogi must go on to find these answers, as he deserves to have these answers. Only after achieving this knowledge can a yogi relate to the deeper unfoldment of consciousness. The key to this great stage of a yogi's journey was revealed to me in just one word, *aparigraha*, the fifth *yama* or restraint.

Aparigraha literally means the observance of 'non-receiving'. Every act of giving commonly has two necessary outcomes, and neither of them is beneficial to mankind. On the part of the giver, it results in a sense of pride and pleasure relating to their capacity to give. As long as the giver is not free from the pride and satisfaction, he is not actually giving anything. He is merely doing a business as he is only purchasing for himself confidence, image, pride, reputation, status, ego and some happiness. Due to the presence of this subtle element of business, the receiver is not fulfilled no matter how much is given. Therefore with every act of receiving, he doles out his own confidence, image, pride, reputation, status, ego and some happiness.

Giving gradually builds up the giver's ego and pride, and the receiver is gradually weighed down with his ever-increasing psychological burden. *Aparigraha* (non-receiving) is not just a term to read and re-read. It is, in fact, the conscious and practical act of non-receiving. Most of us will suffer some form of discomfort at the idea of the non-giving and non-receiving world. One of my friends used to argue, "Receiving is giving itself." To some extent he was right, but we never receive what we give away.

How can a yogi ever be free if he is constantly carrying the psychological burden of gifts and favors? By the actual and habitual practice of *aparigraha*, a yogi enters into the understanding that the giver and the receiver are but one element. The cycle of giving and receiving is endless and perpetual. The act of giving and receiving is only a reflection of the cause and effect of the same cosmic process. The only way to get to that higher truth is to completely withdraw from the give and take business of the mundane world.

The devastating effects of receiving and the psychological turmoil of being the receiver can sometimes exceed measurable limits. The following instance illustrates the effects of giving and receiving, along with its karmic implications.

Once I was traveling by bus to a distant place. Somewhere on the journey, the bus stopped in a small town. It was a kind of tea-and-snack stop. I had a little time in hand whilst everyone disappeared into the nearby tea stalls. I took the opportunity to stretch my legs and look around the little market that had grown around the bus stop. Here I met a man who looked very much like a beggar. He was wearing the usual torn and tattered clothing. He was begging with a pitiful and pathetic plea. As I walked passed him, he stopped me and pleaded, "Please, take this."

In his outstretched hand was a coin. I could not understand what was happening. I had never known of a beggar who offered money rather than asked for it. He again pleaded, "Sir, will you please take this?"

There was a strange and moving desperation in his pleading. I was somewhat bemused and bewildered as I walked away from him.

The beggar sadly walked a few steps closer to someone else and offered the money. Standing at a distance I continued to observe the beggar and his strange behavior. The more I looked at him, the more I became intrigued to know about him. Why would somebody who is obviously not rich try to give money away? His pathetic condition and pitiful pleading amplified my curiosity. I walked over to a nearby tea stall, chose a seat close to where the owner was sitting and started a casual conversation with him. After ordering a glass of milk, I asked the owner, "Could you please tell me something about that beggar? Why is he offering money to people?"

The tea stall man took a glance at the beggar and said, "Sir, that is a long story. He is only trying to pay back what he had received before."

I requested him to continue the story of the beggar at length.

The tea stall owner sighed deeply and continued, "His name is Syam Saran. He was a poor farmer from a nearby village. He had a little land and a small family. He was cultivating his land and somehow managing to support his family. He lived a very humble life, but always nurtured a wish to become rich. He had never imagined millions, but he was constantly looking for any opportunity to stretch his income to a more comfortable level. No one knows how he managed to think of such a silly idea, as he gradually started to moan about his poverty. He would visit his wealthier relatives and friends and try to invoke their pity by describing his misfortune. At the same time he would praise and compliment them for their fortune and wealth. He would invariably and perpetually express his unhappiness about his present state of affairs and indirectly plea for help.

Indian villagers are generally very kind and generous, and they don't *usually mind sharing a little of whatever they may have with someone who is in desperate need. This ploy of Syam Saran paid off, and he gradually accumulated quite a fortune in the process. By then he had taken to the taste of receiving gifts and favors. He was no longer a poor and humble farmer. While he continued to accumulate his pitiful fortune, his family members flaunted their wealth in front of their poorer relatives."*

The owner paused for a moment whilst he took another glance at the beggar.

"Six years ago there was a great and devastating flood. In the flood, Syam Saran lost his house, all his family members and all his fortune. Completely shaken, Syam Saran ran from door to door to gather sympathy and help for his condition. In such a desperate condition he didn't get any sympathy or help from anyone, as everybody in or around his village were more or less aware of his pretence and greed. The time when he needed help the most, all that people offered him was a reminder of how much he was already indebted to the village. Gradually Syam Saran broke down and stopped wandering from door to door. Everyday he was seen sitting at some corner of a street and silently crying. He never spoke to anyone or stopped crying.

Slowly people began taking pity and started to toss a coin or two towards him. Somebody would give him some food, and Syam Saran soon became a permanent part of the village landscape. He would eat the food that was given to him, but began to laugh at the sight of money. For the last four years or so, he has not used any money that has been tossed at him for his own needs. Instead, he is desperately trying to give the money away to people. Maybe he is trying to do a penance for the deeds of his life?"

I stood up, paid for my milk and thanked the tea store owner for the account of the strange beggar. The driver of my bus was honking to get the passengers back into the bus. I looked around and spotted the beggar in the crowd. I walked over to him and held my hand out and asked for his coin. With a wide smile on his face and an obvious sense of satisfaction, he placed the coin in my hand and said, "Thank you."

As I took the coin from him something stirred deep inside me, and I made my way back to the bus.

Syam Saran is a prime example of the psychological debts that one incurs by receiving gifts and favors. Initially the pleasures of the gifts and favors may cloud one's mind and make one forget about the psychic consequences, but sooner or later the accumulated psychological burden becomes far heavier than the superficial pleasures of enjoying it. Today, Syam Saran is considered a lunatic. Well, think again. Imagine what is in store for anyone who is living oblivious to this subtle and tragic truth of life.

The practice of the *yamas* is of great importance for a yogi. The practice of *brahmacharya* and *aparigraha* transcends a yogi to a superhuman state of body and mind, while the practice of *ahimsa, satya* and *asteya* earns him the good will and blessings from mankind. How can the ultimate journey of human life be accomplished without these invaluable advantages? As it is absolutely senseless to ride a horse whilst it is tied to a tree, it is absolutely futile to attempt yogic practices without observing and practising the *yamas*. The exact practices of the *yamas*, like those of *ahimsa, satya* and *asteya*, are to be derived from several ancient texts. Here the guidance of the guru is of utmost importance as a guru is in a better position to know our exact standpoint in the karmic cycle.

Over the next few days, I received lessons on *vairagya* (detachment). The practice of detachment and the *yamas* are very closely related. My guru explained in detail the austere practices of the *yamas*. I then took my first meaningful step in the path of spirituality.

There was a great change in my daily schedule. My practices began at sunrise. I would take a bath, get into my cave, and for the first hour or so, enter into a contemplative composure and stillness. I would then begin to recite in my mind the vows of the *yamas* in the form of concise mantras and incantations. After spending the entire morning in the cave, I would come out for the practice of the second phase of the austerity, which is accomplished by consciously relating to every element in the natural surrounding. Every element that you see is standing as a selfless performer and a silent witness to the cosmic glory. A yogi essentially needs to be one with his surroundings.

Within the first few months of these practices I had witnessed great resistance and unspeakable tumult inside me. I don't know how I could have gone through that phase without the constant support and assurances of my guru. I felt his powerful presence all around me every time I was about to drop my practice. Soon the world around me began to change. In fact, it was only my perception about the surroundings that had actually changed. I began to experience the world as one divine unit.

To achieve complete success in a spiritual practice, the yogi needs to firmly set the foundation disciplines in place. As explained earlier, the *yamas* and *niyamas* form the basis of a yogic practice. As one learns from various ancient spiritual scriptures, including the Yoga Sutras, the destruction of impurities always precedes the gradual performance of the component parts of Yoga. The two most important aspects of this undeniable basis of practice are 'austerity' and 'detachment'. The restraints, as we have already discussed, provide the austere state for the yogi and creates the right kind of psycho-physical state to proceed in the practice. On the other hand the *niyamas* (principles) are designed to give a yogi the right amount of detachment. Detachment is one such quality which alone determines divinity.

Here you may ask, 'Does the Divine need to have a sense of detachment?' Detachment, as commonly understood, is like a rein applied to materially erring people. Let us now examine the importance of detachment, even for the Divine.

Most of us have heard the term *Bhagwan*. Many people have

this common name in India, and many others use this term as a title to decorate their spiritual status. This word is a combination of two expressions, *'Bhag'* and *'wan'*. *'Wan'* stands for 'the one who possesses': for example, *Balwan*, where *'Bal'* stands for 'force'; hence *Balwan* denotes the powerful. Another example is *Dhanwan*, where *'Dhan'* stands for 'wealth'; hence *Dhanwan* denotes the wealthy. Similarly, *Bhagwan* denotes the one who possesses *'Bhag'*. The single word *'Bhag'* stands for five absolute qualities. Anyone who possesses these five qualities in the absolute sense can be called *Bhagwan*. These five qualities are absolute force, absolute wealth, absolute knowledge, absolute fame and most importantly, absolute detachment.

Therefore, without absolute detachment, there cannot even be a *Bhagwan*. Many eastern religions speak of innumerable gods and goddesses. Some of them are worshipped for their strength, wealth or any such material absoluteness and are often described in a very human-like character. However, it is the essential quality of detachment that makes the Divine stand apart from the hoards of lesser gods.

I remember an old ascetic with whom I used to spend my childhood days. I was always curious to ask him why he chose not to live in a house, why he did not have any wealth, and why he did not do anything to earn some money. Did he not know that he could buy so many nice things with money? This old ascetic had given me my first lesson on detachment. At that time it was beyond my understanding, but the simple analogy that he used is still very clear in my memory. It is a pleasure to share it with you.

He asked me, "Do you know some arithmetic?"
"Yes."
"Do you know the difference between numbers and zero?"
"Yes."
With his finger he drew some numbers on the floor and some zeros on the other side and said, "Wealth is like numbers, and the zero stands for

detachment. As you add a zero to a number the value of your wealth becomes ten times more. The more detachment you add to your wealth, the more your wealth increases. If you continue adding detachment to your limited wealth infinitely, you actually end up being the owner of the entire universe. Without adding any detachment, you only enjoy your wealth within its material limits."

It is necessary to have the right amount of detachment to further the spiritual effects of austerity. The first step towards detachment is *saucha* or purity. Guru Nirupanand is the *saucha-master* of my ashram. He seemed to have the right tone to instill this powerful practice in a yogi's life. When he started explaining *saucha*, I didn't jump the gun to blabber how much I had read and was previously taught about it. I behaved properly during his teaching – partly because of his powerful nature, and more importantly, I had already dumped my past notions of *yamas* and *niyamas*, as there was an urgent need to discard them under the light of the pure knowledge that I was now receiving from my masters. The great process of learning in the ashram also involved a great process of un-learning, and over the years I learned to accept the many pains of this process.

The *kriya* of *saucha* can be accomplished through several stages. *Saucha* commences from the purification of the external body and gradually proceeds to the internal body, nervous or psychic centers, and the mind, resulting in the ultimate detachment of the impure physical state from the absolute pure self. Beginning with the external body, keep it clean and free from all impurities. This can simply be achieved by washing the body thoroughly. Bathing once or twice a day keeps the body reasonably clean. A ritualistic early morning bath is not what I am talking about. The actual cleansing effect of the bath is important, not the ritual.

How often one cleans himself can vary from place to place, time to time and person to person. People often apply certain cosmetic condiments on their face or body in order to 'feel' clean and confident, which in reality defeats the whole idea of cleanliness. If you do not feel clean by taking a bath, you are free to keep bathing until you feel really clean. Always remember to wash yourself thoroughly after you go to the toilet.

Not only is it important to make the body clean, it is also important to keep the body clean. The maintenance of the cleanliness of our body largely depends upon what we add to it. If we refrain from adding any superficial substances on our body, we can then proceed to talk about our dietary habits.

Food plays a very important role in the internal cleansing of the body. Foods that give offensive by-products to the body are to be avoided. For example, food that gives you gases, constipation or unpleasant body odor or sweating should be avoided. We cannot actually make a list of food items that can be universally applicable to everybody. Application of a little wisdom on this matter would suffice. If you are still in doubt, consult a good book or an expert in Ayurveda who would determine your physical constitution and suggest a dietary regimen based upon your individual situation. Refraining from inappropriate food and drinks makes it possible to advance in the practice of *saucha*.

The ancient wisdom of Ayurveda contains several proven methods of detoxification of the body. If you have never done any cleansing *kriyas*, it would be useful to go for the Ayurvedic cleansing processes. After proper and thorough cleansing of the internal parts of your body, it is important to adopt the hatha yogic cleansing *kriyas*. The *kriyas* such as *neti, dhauti, nauli, basti* and *kapalabhatti* should be practised under an experienced teacher. The frequency and intensities of such practices are again dependent upon the capacity of the individual. After a while, every individual usually understands their own capacity and limitations and can accordingly set the rhythm of their practices themselves. A clean body has a clean and clear fragrance. The experience of this fragrance gives you the knowledge of the cleanliness of your body. After achieving this cleanliness and fragrance of the body, one can proceed to the more subtle aspects of purification.

The human body has its own subtle channels through which *pranic* energy moves. It can be compared to a complex electrical circuit. As an electrical circuit has to be absolutely flawless for its function, similarly the psychic energy channels of the human body have to be absolutely flawless in order to be manipulated. After the complete physical purity of the body is achieved, we can expect to have a healthy system of psychic channels. The strength of our psychic channels and nervous system plays a very important role in cleansing the *pranic* body. Those who are using any kind of stimulants are likely to have weaker psychic channels. Habitual dependency on certain psychotropic substances can also lead to the weakening of this system. In my own experience, I have seen ex-drug addicts take an enormously long period of time to achieve psychic purification in comparison to normal people.

This *kriya* of purification is known as *nadi sodanham*, *bhuta shuddhi* or *sarvanga nyasa* under different scriptures. There are several kinds of practices available for its accomplishment. Before choosing any one of the systems, it is useful to keep in mind that you have successfully undertaken all the psycho-physical prerequisites mentioned earlier. Only then will your teacher choose the exact dose of the practice that is appropriate for you.

Before we move on to discuss the detailed practice of *saucha*, allow me to briefly refer to some of the alternative methods of this practice. In my days of seeking prior to coming to my ashram, I had spent a couple of months in Varanasi. During the stay I had taken to studying the practices of the *aghora* sadhus, those living in one of the numerous cremation *ghats* along the holy river

Ganges. I am forbidden to disclose the name of the sadhu with whom I had once lived.

These *aghoras* have some ingenious ways to develop the sense of detachment towards their own bodies. They follow various forms of practice and rituals in which they use the human body as any other inanimate object. They use the corpses of the dead as a seat to sit upon whilst meditating. The flesh is used as an offering to their deity, the *maha aghora*. Depending upon the quality and sex of the body, they use it for various purposes ranging from food to sexual intercourse. In the words of my *aghora* companion, the body is simply a lump of matter. There is no use being so attached to it. Whether my body or yours, it all goes up in flames to become an offering to the *maha aghora*.

Nirupanand made no bones about the fact that the kriya of purification has to be taken with absolute clarity and sincerity. He gave innumerable instances of how small misunderstandings about the process render your time and efforts useless. His description of the nerve purification process was akin to the cleaning process of a gun barrel. As the passage inside the barrel of a gun has to be absolutely clean and free from any blockages and impurities, similarly the channels through which our psychic energy moves have to be impeccably clean. Without the correct passage, it would be disastrous to introduce enormous force through it. One can also relate to the example of an electrical circuit in which the connections need to be flawless before the main power source is switched on. Always remember, it will be an unpleasant experience to have a blasted barrel or an exploded electrical appliance or a neuro-physical experience of the same description.

Nirupanand took meticulous care in explaining the nature and behavior of psychic energy in the body. "The body is largely divided into two zones, the left and the right. So is the brain. One-half of the brain controls and regulates the opposite half of the body, and vice versa. All the major components of the body are also available in pairs."

He went on to explain the reason for such a structure of the body and the brain. "The body is a fusion of two different entities, the male and the female. All the masculine and feminine aspects of our body and mind are appropriately arranged in the body as well as in the brain. As modern science has also discovered, the two sides of the brain deal with the masculine and feminine nature of the individual. The right side of the body and the left side of the brain are masculine in nature, whereas the left side of the body and the right side of the brain are feminine in nature. Even though the organs of both sides of the body look very much alike, there is a very definite and subtle difference in their functions.

What makes the difference is the flow of *prana* or cosmic energy through the organs and the behavior and manifestation of the *prana* within them. *Prana* itself is sexless. It is neither masculine nor feminine, but while traveling through the right side of the body, its functions are masculine in nature. Accordingly, it becomes feminine as it traverses through the left side of the body."

Here Nirupanand paused to ask a very funny question that I had never thought before. "Do you know that the entire air passage from the top of the nose until your lungs is but a single tube? If that is the case, why do we have two nostrils?"

All of us listening continued to offer some really funny and absurd guess-works until Nirupanand actually explained the reason.

"The nostrils work as air-intakes, as well as chimneys, of the two sides of the body. When we notice that one of our nostrils is flowing more than the other, we have to understand that the corresponding part of the body mechanism is at work. The flowing of the right nostril denotes the active working of the right and masculine side of the body. At this time the individual feels most active, energetic and willing to function. On the other hand, when the left nostril is flowing more than the right, we can conclude that the left or feminine elements of the body are at work. Under such conditions the individual is in a relaxed state. Sleep, relaxation, rejuvenation, healing and development are some of the functions that the body is undertaking."

One may have noticed that at some time or another during the day, our nostrils do not breathe alike. The peculiar working styles of the nostrils, as well as the different sides of the body, are both a direct outcome of the time of the day. As explained earlier, the solar and lunar movements directly affect the functioning of the body. Hence, at different times of the solar and lunar conditions, the nostrils flow differently. There are certain times during the day when such conditions shift naturally. The primary idea of this purification is to harmonize the energy flow and dynamics of the body by aligning them with the natural changes. These natural changes usually occur four times in a day: at sunrise, at midday, at sunset and at midnight. At these four precise times, everything under the sun or moon undergoes a definite change. The life cycles of the plants and animals very closely depend upon these changes. The effects of these changes can be seen and observed by the opening and closing of flowers and plants or by the natural behavior of many birds and animals. The purification practices are to be performed exactly in line with these natural changes.

The subtle psychic energy travels through the body in two major channels called *ida* and *pingala*. These channels lie close to the spinal cord in the body. Hence, it is of utmost importance to keep the spine very straight and stress-less during the practices. We have to adopt a comfortable posture for the practice of the purification. Nirupanand demonstrated how one should sit down to perform this practice.

After sitting in a comfortable and relaxed position, breathe through your nostrils alternately. One has to use the thumb and ring finger of the hand to close the nostrils. The breathing always begins with the left nostril whilst the right is closed with the help of the thumb. Without any retention of air, one should breathe out through the right nostril while closing the left with the ring finger. This process is repeated in a reverse manner. Left handed people can use the left hand for this practice while the other hand can rest on the lap.

Like most of you, I thought that Nirupanand was talking about the overly used alternative breathing or *anuloma-viloma pranayama*, something most have done in some yoga class or other. I had also done this mindless ritual for several years, and it never helped me in any way. Some popular 'gurus' of India speak highly of the healing effects of this practice. Over several years of experience I had learned not to believe in such crap. I was definitely eager to place my doubts before Nirupanand.

He patiently explained that the practice of a yogic *kriya* is like an experiment in a science laboratory. An absolute clear under-standing of the experiment is required in order to do it effec-tively. The result of the experiment is not dependent upon how long you practise; rather it depends upon how correctly you practise. My curiosity and excitement crossed all boundaries I had known before, as I was about to acquire the secret ingredients of a successful practice.

Nirupanand explained, "It is important to keep the body aligned with the natural energy axis of the earth and sun. With a conflicting gravitational or magnetic field it will be extremely difficult to achieve success of the purification practice. In the precision of the practice lies the key to its success."

The usual length of this purification practice is about sixty days. However, some people accomplish it much earlier, while others take years to experience even the first glimpse of purifi-cation. The entire purification of the subtle energy channels takes place grossly in four phases. The accomplishment of each phase is heralded by some beautiful, super-human experiences called *siddhis*. A practitioner can actually experience and demonstrate his super-human capacities or powers by the blessing and permission of his guru. In my case, the entire purification was accomplished in forty-six days. After its completion I was sent to Nepal.

To conclude, Nirupanand gave us a piece of history as he exclaimed, "In the history of this psychic purification, no one is known to have accomplished it without the presence and constant guidance of the teacher."

Life in the ashram is very strange. I was looking around the ashram and smiling to myself. This place, unknown to almost everybody in the world, lays in a corner of the mountains some five thousand, six hundred meters above sea level. It is perpetually covered by ice. The only inhabitants of this mountain abode are a few half-clad yogis, and there are only a few caves with hard rock floors that serve as our apartments. There is no bathroom, no toilet and no hot water. It is extremely cold up here, as the nighttime temperature in the peak of summer remains below zero. None of us have jackets or overcoats. We eat one simple meal a day. We have nothing one in the modern world would equate to comfort, yet none of us ever have any complaints. We are perfectly and blissfully happy here. I was asking myself what makes us so comfortable here when we have absolutely nothing for such comfort. The irony of the question brought upon my smile.

A friend of mine was passing by. I called him as he came closer and asked, "Have you ever heard of Adam and Eve?"

He hesitated for a moment and then said, "Yes!"

"Do you know in which country Adam and Eve lived?"

He thought for a moment and replied, "I can't say."

I answered, "They lived in India!"

He smiled and said, "I don't think so!"

"Think of this. These two people had no clothes to wear, no house to live, no car to drive, and only one piece of fruit to eat, yet they called it Paradise. They could not have come from anywhere other than India."

He laughed and nodded in agreement. I got up and walked with him to where Acharya Kripanand was sitting. My friend and I enthusiastically asked Kripanand the question about Adam and Eve and also got him to laugh.

Kripanand in turn asked us, "Do you know what could have been the secret of their happiness?"

After thinking for a while, we replied in unison, "I don't know."

Kripanand simply answered, "The answer is contentment. Contentment does not depend upon any material possession. There are no instruments for contentment. Yet it is contentment that is the only difference between this world and Paradise."

Contentment is a state of mind which can be cultivated and practised like any other skill. The practice of contentment mostly depends upon the way we relate to our possessions. Let us examine the small reasons that lie behind every one of our possessions. Each item we have accumulated and surrounded ourselves with is only a superficial attempt to ignore the intrinsic and perpetual sense of unhappiness. Someone in history once said, 'Suffering is a universal truth of life.' Kripanand at once corrected me, "Suffering becomes the universal truth of life as long as you do not live life as it is supposed to be lived. When one lives in accordance with the true purpose of life, one lives a life of contentment. There is no place for suffering in a life of contentment."

I added, "You are talking in the lines of the great Buddha."

He replied, "Who do you think, other than Buddha himself, could have spoken these immortal lines? Buddha was right when he held desire to be the cause of all suffering. Human desire is endless, and endlessly one goes on to accumulate and surround himself with objects. He expects all his possessions to tell him that he is not unhappy. Sitting amidst the material frenzy of the world, everyone pretends to be happy. As soon as the support of the pretense ceases to exist, the suffering again surfaces."

Kripanand concluded, "The true process to destroy desire is to accept and adopt the most humble life."

Here in this ashram we live with the barest of necessities. The food is just enough for survival. The possession of one piece of cloth is just enough for its purpose. The whole idea of living in the ashram is to realize and live life as it is supposed to be lived. I got my answer. Contentment lies deep inside everyone. In order to find contentment you can only detach yourself from all that you possess and all that you desire.

CHAPTER FOUR

Yoga Beyond Fitness

It was the beginning of summer, and people in the ashram were spending more and more time outside in the open. One of my favorite things to do in the morning was to take a quiet walk into the mountains and immerse myself in the blissful surroundings with a soothing and serene contemplation. I slowly developed a growing desire to be lost in the profound silence. The mountains provided me with a silence that was intoxicating and inviting.

I would always attempt to blend my thoughts with the surrounding silence. It was never easy. The silence seemed to be talking to me; I could almost hear it whisper. I always had a strange attraction to what it was saying, but I had never been able to make out exactly what it said.

The more I would take myself into the quest of silence, the more it seemed to fade away. Gradually I became restless and irritated as to why I could not get closer to silence. In my walk, I would sometimes stop in my tracks and sit down in an attempt to have a better perception of it. But the more the mind was racing, the further away seemed this elusive whisper. I soon found that it was not in my control to make my ever-racing mind sit down. I decided to ask my guru for help.

Later that evening, I walked into my guru's cave and sat down without speaking a word. In this cave too, there was a silence, but it was different. This silence was not tormenting or titillating. It seemed as if the silence in my guru's cave was constantly in a vibrant state, as if it were perpetually engaged with my guru in some kind of conversation. After a little while, the silence here began to fade away. Before it turned into a 'dead' silence, my guru spoke to me. "What is troubling you, my young yogi?"

I touched his feet and asked, "Gurudev, please tell me, does silence speak?"

He smiled. "Yes, silence has a voice. The rest of the things that you hear are only noise."

I remained silent for a while. I folded my hands, and with a tone of deep respect, I begged, "Please tell me how I can hear the voice of silence. For the past few weeks I have been constantly trying to follow this whisper everywhere, but it wouldn't come to me. Please tell me what I can do to take myself into that state of silence forever. I am sure that this silence holds the answer to every question I could ask."

My guru replied, "The silence you have been chasing around, in fact, is found everywhere. But it won't be possible for you to run everywhere and grab it. The best way to find silence is to delve right into the depths of your own self. Probably you will be able to do so, but before that, you will need to still your mind. Without quietening the ever-chattering mind, how can you possibly listen to silence? The reason you failed to hear the voice of silence was only because of the incessant chattering of your mind."

I then asked my guru, "How do I make the stupid mind shut-up? Does it not know that I have something better to hear? Is it a good idea to point a gun at my head and squeeze the trigger? Probably that will make the stupid mind shut-up forever."

My guru smiled and said, "Yes, it could be a good idea, but by doing so you won't be able to hear the voice of silence either. The bullet will not only shut-up your chattering mind, it will also shut-up your listening mind."

It took me a few minutes of powerful mental struggle to come out of my notion that I had gathered in Pune from the master of so-called Dynamic Meditation. He had said that 'Yoga is the cessation of mind'. The 'master' had explained in his captivating flowery discourses that a yogi should successfully kill the mind, and Yoga is a state of 'no-mind'. Only now I came to realize such an action would be as foolish as throwing the baby out along with the bathwater. Yoga is about the elimination of the storms from the mental planes. It is never to be misunderstood that it is the elimination of the mind itself. The sutra *'Yogaschittavrittinirodhah'* (1:2) explains about eliminating the *'vritti'* and not the elimination of *'chitta'*. The plane of mind is very necessary in the process of formation of matter. In the reverse process it is the necessary phase of transition between the material plane and the state of enlightenment.

My guru went on to explain clearly, "The secret of a yogi is that he knows the trick to keep aside his chattering mind and immerse himself in the voice of silence. Once he is in the voice of silence, he stays there forever. He comes to know the answer to all his questions. That state is called Meditation."

I jumped up and demanded, "Please teach me Meditation!"

My guru reached forward and hugged me, and in his kind voice he said, "Do you know why I have got you here? It is because I love you so much. I have always loved you so much, ever since the day I came to know you. If Meditation was a bar of chocolate, I would have gathered all the chocolates from all over the world and given them to you. You are certainly going to receive what you are asking for. But you need to have patience. The perpetual state of Meditation is one of the highest things to be achieved. A lifetime is not quite enough for this purpose. If you really want to accomplish such a thing, you have to be prepared to take every step of whatever it may take to get to that point."

I remembered the strength of my resolve and how I had used it to accomplish some of the tough *kriyas* of the past. With a confident tone, I affirmed my resolve before my guru. He closed his eyes for a moment. I felt this could be nothing other than a whole-hearted blessing for me.

He spoke again. "The first step towards your goal will be to go beyond the limits of your physical body. By that you will be able to subjugate your senses, and ultimately, the mind. Tomorrow morning Kripanand will give you your first lesson on the process to break free from your physical limits."

Kripanand seemed to be waiting for me when I approached him the next morning. He walked me into the sunshine. He folded a blanket, placed it on the ground, and made me stand on it facing the sun. He declared, "It's time we learn the 'Asana' of yogic practice."

The mention of asanas came as a shock to me. In bewildered defiance I exclaimed, "What the hell! Why am I supposed to do those silly gymnastics? There is no use of them! Don't you know, so many people in the world have been doing these exercises for ages and never got anywhere? You may not believe that I have done enough of this crap before. I am absolutely sure there is nothing spiritual about it! My guru had told me that you were supposed to teach me how to meditate and how to listen to the voice of silence. That is what I am interested in – I am not interested in doing any more of those gymnastics!"

Without losing his calm, Kripanand answered, "Yogi Manmoyanand, I am going to teach you Asana, which in my understanding, you have never practised before. Not gymnastics."

I stopped short of my outburst and reduced my tone, "What do you mean? Are asanas not just a set of gymnastic gyrations? Do you not do asanas just to gain some physical and health benefits? Is it not true that asanas are meant to give relief from a host of diseases and discomforts, like back pain, diabetes, stress, hypertension, arthritis and the complications of pregnancy? There are a dozen of world famous gurus out there who have been teaching these asanas in every conceivable style to suit the needs of every individual in the world. Dear Sir, I don't consider myself to be one of those fitness freaks who throng to such yoga classes everyday!"

The initial shock of Kripanand gave way to amusement. As soon as I stopped, he started to laugh aloud. He then called out to the people around and asked them to gather in front of me. "Dear Sir," he addressed me with an exaggerated politeness, "would you be kind enough to repeat all that you have just said to me before this congregation?"

After a little more prodding, I timidly repeated everything, which made everyone burst out laughing. In a state of absolute bewilderment, I demanded to know, "Is there something wrong with me, or is there something wrong with everybody here?"

Still laughing, Kripanand answered, "There is nothing wrong with anyone here. You have only just told the joke of the century!"

I still couldn't understand and continued to look silly. As the gathering slowly began to disperse, Kripanand sat next to me and explained. "Now listen to what I have to say very carefully. The physical body is a formidable obstacle for a practitioner and stands in the way of entering into the spiritual realm of the self. The body has innumerable afflictions attached to it. This body and your attachment to it is the root cause of all your desires – and desire is the root cause of all your sufferings.

The real purpose of life is not to limit your experiences to the outcomes of the body. What you are looking for in life actually lies beyond the life of this body. Physically, or humanly, it is impossible to go beyond this obstacle. Asana is a *kriya* that helps you break through the limits of the physical body and allows you to experience the subtler aspects of existence that lie beyond it. This is the reality of an asana. Any practice, no matter what you call it, if it builds and further enriches this obstacle, cannot be termed an asana within the meanings of Yoga."

Each word of Kripanand hit me squarely in the face with considerable impact. It took me a little while to regain my composure. I asked firmly, "Who says that? I have never heard this explanation before from any yoga teacher or master I have met in my life. To make this powerful statement, one has to rely heavily upon some true authority of Yoga or has to be highly experienced or an accomplished master. There is always more than one angle from which to look at it. Maybe whatever you are saying is right, but it is possible that there could be another explanation of Yoga or version of practice which could be equally true."

Kripanand reminded me that I had already told the ultimate joke of the century, and I should save this one for my grandchildren. "Please keep these questions properly saved in your mind, for they will be no more by the time you begin to experience the effects of a true asana."

Kripanand went on to elucidate, "Every principle of Yoga, including those of the asanas, is exact and definite in nature, just like the laws of physics. The science of physics does not create a principle. It only discovers a principle. All the modern science that exists today only attempts to discover and explain the way nature works. For example, the law of gravitation is only a discovery of physics, but the principle of gravitation belongs to nature. Scores of scientists may have explained the laws of gravitation in their own words, according to their own individual understanding. In such cases their explanations are bound to be different from one another. A change in the law of gravitation by man does not change the principle of gravitation in nature.

No matter which school you attend, one plus one always equals two. You can write the numbers in as many different styles as you like, but the formulas of mathematics remain the same. It would be absolutely foolish and absurd to think that a change in the style or performance of an asana changes its precise scientific equation. You are free to change the shape of an asana, but you cannot change the substance of an asana. In the forthcoming days you will be studying the structure, the substance, the effects, as well as the evolution of asanas. For this purpose, you need to have a completely open mind. A clear and complete understanding of asanas is absolutely necessary before you even attempt the first one."

The explanation of the term Asana is like explaining the A to Z and back to A of the evolutionary cycle. The evolutionary process has taken billions of years to develop the first few atoms of matter from an immense non-material void. It took a further few million years more to create the first egg-like unicellular organism. From that day until now, nature has used a further few million years in crafting the final products of creation. We, the Homo sapien sapiens, are so far the ultimate product of this process. In other words, the human beings are the ultimate manifestations of the ever-evolving supreme consciousness.

Do you know why it took the creator such a long time to make us in this way? If being human is all about the form, we could have been manufactured a lot earlier. The only justification for this extensive period of time is due to the constant process of assimilation. It has taken over millions of years of evolutionary development to form this fine, compact and supremely capable specimen. The human body that we see today is the total culmination of all the bodies of all the species that have been created so far. The capacity of the human mind is also the sum total of all the intelligence that has been put to play until today.

Thus arise the natural questions: 'If all of the above is true, then what is the 'big idea' behind the intentions of nature? What does nature expect from us? What could be the purpose behind putting such a capable human body together with such a capable mind? Why are we so ignorant about our true potential and the true nature of ourselves?'

Let us look for the answers in the following story. This story is collected from the old fables of ancient India. If I remember rightly, somebody made a beautiful animation movie of it.

Long, long ago there lived a herd of sheep at the edge of a jungle. Everyday the shepherds would drive the herd into the jungle for grazing. After a day's grazing, the herd would come back to their place to rest for the night. One day while they were grazing in the jungle, a ewe heard a strange and curious noise. After hearing it a few times, she came to understand that it was the noise of a lion cub. She immediately ran away in fright.

The next day she heard the same noise in the jungle. This time the noise appeared more weak and pained than before. She wanted to go and investigate what had befallen this poor lion cub. After gathering some courage, she moved closer to the sound and discovered that a small baby lion was lying under a bush crying pitifully. The pitiful cry of the lion cub filled the ewe with love and compassion, for she was a mother herself. She thought that the cub's mother might have been dead or had deserted the baby. So she decided to feed the baby. After being fed with her milk, the baby lion was happy and soon fell asleep in her lap. The ewe stayed with the baby all day, but in the evening she had to return along with her herd.

From that day on, she would find time everyday to visit the baby lion and feed it. The baby lion would also wait for her return. Many days passed by. The rainy season arrived and now there was plenty of grass everywhere. There was no need for the herd to go into the jungle anymore. This made the mother ewe worried about the baby lion as it became difficult for her to go to the jungle everyday to feed him. So one day she took the baby lion along with her into the herd.

The baby lion lived in the herd and soon grew up to become the ugliest sheep anyone had ever seen. Because of his appearance he had become an object of mockery and ridicule by his fellow sheep. They laughed at him and the ugly growth of wool around his neck and pulled his funny long tail. The lion would often run to his mother and complain about the ill treatment that he suffered from his siblings. The mother ewe always comforted him by saying that he was her eldest son and should not take the play of the smaller children seriously.

One night it so happened, while everybody in the herd was sleeping, a wolf sneaked in amongst them. It grabbed the mother ewe by the leg and began to drag her away. The mother ewe began to scream and bleat loudly for help. The situation mortified the rest of the herd. Every single sheep ran away to hide from the wolf. The lion too was hiding and shivering with fear. As the painful cries of the mother ewe were fading into the darkness, the lion suddenly jumped to his feet. The brutal murder of his mother was too much for him to tolerate. As he remembered her love and kindness towards him, his blood began to boil. He was, after all, a lion! He sprang out from his hiding place and with a tremendous roar ran after the wolf.

The wolf was completely shocked at this sudden change of script, as it saw a massive lion running after him! He got the fright of his life. He simply dropped the ewe and ran away to save his own skin.

The mother ewe was rescued very much to the surprise and disbelief of the other sheep. No one was able to comprehend how one sheep could rescue another from the jaws of a wolf. The mother ewe explained this mystery. She revealed to everybody that her son was not a sheep, but a lion. Since he had grown up amongst the sheep, he never had the opportunity to know that he was a lion.

As long as a lion doesn't know or realize its true nature, it is only another sheep.

Very much like the lion-sheep, an ignorant person pursues a far inferior life than what is appropriate to their true nature. There is an urgent need for everyone to wake up to the reality of the true nature of themselves. Only then can one expect to pursue and achieve the true objectives for which their supreme capabilities are given.

Closely keeping to the path of the evolutionary process, the formulation and practice of yogasanas have evolved. As we have noticed, the practices of many asanas are named and designed after different species of creation. The chief reason why they are so-named or designed is to invoke and make the practitioner realize the physical importance of that species within his own body. The performance of the asana leads to the realization of the relative position and significance of a species in the evolutionary scheme. Before being human, all of us have undergone a very precise and definite process – from being a unicellular organism to the subsequent change into a fish, to an amphibian, to a reptile and lastly to a mammal.

The evolutionary process is millions of years old, but nature does not intend us to forget it. Every time we are born, we undergo the entire process of evolution inside our mother's womb. Within the nine months of gestation, every human being is bound to re-discover and re-live one's evolutionary truth. A human baby is always born with the complete knowledge of his evolutionary journey, but soon he begins to forget this fact in the exact same way the lion forgot he was a lion.

The role of asanas in Yoga is to enable the practitioner to regain his complete evolutionary memory and re-live the nature of his true self. There is a vast difference between an ordinary person and a practitioner of asanas. An ordinary person can be compared to an over-excited animal that has suddenly come to know that there is a world of opportunities to enjoy and indulge his senses. Such people excitedly and blindly pursue the fulfillment of their sensual desires without ever bothering to question the purpose behind the benefits that they are enjoying. However the practitioner of asanas goes on to realize the depths of the human mind and the supreme capacity of his human body. Instead of indulging in the senses, the yogi begins to regulate the senses and proceeds to find out the objective of their unbelievable capacity.

This is only one of the many explanations of the asanas. Apart from regaining the evolutionary experience, asanas play other important roles. As you know, not all asanas are named after animals or species. There are a whole set of asanas which are designed after the effect and symbology of different objects, like *padmasana* or *swastikasana*. Also, quite a few asanas have been added to the list which has been specifically created by some of the ancient yogis and masters in order to deal with the difficulties of their students – for example, *vashisthasana* or *matsyendrasana*.

To understand this evolutionary theory of asanas, let us choose any one asana at random. Take *ushtrasana*, which is popularly known as the 'camel pose' in the West. Like every single species, the camel enjoys a unique place in creation. In this position, the camel is responsible for the deliverance and performance of specific responsibilities. Similarly, in a definite way, all species are responsible in maintaining the balance of nature and ecology, and for that purpose they all have very specific capabilities. In our example of the camel, we see that the life of a camel depends upon dry and desert conditions. The most unique quality of the camel is the ultra-rational use of food and fluid in its body. In order to survive the desert conditions, the camel is equipped with the capacity to eat and drink only once in a while. It saves the food and fluid in its body and can survive without it for a surprisingly long period of time.

Hunger and thirst are two overwhelming physical afflictions for a practitioner. If one is constantly thinking about food and drink, they can never succeed in their practice. After re-living the evolutionary position of the camel, a practitioner, like a camel, can survive with minimum food and drink. The practitioners of the camel pose begin to experience a noticeable change in their food habits. Within a few weeks of correct practice, the practitioner soon enters into a state where his appetite is extremely low. This great loss of appetite has no negative affect on one's taste, preference or liking for food or one's general physical strength or energy. The use of food and fluid in the practitioner's body becomes so modified that they can never again take any food which is more than their physical requirement, no matter how little it is.

Apart from this great benefit, the camel pose also has certain beneficial side-effects. As with any regulated food mechanism, practitioners tend to lose excess weight. It can also regulate and therefore help change the habits of people with anorexia or other eating disorders. One also gets strong and powerful legs, a powerful back, and relief from lower back pain, balanced blood pressure, as well as an improved respiratory system. However, it is very important to keep in mind that the asana can barely be practised with success if one is consciously looking for only the benefits of the side-effects.

Not only the camel pose, but an entire range of asanas are to be practised with conscious understanding of their effects in the appropriate manner. The collection of asanas, bit by bit, provides perfection to the practitioner's body, and ultimately one emerges being in complete control of their physical self. This perfection and complete control is the all-important requirement which enables the practitioner to move beyond his physical limits.

Kripanand never forgot my argument about the correct use of yogasanas, as he recited the yogic scriptures and indicated that they have, in fact, forbidden the use of yogasanas for any purpose other than spiritual development. In the *Upadesa-I* of the *Hathayoga Pradipika* (1:1, 2), it states:

'Sri adinathaya namo stu tasmai yenopadista hathayoga-vidya Vibhrajate pronnatarajayogama-rodhumicchoradhi-rohinival'

(Salute to Sri Adinatha who advised about the great knowledge of hatha yoga which is like a luminous set of steps for the one who is desirous of climbing the great heights of (raja) yoga.)

'Pranamya srigurm natham svatmaramena yogina Kevalam rajayogaya hathavidyopadisyate'

(By Svatmarama, a yogi having worshipped his divine Guru is being taught hatha yoga only for the purpose of (raja) yoga.)

Without giving me any further opportunity to argue, Kripanand declared, "An asana has but one ultimate purpose. If you examine an asana in extreme detail, it reveals a wonderful world of psycho-physical balance. The immortal sutra from Maharshi Patanjali (2:46) gives the ultimate definition of Asana. It reads, '*Sthirasukhamasanam.*' This is a single word. It can be dissected to mean '*Sthiram*' and '*Sukham*' is the '*Asanam*'. This translates as 'steady and pleasurable is the posture'. The word 'steady' denotes a physical condition, and the word 'pleasurable' denotes a psychological condition. Thus, Asana is a state that includes both a specific physical and a specific mental condition."

One may ask, 'If Asana is a state, then it surely defeats the notion of Asana as a process?'

According to the Yoga Sutras, Asana is only a state and not a process. The term 'Asana' within its meaning in the Yoga Sutras does not mean the same as asana found in the *Hathayoga Pradipika* or the *Gheranda Samhita*. Asana as a state is a pre-condition for the practices of the higher component parts of Yoga, like *Pranayama*, *Pratyahara*, etc. At the time the Yoga Sutras was written, there was no need for express instructions for psycho-physical fitness, which has only in the later ages become a difficulty for the common man. Hundreds of years later, yogis like Goraknath, Svatamaram, Maharishi Gherand and Agnivesa came up with the discovery of yogasanas. The practice of asanas as a process is meant to achieve the state of Asana. Such is the reason why all these yogis have taken specific care to limit the use of asanas only for spiritual purposes.

For clarification, the term 'Asana' with a capital 'A' denotes the state of Asana, whereas 'asana' with a lower case 'a' denotes the process of asana.

Let us now study the specific physical and psychological conditions of the state of Asana in detail. The word *sthira* in Sanskrit is derived from the term 'unmoving', or something that is rooted to the ground, like a tree or a mountain. Asana involves a very stable or rock-steady condition of the body. Remember that it is not so easy to get the body into such a condition. It takes enormous effort to accomplish this.

Let us first understand the neuro-physical, as well as pathological dynamics of the body. Every act, behavior or even minor movement of the body occurs as a result of a thought. The thought pattern, in turn, is the outcome of brain waves. The brain waves are generated as a result of discharge of electrical impulses of the brain cells called neurons. The electro-chemical functions of the neurons are triggered by stimuli which could be either internal or external. Thus the root of all the extraordinary acts and behavior of human beings lies at the point of a microscopic trigger. The stillness of the body is possible when we take into consideration the entire process of behavioral manifestations. Let us now see what happens in reality.

Under a normal waking state when we are walking, talking or doing any day-to-day activity, our brain works at a certain frequency called the 'beta level'. Under these conditions the brain produces waves at the rate of about 12-28 cycles per second. If the frequency of brain waves is reduced from that band, the body will not be able to function at the same rate. As the frequencies are reduced, several functions of the body will also be proportionately minimized, and the body will slowly go into a more slackened condition. The more we cause a reduction in brain wave frequency, the more relaxed will be the condition of the body.

Here we observe a very interesting relationship between the level of brain activity and the level of relaxation of the body: the higher the brain activity, the higher the physical activity; conversely, the lower the brain activity, the lower the physical activity - and proportionately the more relaxed the body. If this is the neuro-physical truth of a human body, then let us do something to reduce the level of brain activity. An asana *kriya* involves a conscious and voluntary modification of the electrical discharge rate of the cerebral cortex neurons. However, before attempting your first asana, you should make sure that all your homework of the nerve purification and the *kriyas* of *yama* and *niyama* have been practised and successfully completed. The target level of stillness in this process is to reach a level of brain activity where the frequency of the brain waves is three or less per second.

Don't panic! The great master Maharshi Patanjali has given us the secret of achieving this feat. He has not left us to wander in darkness by placing this enormous and seemingly impossible task before us. Let us remember that Asana is not just a physical state, but the combination of physical, as well as mental states. In his next sutra (2:47), he has explained exactly how to accomplish this combined state of Asana. It states, *'Prayatnasaithilyanantasamapattibhyam.'*

Let us now place this sutra under a microscope and examine its components: *'Prayatna'* means 'level of psycho-physical activity during the waking state'; *'saithilya'* means 'into (absolute) relaxation'; *'ananta'* means 'the infinite proportions'; *'samapattibhyam'* means 'to be placed or established at'.

The sutra in English can more or less mean, 'The usual level of psycho-physical activity to be absolutely relaxed and at the same time shift and establish the mind into the infinite (of the self).'

In this sutra, Maharshi Patanjali has indicated the presence of two elements in the same plane: the density of the form and the infinity of the formless. In the psycho-physical synthesis of Asana, it is important to achieve both these elements together. I have come across many confused practitioners who have not understood this basic rule of yogasanas. Many people have tried to practise asanas only from the physical angle without involving the mental or psychic element. They have attempted to stretch the tolerance level of the body to its extreme in order to achieve its stillness, but such an apparently 'still' body lacks the vital ingredient of pleasure. Therefore there is no difference between such practitioners and people working in the circus, professional gymnasts or even contortionists. Many modern-day yoga teachers try to experience this pleasure of the physical state by following some devotional practices. The use of drugs and psychotropic substances are also not uncommon to support such practices.

Let us now see how both of these vital ingredients are achieved simultaneously. For this purpose you have to study the evolutionary anatomy of the body. The body, as we normally see and experience, is not all that we have. In fact it is only the gross material manifestation of a much larger halo of energy. To explain this to the skeptics, let us go slightly away from the present discussion, only to come back to it later.

Every thing or object that we see around us is only a lump of matter. These lumps of matter are comprised of various kinds of elements which we recognize by their shape, color or function. It could be anything from a piece of rock, wood, water, a tree, a butterfly or a dog. Contrary to popular belief, it is not true that some of these things have life, and some are dead. In truth, as stated earlier, every single particle found in this universe contains life. Any single particle can be examined in extremely close detail only to find within it the incessant activity of protons and electrons. The behavior of these sub-atomic elements goes a long way to prove that a single particle or a lump of matter is only an example of gross representation of energy. Thus our physical body is but a gross manifestation of energy.

While talking about the presence of energy in every single particle of the body, let us do a small calculation. Have you ever wondered how much energy can be produced if all the particles of the body of an average-sized man are 'liberated'? A calculation reveals the amount of potential energy is approximately 7×10 to the power 18 joules. If every particle of this human body can be liberated, it will produce about 3000 times the energy of the atom bomb that was dropped on Hiroshima!

If we try to measure the dimensions of our energy body, we will find that it is more far stretching than the little physical one. Every part and organ of the physical body has its etheric counterpart inside the energy body. If you take a look at the energy body, which is very much possible in these modern days with the invention of Poly-contrast Interference Photography (PIP), the energy of the particles is presented in a color-code through a computer program. Through this technology we can see the energy of different wavelengths as patches in different colors; the brighter the patch, the stronger the energy and the darker the patch, the weaker the energy.

You will also find that there are many little energy whorls throughout the body. These little energy whorls are called 'chakras' in the tantric system. One can see more than three hundred of them in the energy body. They are found at places like the fingertips, centers of each palm, nose, chin, nipples and other such protruding ends of the body. The highest energy activity will be noticed along the spine, which is the neuro-physical energy axis of the body. From the cerebral cortex to the end of the spine you can notice seven large and luminous whorls of energy. The size and luminosity of these whorls differs from person to person on the basis of their psycho-physical health condition. This energy body, which is non-physical and non-material in nature, plays a very important role in the performance of the asanas. In the ongoing chapters of this book, we will study about the amazing functions of these chakras and many more things beyond the limits of the energy body. As in higher stages of yogic practices, we will go on to experience many more subtle to subtler forms of the self.

Let us now go back to our original discussion. We have two things at hand: one is the gross physical body, and the other is the ethereal body along with its subtle and subtler infinities. The gross body is the only one that has an apparent limit and is dense in nature. We have already discussed that the density of the body can be reduced with a corresponding reduction of the mental activities. Now the question is, "Where does one take the mind to give the necessary relaxation and laxity to the body?"

The sutra is self-explanatory in nature. Maharshi Patanjali says that as a necessary condition of Asana, the mind has to be shifted into the infinite dimension, which, as we have now found, is the etheric and subtle energy body. It is actually simpler than it sounds.

Whenever we move any part of the body, a great change occurs in the body. Every time the body moves, the microscopic body cells disintegrate into sub-atomic particles and turn into energy. All of you have noticed that after doing a little work, the body gets warmed up. This is because energy is generated during the process. The amount and direction of the energy depends upon the part of the body which was used. In our daily life we do so many activities, and the un-ending process of creation and utilization of energy goes on. All those body cells which are used up in the process get restored with the help of the food or matter that we add to our body. This natural function of the body forms the basis of an asana practice.

During an asana we do three things: firstly, we take the body into a specific posture in a specific manner; secondly, we focus our attention at a specific part of ourselves; thirdly, we give a specific direction to the breath and mental activities. By physically manipulating the body we end up creating a definite quantity of energy. By the breath and the conscious direction of the mind, we channel this created energy to a specific part of our energy body. We then assimilate the energy in the etheric body. In this process, the mind acts as the pathfinder of the energy, and energy acts as the carrier of the mind. During this mutual movement, energy assimilates into the chakras and the mind gets shifted beyond the physical body. It is this combined effect that satisfies the requirement of an asana.

What we see here is the utilization of the energy dynamics of the body, and the absence of the mind in the body in order not to experience the discomfort. One could ask, 'How does one know the exact position of the energy whorls in the body at the time of doing the asana in order to be able to direct the generated energy to it?'

The answer is simple. The practice of *nadi sodanham* and the other *kriyas* of *yama* and *niyama* already provide the experience of the subtle channels in the body prior to the practice of asanas. It is definitely very difficult to experience the effect of an asana without the successful completion of the prerequisite *kriyas*. The asana does not actually end here. After the entire set of asanas has been performed, one has to lie down, and through active and conscious mental direction and concentration, channel and accumulate the entire etheric energy into the appropriate chakras. Thereafter the practice session of asana becomes complete. This process, by gradual practice, results in the enrichment of the ethereal body and consequently improves the possibility of shifting attention into it.

This shifting has far reaching effects. On one hand, it shifts the mental and psychic elements out of the body resulting in a reduction of brain activity. This reduction of brain activity is experienced as a state of supreme relaxation, wherein the body is absolutely stable. On the other hand, the shifting of the cognitive faculty of the mind detaches it from the perception of any physical discomfort. The combined experience of this process is the absolute stability of body and the pleasurable state of mind. The element of pleasure in the asana will be discussed in the next sutra.

In Yoga, an asana has only one absolute purpose: to achieve the absolutely steady and pleasurable condition of body and mind, which is the basis of further yogic practice. This condition or state is called Asana. Hence care should be taken to ensure that the body is actually developing in the right direction. In the process of practising yogasanas, one usually experiences many temporary and superficial effects. In many scriptures these effects are listed. It should not be mistaken that the ultimate purpose of asanas is to experience these superficial effects. The Yoga Sutras specifically mentions the precise and true nature of the asana effect. However, before going into the details of the effect of asanas, let us in brief study the rules which are the secrets to its success.

These rules, discovered by the ancient yogis, have never been laid out in any book so far. During their extremely austere practices, the masters had come to know and realize these principles. The creation, nature and every single function of the human body is a direct outcome of natural principles. The law of nature plays a very important role in managing the changes of the body. It was discovered that the nature and function of the body is largely dependent upon the environmental and planetary conditions.

We all know to some extent how the influence of the sun and moon changes the weather, the tides, the atmospheric pressure, and as much as the opening and closing of a flower and the habits of a honey bee. The human body, with its complex relationship with nature and cosmos, very intricately reacts to these natural changes. When we are practising asanas, we are dealing with fine and subtle elements of the body. Hence it would be absolutely futile if the subtle natural changes were not taken into account. These rules are not so much applicable to 'exercises', which are primarily performed for the purpose of stretching and flexibility. There is a need to mention these rules for the benefit of the spiritual practitioners.

To understand these rules it would be highly beneficial to understand the effects of seasonal changes. Different parts of the world have different kinds of climatic and seasonal conditions. In broad terms, every place on the planet experiences at least two distinct seasons: one is the northward movement of the sun; the other is the southward movement of the sun. When the sun is traveling from the tropic of Capricorn to the tropic of Cancer, it is usually the dry season. This means that there is a marked reduction of water in the surroundings. Every organism loses moisture, and regions in one of the hemispheres of the planet will experience different degrees of dryness depending upon their geographical location. This happens whilst the other hemisphere experiences the opposite season. When the sun moves down from the tropic of Cancer to the tropic of Capricorn, the exact opposite condition occurs. This is a time when water is replaced back into all the organisms, and we call this the wet season.

The condition of our body as an intrinsic part of this natural scheme also drastically changes alongside the changes of nature. From the ancient times, yogis have provided the exact procedure, schedule and modification of the manner of practice for the yogasanas on the basis of these natural changes. There are seasonal regimens, solar and lunar schedules, as well as daily schedules based upon planetary presence, not to mention the hourly modifications that are applied to the asana *kriyas*.

The asanas can be classified under different headings. The principal classification of asana *kriya* is like a pyramid. At the top end lies only one asana, the essential 'steady and pleasurable' condition. For the sake of convenience, let us call this asana the primary asana. This primary asana can be accomplished through *padmasana* (lotus pose), *siddhasana*, *virasana*, *swastikasana* or *vajrasana*. There is no hard and fast rule as to which of these or any other asana has to be adopted for the subsequent practice of the yogic *kriyas*. I would say it largely depends upon individual capacity and preference. To reach this primary asana, one needs to practise a series of other asanas, the practice of which facilitates the accomplishment of the primary one. Again, for the sake of convenience, let us call these asanas the secondary asanas. The number of secondary asanas is between five and fifteen, consisting of *kriyas* like *ushtrasana, sarvangasana, matsyasana, dhanurasana* and *gomukhasana*.

If the practice of secondary asanas does not prove fruitful in the invoking and channeling of etheric energy, then as per the advice of the guru, one can adopt the third level of asanas from the pyramid structure. These asanas are a little more complex to observe and need a considerable amount of physical manipulation to enable the support and development to the secondary level. Some of the asanas of this level are *ardha-matsyendrasana, mayurasana, halasana* and *sirshasana* (headstand). The individual capacities of each practitioner are not alike, as some people develop the effects of the asana more easily than others. The denser the person's physical conditions, the more difficult it will be to relax his body, and the greater difficulty he will face in shifting the mind. In such cases, under appropriate guidance, the practitioner should move to an even lower level of asana. Some of the fourth level asanas are *brischikasana, padasirasana, garbhasana*. In similar sequence, more and more complex manipulative asanas have been created in the modern times, keeping in view the extreme density of the form and the mounting need for relaxation.

Contrary to popular belief, the lower level asanas are actually the easier to perform. This is so because they are mostly performed by the body only. As one ascends into higher levels of asanas, and after the gradual achievement of the appropriate level of relaxation, more and more of the mental and psychological elements are used, instead of physical stress. Had this not been the case, everyone would have gyrated their way to enlightenment!

It is needless to say that the steady and pleasurable posture at the top of the pyramid is, in fact, the most difficult one to accomplish. You will come to know this with the help of a simple test which can be performed on your own.

Sit down on the floor on a comfortable mat. Keep your body straight. Attempt to make your body absolutely relaxed and motionless. You are required to sit in a comfortable, yet rock-still condition.

Find out how long you can remain in that position. Directly proportionate to your mental activity, your body will begin to revolt. The physical discomfort as well as the mental difficulties will soon render your practice impossible to continue.

If one cannot manage to sit down even for a little amount of time without movement, how can one ever think of getting closer to the voice of silence?

Under the second classification of yogasanas, we can divide all asanas into five groups. They are the standing asanas, the kneeling asanas, the sitting asanas, asanas while lying on the back and asanas while lying on the stomach.

In this classification, the standing asanas are the most stressful of all. The term stressful is used here not on the basis of how people perceive it, but on the basis of their energy dynamics. The least stressful asanas of this classification are the ones that are performed whilst lying on the stomach, and the sequence of these groups, as mentioned, denote their relative levels of stress. During the dry season when the sun is moving towards the tropic of Cancer, it is advisable to arrange the sequence of asanas beginning from the standing postures and finishing with the asanas on the stomach. The reverse process can be followed in the opposite season. It is for this reason that the higher the stress of the asana, the more energy you create in the body, and conversely, the lower the stress of the asana, the more relaxation you experience.

The third method of classification of yogasanas is based upon the planetary conditions of the day. Do you know that the number of days in the year, month, fortnight and week have all been so adjusted because of planetary reasons? As most of us know, the day of Sunday is named after the Sun; this is not due to someone's whimsical choice. For centuries, the specific recurring effect of this day had been observed and studied; as a result of the findings, the effects of this day on life are attributed to the sun. This is a day, under normal conditions, that reduces the water and moisture level of the body. On this day the body is generally weak, usually there is less enthusiasm to work, and the digestive capacity is at its lowest. This is a day when highly stressful asanas are to be avoided. Instead, relaxing asanas that add energy to the solar plexus are performed, as the Sun resides at the *manipura* chakra on that day.

Monday is the day named after the moon. On this day the moon lies at the *swadisthana* or the *hara* chakra. The asanas on that day usually begin with the invocation of the lunar energy, and all the asanas that deal with water or the feminine elements are performed.

Tuesday is the day of planet Mars. Mars on this day rests on the shoulders. It is a good day to introduce new asanas into the schedule. Performance of a large number of asanas on this day is usually beneficial since this is a day of force, courage and vitality.

Wednesday is the day of planet Mercury. This little hot planet lives in the head. On this day the softer, subtler and more contemplative asanas are performed. This day, to a lesser extent, is similar to Sunday.

Thursday is the day of planet Jupiter. It is the largest and heaviest planet and yet holds the key to an intellectual pursuit. Its effects are felt at the forehead. Under normal conditions it is usually difficult to perform asanas on this day. It is ideal to practise less complex asanas on this day and attempt to take more rest.

Friday is the day of planet Venus. Venus lies at the heart. Fast moving asanas and the asanas relating to the *anahata* or heart chakra are the specialties of the day. On this day asanas can be repeatedly practised.

Saturday is named after the planet Saturn. In effect it is very similar to Monday. As Saturn lies at the *mooladhara* chakra, on this day practices like *gomukhasana* and *garudasana* are performed.

To these rules there is one major exception: a person may not experience or suffer the influences of a planet easily if he or she was born on the day of that planet. For example, a person born on a Thursday may not have much difficulty in the performance of asanas, whilst others, due to body stiffness, will be struggling to keep up with the teacher.

Apart from the planetary conditions, the asanas can also be divided into those which are practised in the morning and those which are practised in the evening. Contrary to popular practice, high energy-developing asanas are better performed in the morning since these asanas provide enormous amounts of energy for utilization during the activities of the day. On the other hand, the relaxing asanas are appropriately practised in the evening to provide the conditions for healing and recuperation of the body.

The rules of the asana are not to be taken as a set of guidelines that every society prescribes to ensure the reasonable conduct of its members. Rules and social laws have an entirely different purpose. They serve as a bond to keep the society together within the limits of socially acceptable behavior and also to provide punishments for anyone who breaches the rules. The rules of the asanas neither have any binding effect nor are they prescribed anywhere for an intended set of people. The rules are only techniques that have been discovered by the ancient masters of Yoga. These techniques and secrets were passed down through the tradition and lineage of the yogis. Without any compulsion of any kind, the practitioners have been using them only in order to achieve success in their practice. As stated earlier, the only thing that yields success is the correctness of the practice.

The next rule to keep in mind during practice is regarding sweating or perspiration. The place of practice of yogasanas is to be selected carefully. It should be free from dust, noise, smell and uncomfortable heat or cold – otherwise these factors can take a considerable amount of attention away from your practice. During any workout we generally sweat. Sweating is a natural mechanism of the skin designed to reduce the heat of the body. Let us examine this process.

The work-out of the body breaks body matter into energy, and the energy in the form of heat radiates from the body. As soon as the heat of the body reaches a certain level, the sweat mechanism automatically begins to pour out sweat in order to reduce the heat.

During the *kriya* of asanas, we must keep in mind that the energy of the body is not meant for radiation and subsequent escape. Instead, the *kriya* of the asana is created to harness this energy without allowing it to escape. Thus, ultimately the asana results in the enrichment of the ethereal body at the cost of the physical body. The moment you experience sweating during the performance of asanas, it is time to realize that your focus and concentration is poor, otherwise the energy would not have escaped. Always ensure that you don't lose or waste any amount of energy during the practice of asanas. Asana is a combination of physical relaxation and mental activity. A perspiring workout and relaxation are very much contradictory to each other. How can one justify sweating while working towards relaxation of the body?

Instead, the highly active mind, after reaching a certain limit, can result in the warming of the scalp or forehead. This may result in sweating in that area. The moment your head or forehead begins to perspire, it is time to stop. Any further practice after this point would be highly stressful.

There is a huge myth about the elimination of toxins as a result of asana practice. One of the fundamental differences is that during an asana, the generated energy is harnessed and made to move inwards, whereas in an exercise, the energy is radiated and released outwards, and thus wasted. Let me explain this further. The body has an entire mechanism designed for the sole purpose of the elimination of toxic elements. Our faeces and urine eliminate most of it, and the sweat glands flush out further toxins from the skin. Cleanliness and purity, as we have discussed earlier, form the basis of our practice. It is pure nonsense to arrive at asana practice without the requisite cleanliness and purity. The one who is pure does not need asanas to give his or her skin a beauty treatment. Any practice where perspiration is a desired effect cannot be an asana.

Since the performance of asana involves powerful manipulation of the direction of energy in the body, it is better practised during healthy conditions of the body. When one suffers from a disease or discomfort, the condition of one's body, in most cases, is working towards the cure of the disease. Under such conditions, it is not correct to subject the body to the practice of asanas. There is a widespread belief that practising yogasanas can help during pregnancy. This is not entirely true. What could be helpful during pregnancy is adequate exercise, stretching and flexing of the body, which includes the usual special pregnancy exercises. During pregnancy, the body and energy system are specifically working towards the making of the baby. Asana practice, under such conditions, can result in serious interference in the energy dynamics. Hence, yogasanas are to be avoided during pregnancy, as well as during menstruation.

As one begins the practice of asanas, they generally come to experience the importance of these rules. As Kripanand would often say, "Experience is one of the best teachers." Kripanand was constantly by my side when I started my asana practice. In the beginning I hated the frequent corrections, but I knew that I needed them. He would make me stand for hours facing the sun with my hands outstretched, concentrating on the appropriate chakra. Other students practising asanas in the ashram were not as bad as me. He would walk in front of us and pause briefly to peep at our chakras. He would look in the direction of the chakra and nod his consent, or as it happened most frequently in my case, reprimand me to concentrate better.

Complete practice of the purification and the powerful tantric exercise in Nepal now proved beneficial. In Nepal I had learned how to concentrate and feel the chakras and the subtle energy channels. While practising asanas in my ashram, this ability came to my aid. Only after 'seeing' the pulsation of the chakras in our body with confirmed focus and concentration, would Kripanand allow us to proceed with the movements of the asana.

Old habits die hard. My years of experience of gymnastic asanas were the biggest interference in my practice. Either I was running through the asana too fast, or I would jump into the final posture without following the correct process. In the past no one had told me that the manner in which you get to the posture and the manner in which you return from it are equally as important as the posture itself. From the beginning position of an asana, we begin to concentrate at the appropriate chakra. As soon as we feel the pulsating of the chakra and the energy traveling in that direction, we start to move. Maintaining the focus at the chakra, we slowly and gently move into the posture. If the focus or the balance is disturbed, then we have to go through the whole process again.

I found it particularly difficult to synchronize these three different aspects of the asana. In the beginning I was practising asanas for at least twelve hours a day, and at this rate it took me at least a month to correctly hold the first asana of my life correctly. It was an entirely new and awesome experience. Prior to my arrival into the ashram, I had a strong notion that asana was synonymous with the ability to twist, gyrate and manipulate the body in several wonderful ways. I had never understood how an asana differed from the manipulations that you see in a circus. I was ever curious to know if the mere act of twisting and gyrating contained some kind of hidden health effects. For if this was the case, then why are the people working in a circus not the healthiest, least stressed, wisest, or enlightened?

The biggest shock from my asana activity was yet to come. The first asana I thought I successfully completed was *vajrasana*. To perform this asana, one needs to focus at the solar plexus. Kripanand had explained to me that the solar plexus was the least difficult chakra of all to work upon during asanas. After seeing him appreciate my *vajrasana* a couple of times, I gleefully asked him to give me the next asana. As he smiled and gently slapped my shoulder, he said, "My dear yogi, performance of an asana does not mean the accomplishment of the asana. Every Tom, Dick and Sally practising gymnastics out there, with a little practice, can perform *vajrasana* as cutely as you. The ability to perform an asana takes you nowhere. There is something called *asana-siddhi*, which means the successful accomplishment of an asana. Only after experiencing the *siddhi* of an asana, will you go onto the next one."

I complained, "You are making things too difficult and too discouraging for me."

He smiled and asked, "How many years did you spend going to schools and colleges in order to get a degree?"

"About fifteen years."

"Fifteen years for a piece of paper - a piece of paper on which your name is written next to the word 'degree'. To see your name written somewhere next to another equally insignificant term, you spent fifteen years. Now, to get an absolute and permanent benefit for life, only one month for the asana has become difficult! As far as the discouraging factor goes, let me remind you that as you stand today, you are the sum total psycho-spiritual culmination of a long series of lifetimes. The force that is propelling and moving you towards your spiritual destiny is no ordinary phenomenon. We, the people in the ashram, are only instrumental in providing you with the direction, whereas the cosmic dynamic is playing the most essential role. Do you think under this condition you can be discouraged?"

Kripanand continued, "My boy, the force at which you are moving forward cannot be contained by anyone, including you. Besides, if you want to achieve anything substantial in life, never take shortcuts. What are you trying to prove by your asanas? Do you think that you are participating in some kind of competition where your performance is applauded? Do you think you are expected to showcase your asana to be given a prize, popularity, fame or anything like that? The one and only reason why you are doing asanas is that you, yourself, want a very substantial progress in your spiritual life. Your practice of asana is going to benefit only you. Neither you can give nor can I take its benefits from you."

I then sheepishly replied, "Ok, I am sorry. So tell me, how do I know when the asana becomes accomplished?"

Kripanand answered, "At last! There comes a sensible question. Let me briefly tell you the incredibly good news about asanas. There are generally three kinds of trainings that we go through in life: physical, mental and spiritual. The physical trainings develop the body and its components, but these physical effects are very short-lived and gradually diminish over time. The mental trainings last much longer than the physical trainings. You enjoy its fruits for a lifetime, but with the death of the body, your mental faculties also come to an end. However, the case of spiritual development is different. It never comes to an end because the spirit has no end. In an asana *kriya*, there are some physical, mental and spiritual acts involved. Hence all effects of the asanas do not cease over time or by death.

Let me give you a small example: if I slap you really hard, you can experience at least two kinds of effects – one physical, one mental. The physical pain will finish within a couple of hours, but the pain inflicted upon your mind may last for a lifetime. Even though the physical pain has long disappeared, you may continue to experience and live the effects of the slap for the rest of your life. An asana is very similar in nature, but goes beyond the lifetime, as once the asana affects you at your deep mental and spiritual levels, the effects become ever lasting. The good news is since the effects of the asana are permanent and irreversible in nature, once successfully accomplished, there is no need to practise them again. Not only that, the effects of the asanas are carried forward from life to life because of its ever-lasting spiritual effects."

Kripanand then reminded me of the analogy of cooking and the relationship of the pot and the food. "The accomplishment, or the *siddhi* of asanas, is said to be achieved when your practices have reached the point of no return. This means you should practise the asanas until their permanent effect is achieved. Always remember that you are cooking the food and not the pot. It is complete only when the food is properly cooked, and not overcooked."

I asked, "How do I know that the food is properly cooked? How does the practice of an asana come to an end? Who tastes the food to certify that it is done?"

Kripanand explained, "Since the ultimate purpose of the asana is to achieve one absolutely steady and pleasurable condition, we have to see that the practice of the asana moves in the same direction. Once you have achieved the synchronization of all the ingredients of the *kriya*, you should endeavor to maintain the posture for a longer period of time, which in other words, is the 'cooking time'. Different foods take different times to cook. Similarly, different people with their own peculiar physical density take different amounts of time to arrive at the point of absolute posture.

Until now you have merely learned to synchronize yourself into the posture with all its components. Now it is time you learn to hold the posture for a prolonged period of time, until its effects become permanent and irreversible."

"How long does that usually take?" I asked impatiently.

Kripanand replied, "It depends. In my experience most of the people in this ashram achieve *siddhis* from an entire set of asanas in about a year's time. At the current rate of your practice you should be able to achieve the state of Asana within the next two years."

In my mind I repeated my resolve. With an increased rate of practice, I was sure I would do it in a time much less than two years.

Within a few days, I increased my practice time from the twelve-hour average to an eighteen-hour average. Eighteen hours of practice for an asana per day was excruciating. I had difficulty walking properly, to sit down without fidgeting, and the terrible pain all over my body began to affect my sleep. Instead of having any pleasurable experience, I gradually became weak and sick. Even though my extraordinary efforts were noticed by my teachers, no one came forward to help me. That was until the day when I literally could not move from my sleeping place and my very loving and grandfather-like Kripanand appeared next to me. He said, "You are such a good boy and such a determined yogi. We are all very pleased with your efforts, and if you keep practising like this, very soon you will go beyond the afflictions of the body forever."

I blinked at him as I could not understand what he meant. I asked, "Do you mean to say that I will soon die?"

He answered, "Yes. The 'I' in you will die very soon. This is what, we yogis say, is freedom from the afflictions and imprisonment of the body."

Kripanand had brought with him some herbal preparations that he himself had prepared for my use. Very kindly, without asking where it hurt, he applied the powders and pastes at only those points that actually needed treatment. By the end of the day

I was feeling much better. In about three days time I was back in my practice with renewed confidence and strength. After a few more days of practice, I did the next most stupid thing which I will never forget in my life. With a strong resolve and determination, I decided to hold the asana beyond all limits of time. I was confident that my teachers would not let me die or seriously injure myself.

The next morning after performing all the prerequisites of the asanas, I sat down in *vajrasana* with absolute stillness of the body and a strong determination in the mind. Hours passed by. After over two hours, I began to feel a growing numbness in my legs and lower back. Slowly the numbness and an extraordinary pain began to creep upwards through my spine. Within the next hour or so, my whole back and shoulders were frozen. Yet, still I held my posture without movement. Slowly the pain began to creep upwards through my neck, and I began to see colors. I slowly got into a state of profuse delirium and eventually collapsed. I do not know what happened after that. I was later told that I remained in a state of unconsciousness for more than a day, in a paralytic seizure of the body. After regaining my senses, I still experienced a paralyzing stiffness in the lower parts of my body, so I was asked to rest for the next couple of days.

While lying there on my blanket throughout the day, the agony I suffered was mostly from my inability to visit and spend time with my guru rather than the physical pain. Soon my eyes began to tear, and I started calling my Gurudev in a whispering voice. A short while later he was right there beside me. He asked, "You called me?"

I replied, "Yes, I was kind of desperate to see you."

"Why do you have to be desperate to see me? Do you not know that I am always there with you?"

I hesitated, and trying to conceal my embarrassment said, "I called you because I wanted to ask you something."

My Gurudev sat down next to me, and without a word I put my head on his lap. I asked, "Please tell me Gurudev, what went wrong in my practice?"

He smilingly questioned back, "What was right about it, silly boy? Your practice was extremely stupid and mindless."

My guru explained the folly of my practice. "Firstly, during the *kriya* your mind was not at all focused. Instead, you were thinking about your own proud capability of performing the asana and because of the non-application of the psychological faculty, your whole practice was reduced to only a tolerance test. You subjected your body to extreme levels of tolerance and even forced to stretch it infinitely. Your body is not yet fit to endure such treatment. One has to go to the accomplishments of the asana, not with blind courage and determination, but with cool confidence and the correct process. How many times have I told you before that the *kriyas* of Yoga are like complex scientific experiments? It is absolutely necessary to understand the experiment clearly and practise it with competent guidance. Just because you have seen your body for twenty years does not mean that you know it. Knowing the body itself is still not enough if you fail to realize its cosmic nature. I hope you will not do such kind of misadventures again."

I smilingly assured him that I would not.

After that day, my guru made it a point to monitor my asana development himself. With steady, determined and patient practice, I slowly began to yield the proper results. My *vajrasana* crossed a whopping eight-hour marathon without absolutely any physical discomfort. Pleased with my achievement, Kripanand gave me a series of seven secondary level asanas to be accomplished in the same manner as *vajrasana*. Years later I learnt that these asanas were chosen on the basis of the astrological conditions which specifically supported my body. The present set of asanas got all the chakras involved. Each day before I started the asanas, Kripanand would tell me the sequence of their practice.

And the sequence changed every day.

After a few months of practice, I slowly began to feel as if I was full of energy. After the end of each day's practice, I would have an ecstatic evening. I would run around the ashram and talk to people excitedly, jump or dance in sheer happiness or do some other form of hyper-activity.

One day my teacher sat me down and explained to me the reason for such hyperactive behavior. "You are experiencing the effect called *prana-prabalya*. This occurs when all the *prana* is not appropriately channeled or contained in the correct manner. Hence, it tends to express itself in such monkey-like activities. It is not the *prana* which is the monkey, but it is you who becomes a monkey as a result of this overflowing and uncontrolled force inside you."

My guru continued to explain, "Some people are known to laugh or cry, turn around like a 'top' or run hither and thither in a feat of sheer joy or madness. These effects of this uncontrolled *pranic* behavior are as far reaching as the controlled effects of the asana."

As my guru was explaining this, yet another myth about asanas cleared from my mind. Common people generally look forward to achieving a joyful effect from the asanas. An incorrectly practised asana, or even a series of asana-like physical exercises, can in fact result in this effect of *prana-prabalya*. In the excessively stressful modern life, this comes as a great relief for people to whom a moment of joy is the worth of a lifetime. As soon as they experience the tiniest amount of this effect they are enormously happy with the 'success' of their practice. The ultimate effect of a yogasana in the modern-day understanding is, in reality, an insignificant side-effect that constitutes no amount of spiritual development.

In order to contain the overflow of energy, my guru added a new *kriya* to my schedule. This was called the *chakra-dharana kriya*.

After every bout of asana practice, I would lie down on the floor, keeping my body aligned with the energy axis of the earth and with conscious practice, sweep all my energy output into my different chakras. After about two hours of this *kriya* of the assimilation of energy, I would no longer jump around like a monkey.

One day out of curiosity, I asked my guru, "What could be the capacity of the chakras to hold the energy that I have been piling into them over such a long period of time? Do the chakras have a bursting point?"

My guru got up and asked me to walk with him outside his cave. He looked briefly into the night sky. Pointing his finger he said, "Can you see that star-like object up there?"

After a little difficulty, I saw what he was pointing at. Yes, it was a star, but I could not understand why he had taken me out of the cave to show me that particular star.

He said, "That is not a star, it is a galaxy."

My guru went on to explain, "The chakras that you feel in your body are like little galaxies. They do not just function like a galaxy: let us say that they are virtual galaxies. The chakras in your body and the galaxy up there are actually one and the same thing. The arrangement of all the galaxies in the sky and their interrelationship are the same and identical with the chakras of your body. The galaxies do not have a bursting point. Since the day of their creation they have been a self-evolving mechanism. They play a very important role in the life of the universe. The chakras in you, similarly, are responsible for the creation, preservation and destruction of your physical body. Since the living body of yours needs a great deal of energy for its daily requirement, the chakras individually and collectively provide your body with the appropriate *pranic* nourishment. Even though the chakras are not part of the physical body, they are closely related to the physical counterparts in the body."

We walked back into a cave which had no burning fire pit. It was quite dark inside, and my guru called out to a young yogi a few years senior to me in practice. The three of us entered the cave and took seat. My guru asked him to demonstrate and show me what happens when a yogi keeps on piling energy into the chakras. The young yogi bent down to touch the feet of my teacher before proceeding in his demonstration. A little distance away, he sat down facing us.

All I could see and hear was his rock-still posture and deep rhythmic breathing. Soon the breathing became heavier and faster. Without my guru's presence I would have concluded that the poor fellow was getting sick, but soon his body started to light up as if there was a powerful light bulb inside him. In the next few minutes, his body began to glow in a semi-translucent form. I was seeing all his physical features very clearly. He stopped his breathing and very slowly the light began to fade out until he regained his previous color. I was delighted and excitedly asked my guru, "Will you teach me how to do this?"

"I will, but only if you promise not to show off this capacity to people."

That, I promised.

One day, six months after this event, Kripanand broke the news that I was nearly ready to attempt my first Asana test. The test was about getting a comfortable sitting position and maintaining the position, absolutely still, for at least twenty-four hours. It was difficult to fathom the possibility of such a feat, but my guru assured me that once you have the ability to detach your feelings from your body, there was no difference between twenty-four minutes and twenty-four hours. The achievement of the steady and pleasurable condition of Asana necessarily includes the surpassing of the limits of pain and pleasure, heat or cold and happiness or sorrow. I began my journey of reaping the benefits of my one-and-a-half year's grueling schedule of asana practice.

It was much easier than I had anticipated. Kripanand would

take me to a silent cave to give me these lessons alone. After a few cycles of *chakra-dharana* practices, I began to concentrate and build a complete, clear and separate image of my ethereal self. The practice was not difficult, in terms of the pain that was involved in the *kriya* of the asanas, but it was difficult to experience a completely different phenomenon than my own body. A few weeks later, Kripanand instructed me upon the psycho-physical conditions and what exactly had to be done with them during this maneouvre.

It was a fine and bright Saturday morning, and as usual I followed Kripanand into that cave. This time he advised me to go as deep as I could into my ethereal body and not worry about the physical body anymore. He told me that he would remain next to me all the time and that I didn't have to give him an account of my experience. I touched his feet in a mark of respect, and then joined my hands together in a silent prayer to my guru. I began to whisper the sacred verse to surpass my material body, which I had been practising for the last few days. After the verse, I settled and made myself comfortable in my seat and continued the kriyas. Gradually I drifted into an utterly blissful state of body and mind, but remained aware about my surroundings. I didn't feel my body at all. I was not feeling any particular thought or sensation. I tried to remember the instructions given to me. I was then surprised as I very clearly heard them being spoken to me. I started to think about my guru. I felt the same joy that I always experienced in his company. In my opinion I was completely aware of things, and after some time I decided to return back to my normal condition. I remembered the instructions and began to whisper the incantations for my return journey.

After a little while, I opened my eyes and found Kripanand sitting at a distance. I smiled at him and asked, "Did I keep you waiting for long?"

The place where the author received his first lessons from his guru and later experienced the voice of silence.

"No, not at all."

"Do you think I did anything right?"

"You did perfectly right, just as I had expected."

I thanked him, and we walked out of the cave together. The bright sunlight outside nearly blinded me for a moment. It was noon time. Kripanand asked me to go and take a walk with a restful mind. He told me that I needed to spend some time with myself. Before taking my favorite trail, I wanted to meet my guru for a moment. I went to him and paid my respects. He said, "Manmoyanand, I am so happy with you. I actually wanted to be with you yesterday when you started the practice."

I was shocked. "Hold on! What do you mean by 'yesterday'?"

My guru smilingly answered, "Yes my son, it was yesterday early in the morning that you had started your practice."

Kripanand was right. I actually needed to spend some time with myself. I had realized this on two accounts. Firstly, I would have bothered everybody in sight by talking about my experience. Secondly, I needed to immerse myself in my contemplation and reflections. I took a walk to the same point where I had once tried to run after the voice of silence. I sat down and lost myself in the breathtaking view. The never-ending array of snowcapped mountains lay before me with a bright striking contrast against the blue sky. I was watching in wonder the rolling clouds and their beautiful formations. I suddenly felt that I had grown into a very tiny particle of something. Everything around me appeared enormously large. Strangely, I didn't experience any fear or any other overwhelming thought or emotion. The perception of myself being so tiny gave me a strange melancholy, but there was no suffering in it. I closed my eyes and allowed the moment to take full possession of me. It was the bliss that I had never before experienced: the bliss of surrender.

After a long time of being immersed in this blissful moment, I slowly retraced my steps back into my guru's presence. As I appeared next to him, he told me, "It is time for you to take a vacation."

"Vacation! Where do you want me to go? Do you think I need a vacation from what I am doing? Please believe me. Nothing that I am doing is stressful for me. I don't need a vacation from this most blessed phase of my life."

He was obviously amused with my desperate pleading, but firmly maintained that I go on a vacation for at least two years. I was perfectly bewildered as to why he would want to send me away. The thought of being lost in the outside world was terrifying. Before I burst into tears, he consoled me and said, "I was not going to send you out alone. Kripanand will also be going with you."

My bewilderment gave way to amusement, but my surprise was doubled with a chuckle as I asked, "Now what did Kripanand do to get himself banished from the ashram?"

This was enough to make my guru laugh. "My little fellow, why do you think you are getting banished from the ashram? If that is what you are thinking, then relax."

My guru went on to explain the reason for my 'vacation'. "With the achievement of the *siddhi* of Asana, the first phase of a yogi's life is over. There are three phases in a yogi's life: the *aarambha*, the *ghata* and the *nishpatti*. We can call them the liberal, the moderate and the courageous. With the accomplishment of Asana you have arrived at the accomplishment of the first stage. Before the snowfall of the coming winter begins, you, along with a small group of others, will walk downhill back into human society. It is in human society where you will perform the next phase of your *tapah* and practice. It is very necessary for you to live, experience, and learn the ways of an ascetic, right in the midst of human pain and suffering."

Until then, my guru asked me to experience the *siddhi* of my Asana at least twice a week. After the initial few days, I did not need any support or instigation to go into the blissful state of Asana. I was becoming one with my practice. Barely had I felt that I was ever born for anything else.

CHAPTER FIVE

Spontaneous Meditation

It was the month of July, and the plains of India were already getting the monsoon rain. Up in the mountains, the temperature slowly began to drop. Chilly and freezing winds were blowing in from Tibet. Eight young yogis from my ashram, including myself, were getting prepared to enter the stage of hard asceticism, the second necessary phase of yogic life. I didn't have much to pack. The backpack with which I had arrived at the ashram was still lying untouched in a corner of the cave. After more than two years, I pulled it out and dusted it. Inside I found my once favorite pair of jeans and some t-shirts with 'Kalvin Clein' written on them. I found my wallet; it had about two hundred rupees in it. I asked someone if I needed to carry anything with me. There was nothing to be carried. However I took the money out of my wallet and decided to take it with me, just in case. My backpack, with its contents, was then again shoved back into its place for the next eternal waiting period.

One day at three in the morning, we were given our marching orders. I was surprised to find that my guru was accompanying this trip. A total of ten of us, including my guru and Kripanand, started our long trek towards Gangotri. On that day I asked my guru, "Why did you decide to join us at the last moment?"

"I wanted to join you because you were all about to cry and roll on the ground in abject desperation. I also wanted to see how my children would behave in the wild."

I asked, "Do you mean to say we are going to some forest?"

He replied, "No. Forests are not wild places. We are going to places that are not forests, but cities and villages. These are not forests, but they are very wild. In the forests, animals live in perfect harmony with nature. No animal kills another through envy or jealousy. They don't do business with other animals' lives. They don't destroy the nature that is the basis of their own sustenance. How can you call the forest, with its animals, a wild place? Where we are going is wild in the true sense of the term. There you will see people hurting each other for no reason. There you will see the entire society propelled by only one attitude: greed! The situation there is so mad that dogs are treated like human beings and human beings are treated like dogs."

We all laughed at his statement.

I was creating pictures in my mind about a dog lying in luxurious human conditions, being pampered with all kinds of expensive food - for which the bottom ninety percent of the Indian population would die. The dog in my imagination seemed to be very comfortable in these conditions. Does the dog know that it is a dog? Probably it knows, but it surely doesn't care. Like the lion in the story, it must have forgotten the nature of its species. The dog even carried a smug expression on its face, exactly the same as that of its owner. Poor dog!

I might have said these words a little audibly, as Kripanand asked, "Why poor dog and not poor man? So much sympathy for the dog and nothing for its owner?!"

All of us laughed out loud again.

The sun was about to set as we reached Rajpadao. This was to be our night's resting place. Walking in single file, we moved towards a cave where we would spend the night. My guru and Kripanand comfortably sat down next to each other, closed their eyes and remained still, while the rest of us walked around pretending to relish the great surrounding view. I was sure that none of the young yogis had any intention of enjoying the view.

The thought running through my mind was not of the view,

but the next phase of my practice. A fifteen-hour walk in the mountains had given me a hunger like I had never before experienced. I had no clue if we had anything with us to eat. I hesitated a little before approaching my guru. I interrupted him by saying, "What can I do when I am so hungry?"

Without opening his eyes he replied, "Sit down in Asana."

At first I was a little confused, then slowly I realized that it was the only option I had under these conditions. After touching his feet for blessing, like Kripanand I sat down on the other side of my guru. Before closing my eyes, I had a glimpse of the others staring blankly at us.

In my absolute blissful state, I suddenly heard somebody calling my name. I slowly began to come out of my Asana. It was Kripanand who was calling out for me. It was already the next morning, and everyone else was ready to continue the walk.

I came out of the cave and joined them. I noticed that there was no trace of tiredness or pain from the previous day. Instead, there was a pleasant sense of freshness. I wasn't feeling the weakness or hunger that I had experienced the day before. The feeling of hunger had completely gone, but I could still feel a slight weakness. We began our walk again. We walked beyond evening and into the night. Eventually we stopped at a cave in which two sadhus were living. These sadhus welcomed us, and we all happily squeezed ourselves into the tiny cave.

My tiredness and weakness were unbelievable. As I was contemplating getting into my Asana reverie, Kripanand called out, "Gentlemen, it's time for dinner. Come and have some food before you go to sleep."

Our host sadhus had prepared some kind of soup for their guests, and Kripanand produced some dry fruit from the little cloth bag he was carrying. This was all distributed amongst us, but Kripanand and my guru did not eat anything. Before starting to eat, I went to my guru and offered him my food. I said, "Gurudev, you have also not eaten for the last two days. Please eat something yourself."

Before my guru could speak, the sudden roars of laughter startled me. I looked around and found the host sadhus laughing like crazy. In the dim firelight, I noticed that neither of the sadhus had any teeth. I felt a little confused and annoyed. One of the sadhus asked me, "How long have you been staying at the ashram?"

"More than two years."

"During that time have you ever seen the masters, like your guru or Nirupanand, eat anything?"

That was a strange question. I tried to remember if I had seen them eating anything; I tried hard, but I could not remember having seen them take any food. Slowly my eyes were getting larger, as I was beginning to think that these people were surviving without any food for all these years.

Seeing my silence and surprise, the sadhus told me in a matter-of-fact way, "Young man, these masters of yours are nothing like you or me. Objects like food lost their importance long ago."

Pointing at my guru, the sadhu said, "Ask him when was the last time he had eaten any food."

I looked back and forth at my guru and the sadhus; I had no words to speak. It will be very hard for me to explain what was going through my mind, so I just kept mum and gaped at them. My guru and Kripanand didn't say anything, but the sadhus told me in their experience of the last thirty years, they had never known any of my masters to take any food. I looked down at the food in my hand. It appeared so strange to me, and for the next few minutes I was looking at my food and my guru alternately. I slowly placed the food on the floor without knowing what to do with it.

In a gentle voice my guru said, "Manmoyanand, please have your food. That time is yet to come when, like us, you will not need any food for your survival."

I began to nibble at my food. I would not say that there was any particular thought that was in my mind; rather a whole cyclone of thoughts, emotions and confusions were blowing around inside my head. Without finishing my food, I went to sleep.

Towards the evening of the next day we reached Gangotri. We went to the bathing *ghat* in front of the temple and washed ourselves. We briefly paused to pay regards at the temple of Mother Ganges before continuing our journey. I looked at the restaurants and food stalls along the path and remembered my hunger. Since the previous night I had developed a strange attitude towards food. Suddenly this one instance had killed most of my desire for this lump of matter which the common man struggles all his life to acquire.

Deep in my thoughts, I walked the narrow lanes leading away from the temple. Unintentionally my hand went to my waist and loosened the small roll of currency notes I had tucked there. I touched the money with my fingers and felt an overwhelming sense of disgust at the sight and thought of it. I looked at the long line of beggars defining the narrow path, only to read the lines of desire and greed in their faces. I dropped the role of notes into one of their waiting bowls. There was an instant frenzy amongst them as a couple of beggars jumped and clawed each other to grab some portion of the money. I walked on and looked up to see if my guru had noticed my behavior.

We walked to a quiet place a short distance away from the village of Gangotri. Everyone was asked to go around and gather something to eat for himself if they wished to do so. I stayed back with my teacher. It was not that I wasn't hungry - rather the hunger that my mind had posed for me was many times stronger than the one in my stomach.

I casually asked my guru, "Do you think it was right on my part to give the money away to the beggars?"

After a moment's silence he answered, "I would not say it was either right or wrong, but what did you expect others to gain by receiving something that you were disgusted about? You didn't give the money with love or a sense of good wishes. They are just as likely to be as disgusted with the money as you are. Do you actually think they don't have any money? You can't imagine how much money each of them possesses. They are begging because they are beggars, it is their profession, and it has proven profitable for them. Your money is not going to make any change in their lives. You only unconsciously supported and encouraged their profession, which is based upon the principle of taking advantage of people's religious beliefs. As you already know, by giving you are only buying your own ego, pride, status and satisfaction. However in this particular case, I didn't stop you from giving because I had noticed your indifference and disgust about the money that you carried."

I touched my guru's feet in reverence and as a mark of saying thank you.

Pointing towards the other side of the river, my guru said, "Can you see that house up there?"

"Yes, I can."

"Go to that house, and an old man will give you some food. You will need that food to continue with your journey."

Without a word I walked to the house, and as soon as I arrived at the door, an old man came out, as if he was waiting for me. He gave me some fresh, hot chapattis and pulao wrapped in a leaf plate.

I thanked him and walked back to my guru. I could not eat more than one chapatti and drank only a little water. Soon it was night; I went to sleep along with the others, while my guru and Kripanand continued to sit there as usual, with their eyes closed.

It took us a week to walk all the way to Rishikesh. Somewhere during the beginning of the walk, the only pair of slippers in the whole group (owned by me) had given up. Like the others, I was now walking barefoot. We walked throughout the day and stopped in the late afternoon in some village along the way. Somebody or other would give us some food, which was usually sufficient for the eight of us who still needed food for survival. The initial pain and tiredness had long since disappeared, and it slowly began to feel as if I had been walking my whole life.

Upon reaching Rishikesh, my guru walked straight to the place where I usually sat in the days of my seeking and wandering, prior to arriving at my ashram. I was feeling as if this place had some significance in my life. Maybe my guru had chosen that place for me to sit and contemplate long before meeting me.

We lived in Rishikesh for a few days. It was here that I realized the true purpose of this 'vacation'. The study and the practice of *tapah* (austerity) in the ashram was only half the achievement. The practice of *tapah* is not at its best and most challenging when the practitioner is living in the most beautiful and blissful ashram environment. There is no other blessing or advantage of life which can be valued more than the presence of the teacher next to the practitioner. According to Kripanand, young practitioners sometimes get spoiled under the constant care and attention of the teachers. In order to emerge perfectly pure, it is necessary for the yogi to step outside the comforting circle of the ashram. In the midst of the wild human civilization, the *tapah* and self-control of the yogi is put to the test.

It was frightening to learn that there are successive stages of *tapah* which a yogi has to perform in his process of self-realization. The strength of *tapah* and purity could only be meaningful when one is surrounded by constant provocation. This was to be the real examination of all that we had learnt and studied in the ashram. At the end of our stay in Rishikesh, my guru left us and walked away without telling us where he was going. The rest of us walked to Haridwar with Kripanand.

Since the moment I left the ashram, something inside me seemed to understand the meaning of all that was happening. I had complete faith and trust in the process of my learning and was absolutely sure that nothing could go wrong in my life as long as it was in the hands of my masters. At the same time there was another part of me that was secretly trying to decipher the meaning of everything. I never liked to remain ignorant about even the smallest of facts; the one and only reason for this, as it appeared to me, was for the sole purpose of knowledge and the realization of the absolute. I naturally began to wonder if there could be any other practice or process that was as perfect as the one I was doing. What could be the highest point of my achievement in this incredible process of learning? My sense of satisfaction was always leading me deeper into the quest.

One day Kripanand said, "We are going to stop at a village for a few days."

We took shelter in a temple near the village, and Kripanand asked us to go into the village and beg.

"Begging?!" I asked Kripanand in complete surprise, "Why should we go out begging?"

The thought of begging gave me uncomfortable feelings. Kripanand, in response to my reaction, took the opportunity to tell us the following story:

"In the ancient past, there lived a young man. His name was Vinod. He came from a fairly well-to-do family and was very hard working in nature. Vinod had an insatiable hunger for knowledge. After he passed out from his village school, he took permission from his parents and traveled to distant places in the country. He went to Avanti and Ujjain, both renowned for their great universities.

Within a few years he emerged as a scholar from both universities with the highest possible degrees. He then went on to Taxila. In the old times, Taxila used to be the place of highest learning. Here he would study the most difficult subjects of all. In the quest of life, he simply wanted to learn everything under the sun. At the end of his study, he emerged with the most respectable degree that any university in India could offer.

At the time of leaving the university, he went to meet his professor to thank him for all his help. The professor congratulated him for the success in his studies and asked Vinod what he would do next. Vinod replied, "Please tell me, is there any other university in the world which offers anything more than what I have already achieved? I just want to learn everything."

His professor thought for a moment and replied, "I know of one such great master. I think you should go to him to complete the rest of your learning."

Vinod was happy to know this. The professor gave him a piece of paper in which he had written the name and address of the master. The professor blessed him, and Vinod started his journey to find the great master who would teach him some of the highest lessons of life.

Vinod discovered that the place where the master lived was not a big city, only a small hamlet. The place didn't look as though it had a university or institution, and no one seemed to know the master by his name.

After moving throughout the village, he still couldn't locate the master anywhere. At last one villager told him that he didn't know of any great master of that name, but he surely knew of a blacksmith by that name who lived at the end of the village. Vinod took the directions and went to the little workshop of the blacksmith.

Upon his arrival he showed the paper to the blacksmith and said that he was looking for this man. The blacksmith took the paper and after a quick glance asked, "Did the good professor of the University of Taxila send you here?"

Vinod enthusiastically replied, "Yes!"

He was happy that at last he had found the man, but he was highly confused as to what lesson this rustic blacksmith could possibly teach him over and above the degrees that he had earned thus far. The blacksmith asked Vinod to sit down and gave him some water to drink. Vinod settled down to relax after the long journey and the blacksmith went back to his work. He watched the old frail figure of the blacksmith hammering away a piece of hot iron to the mould of some garden tool. After a while the blacksmith asked Vinod, "Can you please help me keep the fire going? If you could, please turn the wheel of the bellow slowly."

Vinod went and sat next to the wheel and began to turn it slowly. In the evening the blacksmith wound up his work and got up to go home. Vinod also got up and asked respectfully, "Master, when are you going to start my lessons?"

He replied, "There is time for your lessons. Let's go and rest for the day. We will talk about it later."

Vinod went with the blacksmith to his house. In the night, they had food together and slept in a little cottage on the bare mud floor. Vinod got up the next day in the early hours of the morning. He took a bath and changed into some fresh clean clothes and waited expectantly for his lessons. The blacksmith cooked some food for the midday meal, gathered his tools and asked Vinod to follow him to his little workshop. As the blacksmith started his usual work, Vinod interrupted and asked, "Master, what about my lessons?"

The blacksmith replied, "Don't worry. I am planning your lessons now. Sit down there and run the wheel again."

Vinod had no other option but to sit down and run the wheel. The old blacksmith worked throughout the day and made him run the wheel and feed the fire for the entire day. Vinod's new and clean clothes turned into a dirty mess. As evening approached, they gathered up their work and went home.

The next day was exactly the same. The old man worked, and Vinod ran the wheel and tended to the fire. Only once during the day had Vinod reminded the old man about his lessons. Without giving him an answer the old man asked him to continue running the wheel.

Weeks passed, months passed and years passed. In the meanwhile, Vinod had given up all ideas and hopes of reminding the blacksmith about his lessons. He was taken to the task of running the wheel and was *no longer bothered about how clean or dirty his clothes appeared. His days were spent amongst the poorest of the poor people, who had no wealth and no pride. Vinod never had an opportunity to speak about his high education or the great degrees that he had.*

Two years passed. One day whilst Vinod was by the fire and turning the wheel, he felt the loving and gentle hand of his master on his shoulder. He stopped for a moment and turned to the old man and respectfully said, "Please tell me, master, if I can do something for you."

The old man wiped Vinod's dirty hands with his cloth and replied in a very gentle tone, "My dear son, I am happy to tell you that your lessons are over."

Vinod could not understand. He never knew that the lessons had ever started.

Seeing his confusion the old man said, "Vinod, during the past two years you have learnt some of the greatest lessons of your life. They are humility and patience. Without these two important lessons, all the university degrees are quite useless. Now with these new lessons, you can go and enjoy the fruits of all the degrees you have earned in your life."

Vinod's mind was overwhelmed with gratitude. After paying his respects to the old man, the greatest master of his experience, Vinod walked away into the world."

The moral of the story held my heart in a tight grip. I asked no further questions about begging. The next morning I was the first to go into the village with a begging bowl. Kripanand had given us explicit instructions not to speak a word or even open our mouths regarding our personal or ashram background. We also had the firm instruction to stop begging as soon as we collected enough money for just one meal. Begging was meant for survival and was never to be our profession or business for the purpose of accumulation. We were allowed to beg for only as much as was required for the one meal of the day.

I would say begging was an overwhelming experience for me,

as it gave me immense pleasure to bow down before every man in the street. There was no discrimination in my eyes. Each of these people who threw me a coin was respectable to me. Sometimes small children came to give me alms with their tiny hands. Since I was forbidden to talk or express any emotion, I could only thank each of the givers with a genuine and deep sense of respect. Sometimes people offered us water or fruits to eat. To my surprise, I began to notice that mostly people treated us with respect and never with contempt. Kripanand explained the reason for this.

"There is such a difference between your begging and the activity of a typical beggar. Most beggars beg in order to accumulate. It is greed that instigates and propels their begging. They lack the respect for the giver and are often nagging and irritable. Who will treat these beggars with kindness if their intentions are very clear and apparent? When you beg, never carry yourself as a beggar. Your begging is only meant for the greatest lessons of life: humility and patience. That is why you receive an entirely different treatment when in the act of begging."

In the first six months of traveling we had walked most of the regions of Uttaranchal and northern Uttar Pradesh. As soon as the weather became warm, Kripanand told us that he would be going back to the ashram. The senior amongst us was Brother Sadanand. He was asked to lead us further in our journey. Under his guidance we traveled into the eastern and southern parts of India. The absence of Guru Kripanand had left us a little directionless, but soon we began to learn how to handle our ascetic life individually. We always walked together from place to place. When we would approach a village or city, we would separate and move around on our own. The old tourist in me had not died. I always visited the historical sites of each place as I was particularly interested in acquainting myself with the history and culture of the area. I was forever curious to know the religious and spiritual beliefs of the people.

I mostly begged near the temples for about an hour in the morning. I would never beg in front of places that offered easy food to beggars. One thing was also for certain. I learnt not to stay at one place for more than a few hours. Villagers in India have a peculiar habit; they constantly flock around ascetics to pile their woes on them. I would always listen to them in earnest as they would tell me about their land, their cattle and their wives. Every single one of them had some difficulty or other in life. In order to get remedy and solace, they always brought some fruit or clothing, something they felt I would need. Kripanand had warned me about the attachment these villagers could create in a yogi. It is very likely for an ascetic to fall for the unlimited offerings of the villagers, and if one is not careful, it becomes a wonderful opportunity to develop a God-like feeling and end up accumulating all the material pleasures of life.

We were always careful not to allow any incitement to affect our ascetic life. Many of the ascetics were offered wealth, work, residence, occupation or even daughters in marriage! Things that could appear very valuable to a common man were humbly rejected. None of the offerings carried any value in comparison to what we were looking for in life. This wandering ascetic phase of our lives continued for about eighteen months. During this time we had returned to the ashram on only two brief occasions. The eighteen months had given me the experiences of a lifetime. Living on the streets without any possession had revealed to me the true worth of myself. It was absolutely joyful to realize that I didn't belong to anyone or anything in as much as no one or nothing belonged to me.

I experienced the gradual process of my spiritual unfoldment as I continued to realize the true nature of human existence. Nothing defined my humanness. Nothing was there as a limit. I gradually became free from the afflictions of all human thoughts and emotions. I began to develop a strong restlessness similar to that which I had experienced a long time ago. It was the restless and insatiable desire to open myself up further. I was experiencing a deep yearning to become one with my surroundings, to become one with the supreme joy that I was looking for deep within myself.

Gradually, this feeling became more and more intensified. During this time we were traveling through the southern coast of India. I disclosed my intention of returning to the ashram to the rest of the group. I told them about my feelings and condition, and asked for their permission to leave.

I walked on with a growing and urging sense of desperation in my heart, to cover the approximate two thousand, six hundred kilometers that separated me from my guru. I walked day and night. There was only one prayer in my mind: the name of my guru and a pleading request to help me reach him as quickly as possible. I covered the journey in less than two months.

Upon reaching Gangotri, I found two companions from my ashram waiting there for me. They told me they were sent by my teacher to accompany me through the mountain path back to my ashram, since I was not very well acquainted with that particular path. Without stopping in Gangotri we proceeded towards our ashram. If it had not been for the help of my companions, I realized I surely would have lost my path and died in some remote corner of the Himalayas. All the way to my ashram, tears of gratitude were rolling down from my eyes. My guru was extremely pleased to see me. I threw myself into his arms and began to cry.

After a few days rest, I was given the complete understanding of the past eighteen-month ordeal. My guru explained to me that this time was necessary for me to experience the outcomes of my asana practice. The practice and accomplishment of Asana is only a passing phase in the life of a yogi. The accomplishment of

Asana results in a stage where the yogi is free from the conflict of dualities. The conflicting opposites of every aspect of life come to an end with the achievement of this stage.

The effect of the accomplishment of Asana is indicated in the Yoga Sutras. Maharshi Patanjali has clearly explained in his sutra, *'Tatah Dvandvanabhighatah'* (2:48), which means 'Thence (i.e. - on the achievement of the laxity of the body and the transformation of thought) ceases the conflict from the pairs of opposites (i.e. - the yogi becomes free from the disturbances arising out of the conflict of dualities)'.

The practice of the next yogic *kriya*, very importantly, is based upon the conditions of achievement of this stage. After the completion of any asana *kriya*, it was necessary for me to undergo the testing conditions that led to the assertion of this stage.

I don't know why I began to smile as my guru was explaining this to me. The eighteen months of hardship had definitely sobered me up. I had learnt the lessons of humility and detachment, but the process appeared a bit harsh, as it was only meant to be a test.

My guru firmly pointed out, "The next *kriya* that you are going to do is *pranayama*. This is the invaluable practice that will reveal to you the complete intellective knowledge. The conditions for its practice and teaching are very rigorous, and only a handful of extremely fortunate *sadhaks* get to know this *kriya*. The practice of *pranayama* has the capacity to cleanse the yogi from all negative afflictions of his entire karmic cycle. This super-powerful *kriya* is to be approached with absolute respect and caution. It could be really harmful to practise *pranayama* without the prerequisite psycho-physical eligibility."

Mahatma Vyasa, as well as commentators like Vachaspati Mishra, have explained the ill effects of the incorrect practice of pranayama. One may incur various kinds of diseases or permanent incapacity of the body if *pranayama* is attempted without its absolute foundation. My guru continued that it was very necessary for him to have subjected me to such a powerful test of refinement before I was introduced to the practice of *pranayama*. With this explanation my eighteen-month long tiredness disappeared within a moment. Without showing any undue excitement, I waited patiently for my lessons to begin.

∞∞∞

Pranayama, as a component *kriya* of the eightfold practice of Yoga, is actually a product of Tantra. Thousands of years before the writing of the first yogic scripture, Tantra had explained the cosmic nature of the human body to be exactly the same and identical as the external universe. Ancient tantric studies revealed *pranayama* was used by the tantrists as a vehicle to navigate through the subtle pathways of the universe. There are a great collection of myths and legends about some *rishis* that traveled into the higher realms of the cosmos and returned only to see that thousands of years had passed on earth in the meantime.

The great tantric, Yogi Nirupanand, explained the practice of *pranayama* in a manner that triggered thoughts of movies like Star Wars and Star Trek. Imagine yourself as a cosmonaut. You are navigating amongst the galaxies in a spaceship. The dark expanse of outer space has astral bodies traveling in all directions. You are trying to fly your spaceship to a certain cosmic destination. The chances of colliding into any of the flying objects are extremely high. Your space map indicates only two spiraling pathways. You are cautiously trying to negotiate these extremely complex space manoeuvres. These paths lie in the orbits of large bodies like the sun and moon.

Your years of cosmonaut training and a properly equipped spaceship are all you have to rely upon. Gradually you begin to steer your spaceship through the solar and lunar paths. As you cautiously move forward, you begin to realize these are the only possible pathways available in space that are not clogged by the wandering asteroids. In your mind, you begin to feel thankful for the efforts of other spaceships that were sent prior to you to clear the asteroids from your path. Slowly you build more confidence and begin to accelerate your spaceship. Soon you are cruising at macrocosmic velocity. Traveling at the speed of light, you complete the voyage through the spiraling loop of your path. Back at your original space station, you have a safe landing. You come out of your spaceship and notice that the world looks so different.

Within the short time that you spent in outer space, many years have passed on earth. While your body did not change much during the last few days in space, you have found that all of your friends and relatives have grown old. Some have even died. Your mission has been successful. You have experienced the realm of timelessness and in the process, transcended the limitations of time on earth. You write in your diary: 'I have proven the possibilities of transcending time and will live to see the final stage of evolution on this planet.'

The subject of *Pranayama* can have three major approaches. They depend upon the source from which they are derived. The yogic explanation of *Pranayama* will be the chief subject of discussion. Apart from the yogic approach, the other two explanations are *vedantic* and tantric. Within the meanings of *Vedanta*, there are five types of *vayu* or 'air' present in the body. *Pranayama* is the *kriya* of the fusion of *prana* and *apana vayus*.

Apana vayu is found at the lower part of the abdomen that lies between the navel and the perineum. The place of *samana vayu* is the area of the solar plexus. The place of *prana vayu* is the area around the heart and chest cavity. *Udana vayu* is explained to reside at the area above the shoulders and head. The fifth, *vyana vayu*, surrounds and engulfs the other four *vayus*.

Pranayama kriyas have been explained as the fusion of *apana* and *prana vayu* together. The *kriya* of *pranayama* can also be accomplished by the successful fusion of *apana* with the other *vayus*, as per desire or necessity.

To accomplish this purpose, several *kriyas* need to be mastered. These are called *bandhas* (locks). There are three kinds of *bandhas*. After the successful destruction of physical impurities, the *moola bandha* is applied to move the *apana vayu* upwards to meet and fuse with the *samana vayu*. After the successful accomplishment of this, the *uddiyana bandha* is practised to move the *apana* and *samana vayus* to merge with the *prana vayu* at the heart. *Jalandhara bandha* is performed to provide a check to prevent the escape of the *prana vayu* through the facial openings. Without the correct practice of *jalandhara bandha*, one is likely to give up his ghost during his practices.

After the successful fusion of *apana* and *prana*, the *kriya* of *pranayama* is said to be accomplished. Since the *vedantic* practices have highly contributed to the *kriyas* of yoga, we find the mention of the fusion of *apana* in several yogic scriptures. Maharshi Patanjali also refers to the superhuman capacities (*siddhis*) that one can achieve by the fusion of these *vayus*.

The tantric explanation of *Pranayama* refers to a powerful force of psychic or *pranic* energy which is channeled to the base of the spine to stimulate the polar energy of that area. The base of the spine acts as the south pole of the energy axis of the body. The spinal column, along with the sets of *nadis* (channels), forms the primordial energy axis of the body-universe. The cerebral cortex is the seat of the masculine *purusha* or *shiva*, whereas the bottom of the spine represents the house of *shakti* or *kundalini*. The tantric scriptures have explained *kundalini* as a golden serpent that is sleeping in three-and-a-half coils. The pathways to approach the seat of *kundalini* are through the solar and lunar channels. After the purification of these channels, the *kundalini* can be approached very carefully. Appropriate practice of *brahmacharya* and worship of the goddess of feminine energy are the necessary practices to appease and invoke the blessings of *kundalini.*

The tantric *kriya* of the ritual copulation of the male, symbolizing *shiva,* and the female, symbolizing *shakti,* is practised to achieve the unity and harmony of these powers. As a result of the stimulation of *kundalini* and the correct accomplishment of the *kriyas,* the latent energy at the base of the spine 'wakes up' and travels upwards through the spine. The practice has to be done under correct and competent guidance to contain the consequences of this energy movement as it travels to the seat of *shiva* by piercing through the chakras in the way. The stimulation and movement of *kundalini* is the most extreme example of electrochemical activity of the nervous system. It can be compared to an extremely powerful and prolonged orgasm. The impact of this reaction is carried upward through the spine and nervous system to the cerebral cortex to accomplish the final goals of the tantric ritual.

The fusion between the feminine and masculine energies, in a technical way, completes the circuit and the full cycle of evolution. The tendency of creation and the seed of creation merge completely to take the practising tantrist to the pre-evolutionary primordial state. The realization of the *Ardhanariswara* nature of the cosmos is the primary objective of the tantric practice of *pranayama.*

Many yogis practise *pranayama* for various purposes, but whichever purpose one chooses for practice, the prerequisites of *pranayama* are essential. Another important rule of *pranayama* is that the practice of *pranayama* should not be mixed with the incorrect system. People practising the *vedantic* process of *pranayama* should not confuse and mix up the tantric explanation, nor should the tantric practitioners confuse their practices with the yogic process.

Prior to this understanding, I too had a strange and mixed-up notion of '*kundalini yoga*'. It should be clearly note that the term *kundalini* has no place within yogic terminology. The practice of Yoga in its purest meaning does not contain any complete tantric practice. The whole idea of Yoga is a complete walk away from the fundamental nature of tantric practice, where essentially a male and a female practitioner are involved. The practice of Tantra requires two different and opposite physical entities to excite and stimulate the *kundalini* energy. Here, the union of two bodies of the opposite sex is absolutely necessary to buffer the impact of *kundalini* stimulation. Any attempt to handle *kundalini* without the buffer of the partner's body could be dangerous. No scripture of tantric *kundalini* practice supports or encourages the practice of *kundalini* without the ritual copulation.

The explanation of *Pranayama* in the yogic scriptures has been derived from both *vedic* and tantric sources. However in Yoga we find no mention of the ritual copulation. Yoga is like an ultra-modern spiritual technology. The master scientists of Yoga have not differed from the cosmic explanation of the body and *pranic* energy. Instead, the gross and ritual aspects of the practice were eliminated to explain the subtle, underlying equation, which is actually the sole reason for the success of its practice. By this, they also eliminated the inherent risks by explaining *Pranayama* in terms of quantum physics and the theory of relativity.

It was absolutely surreal and unbelievable to hear of quantum physics from the half-clad ascetics of the mountains. I had never studied physics in my life, and Yogi Nirupanand, who was to teach me *Pranayama*, had never been to a school in this life. After being introduced to the latest explanations of quantum physics, it became one of the dearest subjects in my life. Unbelievable as it may sound, the Yoga Sutras of Patanjali is undoubtedly the first book on quantum physics.

The simple definition of *Pranayama* as per the Yoga Sutras is 'the disconnection of the inward and outward movement of cosmic energy'. Referring to the previous sutra that underlined the effects of Asana, Maharshi Patanjali stated in sutra 2:49: *'Tasminsati svasaprasvasayorgativichhedah pranayamah,'* which broadly translates as 'On the achievement of the effects of Asana the disconnection of the movement of inspiration and expiration is *Pranayama'*. He never meant that you practise a few gymnastic postures and with a small interlude, jump into some breathing exercises.

Maharshi Patanjali has written two words about the process of disconnection: *yama* and *vichhedah*. *Yama* carries a similar meaning as it stands in sutra 2:29, broadly meaning 'restraint', 'conscious control or modification', or 'check'. *Vichhedah* denotes 'detach' or 'disconnection'. In sutra 2:49, Maharshi Patanjali describes the breath or air intake as 'the carrier of *prana'*. Within the meaning of this sutra, *pranayama* does not denote the manipulation of breath. *Pranayama* is the manipulation of *'prana'*.

Prana, in its purest form, largely differs from any other life-giving object. The explanations of food, water or oxygen as *'prana'* are incorrect. However, these articles can be taken as carriers of *prana*. *Prana* constantly moves into and out of the microcosmic entity of our body through the physical particles of food, water or air. Within this meaning, the restraint of *prana* within the body should be possible by the regulation of even food and water intake.

The science of *Pranayama* has evolved from the regulation of breath, accepting air as the most fluid and versatile carrier of *prana*. The restraint of *prana* is what the practitioner should look for, not the mere restraint or manipulation of breath. *Prana* is a spiritual or cosmic element. The correct harmony with *prana* and its acceleration has a spiritual outcome, whereas the mindless manipulation of breath can seriously and harmfully interfere with our physical and psychological health. Hence, the Yoga Sutras has placed so many prerequisites for the correct practice of *pranayama*.

The next sutra of Maharshi Patanajli necessitates a microscopic examination. *'Bahyaabhyantarastambhavrittir desakalasamkhyabhih paridrsto dirghasukhmah'* (2:50), broadly translates as 'When *pranayama* is practised with the external, internal and confining operations, being regulated by space-time and frequency, it becomes prolonged and subtle'. *Pranayama* is not the gross act of breath regulation. In order to be *pranayama*, the *kriya* has to be subtle. Since *prana* is a subtle element, *pranayama* cannot be a gross physical act. In order to attain the subtle nature of *pranayama*, the conscious physical practice needs to be prolonged beyond the physical limits. The technique to accomplish this prolonged and subtle nature of *pranayama* practice is by the 'regulation of space-time and frequency'. Here lies the secret key to the *kriya* of macrocosmic velocity.

What does Maharshi Patanjali mean when he states that we need the space-time and frequency regulation of *prana*? We have seen that *prana* is a cosmic element. It is this element which constantly flows in and out of the human body and acts as an integral connection between the body and the external universe. *Prana* plays the role of the creating, sustaining and destroying force in the physical body. The behavior of *prana*, in the total scheme of the universe, is also responsible for the evolutionary growth and progress of the body.

The *kriya* of macrocosmic velocity is to tune the behavior of *prana* inside the body to the space-time frequency of the external universe. The function of *prana* in the external universe is extremely fine and subtle, but in the human body, it is shrouded by the gross processes of breathing, drinking and digestion. Maharshi Patanjali intends to take the yogi to the exact *pranic* rhythm available in both the internal and external universe. This modification and tuning of the *pranic* rhythm to macrocosmic space-time dynamics is what Patanjali means by *Pranayama*. It is, in fact, the only proven way through which one can accelerate the spiritual and evolutionary progress of the subtle body.

Neither the micro nor the macrocosmic universe has a single or constant space-time dynamic. Like the body, the external universe witnesses a different space-time ratio at different points of the universe. Hence it gives one no reason to panic about the exact space-time ratio of both the cosmic bodies. All that is required in the practice of *pranayama* is only to increase the current ratio. This is accomplished by taking into account the space-time dynamics of the body. Now let me ask you: 'What is the space-time dynamic by which the spiritual and evolutionary growth of the body is determined?'

Let us remind ourselves of something that was explained earlier. The space-time dynamics are experienced through the solar and lunar cycles of the body. There are four stages of the lunar cycle of twenty-eight days, and thirteen such lunar cycles make a solar cycle of three hundred sixty-five days. Three hundred sixty-five days, or one solar year, takes the body into one year of evolutionary process. Let us examine the inner meaning of this.

When *prana* travels in the solar and lunar channels of the body at the speed of three hundred sixty-five days per cycle, the outcome is one year of evolution. Now let us practise to accelerate the speed of *pranic* movement through the same channels. The initial practice will appear like a conscious breathing manipulation. The purpose of this practice is to enhance the space-time ratio of this movement. With gradual increase of this ratio, the practice no longer remains a gross 'huffing and puffing'. Over a sustained period of practice, the velocity of *prana* can be accelerated, and according to Maharshi Patanajli, it becomes 'prolonged and subtle'.

The great master of Yoga did not end the explanation of *Pranayama* at this point. In the next sutra, *'Bahyabhyantaravisayaksepi caturthah'* (2:51), he talks about the transcendence beyond the three-dimensional limits of the *pranayama kriya*. In the microcosmic body, the *prana* has three-dimensional functions. All that the *prana* can accomplish is the extreme limits of three-dimensional manifestations within the limits of three-dimensional space. As per the meanings of sutra 2:51, when the *kriya*, or the *pranic* activity, is made to transcend three-dimensional limits, the *kriya* becomes four-dimensional. Under the fourth dimensional velocity of *prana*, the yogi enters and experiences the fourth dimension of existence.

Yogi Nirupanand's explanation of the *kriya* of *pranayama* seemed to be very clear and simple. But it did not create an instant image in my mind, even though the lines he spoke became engraved in my memory. I withdrew myself for a few days' silent contemplation. I began to toss and turn the powerful words of Nirupanand in my mind. A few times in the process, I even talked to my guru. As I contemplated more and more upon the feasibility of the *Pranayama* theory, the more sense it began to make. I so wished to have some book of modern physics which would have helped me decipher the scientific implications of *Pranayama*. It took quite a few days of serious brainstorming as I began to prepare myself to enter into the actual practice of it. I expressed my desire and readiness before Nirupanand. He informed me that the practice of *pranayama* could be as technical as its explanation. I requested him to teach me in the best possible ways, as I was absolutely ready and undeterred.

Nirupanand disclosed that for the complete and successful practice of *pranayama*, one has to live under a very specific condition that includes zero human contact. He told me that I would have to go far away to a cave where I could see no one and where no one could see me. Later I found that almost all scriptures of Yoga, including *Hathayoga Pradipika*, *Gheranda Samhita* and *Siva Samhita*, actually prescribe this requirement of *Pranayama*. I had absolutely no doubts about the process or the practice. I began my preparation for my 'solitary confinement'.

(Many a time I had referred to my ashram as a 'concentration camp' which, in my definition, is a place where one concentrates, and did not have any Second World War implications.) Nirupanand taught me the *pranayama* practices and gave the exact schedule of practice for each and every day. After explaining the *kriyas*, it was now time to learn and accomplish *surya namaskar*, the 'sun salutation'.

Under pre-ashram conditions, I would have easily jumped up at the mention of sun salutation. I performed enough of these gymnastics in my early days. Most yoga classes in Rishikesh began the morning asanas with a round of 'warm up' exercises in a similar manner as bodybuilders enter the gym and do not start pumping iron until they have sufficiently warmed up. A couple of cycles of *surya namaskar* would serve as a warm-up tool before proceeding into other exercises. At this point in time, my old notion of asanas was completely shattered, and in its place an entirely new and unshakable knowledge of asanas had been formed. With Nirupanand, I could not repeat what Kripanand had labeled the 'joke of the century'. I was only too willing to learn the true practice of this great sadhana. As Nirupananad explained the practice in great scientific detail, all the modern beliefs about *surya namaskar* slowly began to crumble.

"The human body needs energy for survival. People eat food to provide energy to the body. However if one can provide the required amount of energy to the body without the help of food, then there is no need for food.

Whenever we eat some food, depending upon its nature, it takes a certain amount of effort to digest. The body also uses a certain amount of energy in the process. After digestion, the food creates energy in return, and this energy is used by the body for its maintenance and healing. The more you eat or the more frequently you eat, the more the body becomes perpetually entangled in the never-ending cycle of food processing, digestion and energy generation.

During the most austere periods of practice, it is always useful to reduce the activity of the stomach considerably. One has to take as little food as possible to make the practice more fruitful."

I was not aghast at this seemingly impossible condition. I just repeated my willingness, "I will continue my practices without food until the end of my human endurance."

Nirupanand smiled, which was one of the rarest expressions of his face, and comforted me by replying, "The *pranayamas* are done for a specific purpose. Dying a slow and starved death is not the *kriya* of macrocosmic velocity."

He reminded me that the ordinary use of the human body requires ordinary food; but for the extraordinary use of the human body, we need extraordinary fuel. In just the same way as a spaceship cannot rely upon organic fuel in its space missions, the human body cannot take normal organic food for its *kriya* of macrocosmic velocity. A spaceship derives its energy from small reserves as well as solar power. Very similarly, the energy requirement of a yogi comes through the practice of *surya namaskar*. A yogi practising *surya namaskar* does not need any other food for survival.

The solar energy perceived as light has seven wavelengths. When sunlight is broken through a prism, we see seven wavelengths as seven different and distinct colors. Violet has the smallest wavelength and the highest frequency. On the other end of the spectrum, red has the highest wavelength and the smallest frequency. The extreme wavelengths like ultraviolet and infrared have harmful effects on the body and remain unperceivable. The seven wavelengths provide nourishment to all forms of life under the sun. Every living thing directly or indirectly depends upon solar energy for its sustenance. Exposure to sunlight in the morning and evening gives us an important food ingredient, vitamin D. The human body has been intelligently designed to receive and assimilate each wavelength of the sun.

The function and mechanism of the body largely depends upon seven systems: the nervous system, cardiovascular system, respiratory system, excretory system, reproductive system, lymphatic system and digestive system. Each of these systems are in turn governed and regulated by seven specific endocrine glands. These endocrine glands are located along a vertical axis in the body, at more or less the same place where the chakras or energy whorls are situated. As mentioned earlier, there are seven chakras, and their positions lie from the crown of the head to the bottom of the spinal column. The endocrine glands function with the back-up energy that is supplied through the chakras. It is interesting to note that the energy frequencies of these chakras are exactly the same as the seven different wavelengths of the sunlight. The crown chakra corresponds to the violet wavelength, and in that order, the base chakra functions with the red wavelength. Thus the functions of the entire body are directly related to the frequencies of sunlight.

Surya namaskar is not an asana, as technically it does not function to provide the 'steady and pleasurable' state of Asana. It is an important *kriya* used for the support and sustenance of the body. It has seven *kriyas* arranged in a sequence of twelve steps corresponding to the number of zodiacs of the sun. These seven *kriyas* are individually designed to assimilate each of the individual wavelengths of solar energy. The practice of *surya namaskar* is a process where seven *kriyas* acquire and assimilate the seven individual wavelengths of solar energy into the seven specific and corresponding chakras of the body. As a result, the seven physio-pathological systems of the body are nourished and sustained.

The practice of *surya namaskar* involves the practice of mantras. Mantras are usually a sound or syllable, a word or sentence, created on the basis of the sound frequency which is exactly the same as the meaning and implication of the mantra. Mantras have been used as effective tools of spiritual practice for ages by different civilizations across the world. The mantras are usually available in the language of Sanskrit. Mantras can technically be created by the help of any language since it is 'sound' that is used in the mantra and not the linguistic phraseology. Sanskrit is the most suitable language that can be used for the formulation of mantras as the language is highly phonetic in nature, and the words and sounds of this language stand to denote the meaning and objects of the language.

Sound is a form of energy. Like any other form of energy, it can travel as long as a medium is available. Ether is the medium through which sound travels. Depending upon the frequency of the original sound, it can travel through almost anything in the universe since everything in the universe contains the necessary element of ether in it. Simple experiments can be conducted to understand the behavior of sound. Most of us are acquainted with the experiment of the tuning fork. To explain the formulation of mantras, let us take the example of a musical instrument.

If you strike a musical instrument randomly, it will give out a random note. But if you wish to bring out a definite note, you have to strike the instrument in a definite way. Different musical instruments are capable of creating different kinds of sound, but we need the most versatile of all musical instruments to create the notes and vibrations of a mantra. Millions of years of perfection and fine craftsmanship have given us the most versatile of all the musical instruments: our vocal cords. They have the capacity to produce all the notes and sounds that we can humanly imagine.

When a mantra is spoken, a definite frequency of energy emanates from the throat and spreads out in the universe, both internally and externally. The energy travels enormous distances and continues to reverberate. In the process of its transition and propagation it affects those elements for which the specific frequency was intended. The note and rhythm of the mantra can be regulated to create the desired effect in the element to which it is directed. In *surya namaskar*, seven such mantras are used. The frequencies of the mantras are chosen to correspond to the energy dynamics of the seven individual wavelengths. The function of each of these mantras is to invoke and attract the seven different energies of the sun.

For the practice of *surya namaskar*, one needs to face the rising sun and expose as much of the body as possible. The *kriya* is not very useful when practised indoors or with a covered body. Standing in the energy-invoking position, one has to keep chanting the first mantra until the corresponding chakra of the body begins to pulsate very strongly. Keeping the attention on this receiving pulsation and maintaining the chanting of the mantra, one has to perform all seven *kriyas* of *surya namaskar* in the correct sequence of twelve steps. This invokes, receives and assimilates the intended wavelength of solar energy into the corresponding chakra. In order to acquire and assimilate the seven wavelengths of the sun, one has to perform the whole process seven times with the chanting of the appropriate mantra and the concentration at the appropriate chakra. This becomes one cycle of the *kriya* of *surya namaskar*. The effect of one cycle of *surya namaskar* helps the yogi to nourish and sustain himself for twenty-four hours. This is how the yogi surpasses the need of food for a full day.

After the years of practice and hard discipline at the ashram, the *kriya* of *surya namaskar* did not pose much difficulty as its physical gymnastics were already known to me. It was only a matter of time until I learnt to infuse the true essence of the practice into my already known gymnastics. This was no easy job. I needed the constant guidance of Nirupanand in the invocation and assimilation of energy. Gradually I began to experience the secret of the ancient yogis who lived without food for years. I grew more excited and delighted as I soon mastered the art of living without

Lake Vasuki Tal - The place where the author spent six months in isolation to practise pranayama. Bhagirathi peaks in the background.

food.

During the practice periods, I sometimes dropped even the only meal of the day. The nourishment of the body by solar energy has absolutely no side-effects. It does not result in any hunger, fatigue or reduction in the general level of one's strength. Here I should remind the readers not to attempt to live without food as long as they have a secondary use of their body. If the machinery of the body is used in any purpose other than the practice of yogic *kriyas*, it would need an appropriate amount of fuel for its function.

One day Nirupanand escorted me to a cave that lay close to Vasuki Tal and Chandra Parvat. The location of this cave was chosen keeping in mind the occasional food supply that would come from Gangotri, which would be left at a place approximately one kilometer away. The second important reason this cave was chosen is because it was used by many great and successful yogis in the practice of their *sadhana* and thus highly recommended. This cave was very small in comparison with the caves of my ashram. Apart from a blanket, a water pot and a piece of paper containing Nirupanand's instructions, I had no other material possessions. Here I started my *tapah* of *pranayama*.

The schedule of practice was one hour per sitting four times a day. Every day at sunrise, noon, sunset and midnight, I began to practise my *pranayama* with the strict adherence to all the rules of the *kriya*. After the *pranayama* at sunrise, I would go out into the open and perform *surya namaskar*. This always helped me remain in high spirits. Gradually my practice increased to twelve hours a day. On the days I felt a little tired and exhausted, I would take more rest. Once in a while, I would go to the food collection point to collect some roasted grams, lumps of *jaggery* and on occasion, some dry fruits. The food usually sat there for a few days before it was collected.

In the third month of my practice, I began to experience a variety of strange sensations in my body. They were not pains of any kind, but they also did not reflect spiritual health. At times my body would shiver uncontrollably, and I would break into a sweat. Whenever this happened, I stopped the practice and took rest. Sometimes I would get strange feelings in the night and get up with a start. One day, I suddenly began to hear voices. I could not find where they were coming from; neither could I decipher what was spoken nor what they were saying. They just seemed to be coming from everywhere. Many times I would get up from my practice and go around looking for the people who I thought were making some noise. I never found anyone, for there was not a soul around. The voices came every time I was immersed in my practice, and it seemed as if they were bent on disturbing my *sadhana*. There was nothing I could do about these voices. I simply started to pray whenever I faced such kind of disturbances. Within a few weeks of urgent prayer, the voices gradually disappeared.

Slowly I began to realize that I was probably a little over-enthusiastic about my practices. I prayed to my guru and Nirupanand to forgive me for my childlike enterprises and resolved to follow the instructions more sensibly. I had given myself a thorough and perfect schedule of practice. In the process, I reduced the use of my body as much as possible. I did not do anything that would exhaust or tire me. I had a secret wish to completely stop taking food. Keeping to a careful regime, I completely stopped my food intake. For this purpose, I began to do *surya namaskar* twice a day: both in the morning and evening. At this time I stopped eating food, and gradually even stopped drinking water. During this phase of practice, I lived for sixty-five days in one stretch without food.

Six months later Guru Nirupanand came to see me. He had a big and happy smile on his face. I was delighted to see him. As he approached, he folded his hands as a mark of respect. Before I could express my surprise he said, "Please let me salute the fine yogi that is Manmoyanand."

I thought he was joking.

He then said with a note of confirmation in his voice, "You may not believe it, but the effects of your sadhana have reached far and wide, and at the ashram we can easily feel its fragrance."

He took a deep breath and looked around. He entered my cave, walked around, and with a sense of satisfaction declared, "This is what the surroundings of a *sadhak's* presence should feel like."

We talked for some time. He explained that the outcomes of the past six months were definitely more than satisfactory. I could stay in the cave longer with my practice, if I so wished. But I didn't see much reason for it. I was eager to return to the ashram as I was growing a little anxious to see my teacher.

That night Nirupanand stayed in my cave, and I talked to him in detail about my experiences during the last six months. I told him in particular about the voices and the restlessness. He just brushed away those questions without paying much attention to them. But I knew they definitely had a meaning, and some day I would find them out.

The next day we walked back to my ashram. In my childhood days, whenever I went on long walks, a peculiar habit of mine would surface. I would pick up a roundish piece of rock, run with it on the road and throw it in the manner of a bowler in a game of cricket, aiming at some imaginary wicket on the path. I would then run after it to retrieve it. I can't say why I did this bowling along the way, but it always gave me a sense of innocent joy and pleasure. Today, walking with Nirupanand back to my ashram, I felt no more than just a happy little boy. I picked up stones, and much to Nirupanand's surprise, started bowling my way to the ashram.

Back in my ashram I was given an entirely different kind of regime for my practice. Every now and then it was readjusted and modified. Nirupanand was a close guard through every step of my practice. He was no longer a serious and straight-faced school-master towards me, as he began to treat me more like a friend and contemporary than a freaky-monkey pupil.

One day I was reciting the verses of the Yoga Sutras, and at the end of the explanation of *Pranayama* in the second chapter, I came upon the sutra that reveals the effects of *Pranayama*: '*Tatah ksiyate prakasavaranam*' (2:52). After pondering over this line for some time, I decided to go and meet my guru. Within the literal meanings of Sanskrit, this sutra simply said, 'Thence, the covering impurities of light fall away.' This didn't make much sense to me. Here, the term *prakasa* denotes 'light that reveals'. It could also probably mean 'intellective knowledge'. All that I could make out was that the effect of *Pranayama* was 'the emergence of the intellective knowledge by the destruction of cognitive impurities'. But I wanted to get a clear picture of the effect of *Pranayama*.

In a kind and loving manner my guru said, "At least there is one effect that is apparent with you. You are no longer coming to ask so many questions."

I replied, "I am sorry if you missed me on these occasions, but what does that have to do with my *Pranayama*?"

My guru said, "As you proceed in the practice of this *kriya*, you will have less and less questions that need to be answered. I am very happy to see you moving towards the point where there will be no question in your mind unanswered."

I continued to ask with childlike innocence, "Where do all the questions come from? And where do all the answers live? There must be light years of difference between these two places."

He appeared to be pleased with my questions, and very affectionately answered, "Do you know that all questions and answers actually live at the same place? They are not exactly questions and answers as such. It all depends upon the angle from which you look at it. A question could be more of an answer, and an answer could give you a whole lot of questions. Every cell of your body, in itself, is a storehouse of information. To some people, their existence is an endless series of questions, whereas to some others, their existence is the ultimate answer. All that one can do is turn away from the question end and move towards the answer end."

I again asked, "What is the use of having so much information if we can't remember it?"

My guru answered, "The availability of all this information in our body is definitely not without a purpose. It gives a definite indication that there is a possibility of accessing it. A normal person cannot access this information because his cognitive faculties are thickly covered with impurities. Every person knows only that much about himself which he wants to know. When someone intends to access this enormous amount of information, one has to systematically cleanse his or her impurities. Only after this can one access this information and come to know the truth of their existence. Nothing remains unknown to this person, who in other words is called an accomplished yogi. *Pranayama* is a *kriya* and, like the purifying effects of fire, cleanses all the cognitive impurities and helps to reveal the true and effulgent light of intellective faculties. That is why the *kriya* is performed after the cleansing of physical impurities through Asana. In sutra 2:52, the great Maharshi Patanjali only refers to 'the revealing of this effulgent source of information and knowledge'.

After a little hesitation I asked, "Is this the same as what they call 'enlightenment'?"

My teacher smiled and said, "Where did you pick up that expression? I can't say what others mean by the expression 'enlightenment'. People found using this term are far from the comprehension of what it could mean. In the modern world, you can find hundreds of people claiming to be 'enlightened'. If enlightenment was meant for so many people, then I would say that this sutra of Maharshi Patanjali does not refer to anything of that kind.

As one of the eightfold path of Yoga, *Pranayama* is only the fourth step and not yet the final one. After achieving the best effects of *Pranayama*, there is still a long way to go. Gaining access to the source of all knowledge is not yet the ultimate objective of spiritual practice. At this moment you are only beginning to realize the existence of this knowledge. Soon you will delve deep into its infinite universe. When you and your realization are no longer separate but are merged to form only one phenomenon, we call that state *Samadhi*. It is not yet your time to worry about that stage of your practice. I am very confident that day is not very far away from you."

Listening to the words of my teacher, I thought to myself that I was far from prepared to leave his company.

While I continued to sit there, I was planning an appropriate way to ask about those voices that I had heard during my practices. After a little while, my guru casually asked, "Are you still wondering about those voices?"

"Yes, but now I think I know the answer. I remembered some religious stories that I had heard during my childhood. The practices of yogis and *rishis* always somehow tormented the ogres, demons and evil spirits that lived in the area, and often they would come and disturb the concentration of the practitioner. Sometimes they would scream and shout. If that failed, they appeared physically and destroyed the whole institution of practice. Perhaps this is what I had experienced. I consider myself fortunate because in my opinion, Nirupanand had sensed my troubles and came to rescue me before these evil beings manifested before me."

Listening to my explanation, my guru laughed heartily. "My dear yogi, there are no such spirits in that area who would have dared to come and trouble you, especially when Yogi Nirupanand is in charge of your training."

I felt a little ashamed to have overlooked the tantric prowess of Nirupanand.

"Then what do you think those voices were about?"

My question sent my teacher into a long, thoughtful silence. Eventually he replied, "It is a bit premature to reveal to you the meaning of those voices, but I would not like you to arrive at incorrect conclusions or inferences. All that I can tell you now is that those voices are the reminiscence of your past life. During the process of your practice you unintentionally uncovered some of the memories of your past which triggered these experiences. As I have already mentioned, you are in the process of uncovering the long-lost memories of several lifetimes. After the death of your body, there is no end to the deep-rooted memories in your mind. Every time you are reborn, you are born with all these memories. As a newborn baby your memories are very fresh, but as you grow up, gradually day-to-day experiences eclipse your past-life memories. As an adult you identify yourself as the product of the experiences of only the present life. But the truth is that you are the product of the experiences of hundreds and thousands of lifetimes. As a result of the spiritual practices, the coverings of your latent memory get washed away, and you begin to re-live as the complete product of so many lifetimes."

I was completely mesmerized and began to wonder, 'Does the invocation of past-life memories serve any purpose in the present life?'

After a little while, I spoke of my thoughts.

My guru replied, "For a common man, the knowledge of one's past life serves no useful purpose. Rather, it can result in endless torment for them, as one can never endure the memory of an enormously long account of his own pains and sufferings. One can neither 're-live' nor withstand the multiple traumas of his own past deaths or the deaths of all his loved ones. If any of them are still living, he will end up with multiplicity of relations. Imagine a life with multiple parents, children or spouses. Furthermore it is difficult to control the rage against injustices suffered in the past life. It would be absolutely disastrous if you were to start settling scores today with innocent people.

However, the knowledge of past life serves a different purpose for a yogi. A yogi is a person who is in the path and process of realizing his entire celestial journey, not as a human being, but as an eternal being. The time phase between birth and death merely denotes the journey of the body, but life exists beyond the points of birth and death of the body. This realization is extremely important for a yogi. Hence it is only for a yogi on the journey to transcend all the barriers of life, death and physical existences, to know and remember the entire journey of his past. Every step of the yogic practice gives a glimpse of realization about the eternal nature of the yogi. Arriving at this point of your practice, you are indeed in a position to recollect the events of several of your past lives. But let me caution you of the dangers of premature finding of past-life events. I don't want you to suffer any trauma which may come as a result of your investigations."

Curiosity is a term applicable to all living beings in this world, and I was no exception. The more I tried to forget, the more restless I became. I continued my practice in earnest. I prayed to the Divine and to my masters to help me overcome these difficulties, but still I found it difficult to free myself from the thoughts of my past life. I was once again beginning to hear those voices, and at times I began to see glimpses of images. Sometimes there were faces. Sometimes it appeared as if I was lying in a dimly lit room with a lot of noise outside. At times I often tried to recognize the faces, but could not remember seeing anyone to whom they matched. I often saw the face of a woman who looked very much like me, but I could not remember her. The time I had lived in my ashram nearly wiped out the memories of most of the faces I bothered to know in my life. Slowly, I began to reconstruct all these faces again in my memory. Gradually, I came to remember all my childhood friends, school teachers, relatives and acquaintances. For quite a few days I remembered the peculiar qualities of each personality and my relationship to them.

A particular instance of my past began to emerge very prominently amongst all my memories. I remembered meeting a particular woman who had a very similar appearance as me: tall, thin and dark, with a sharp face. She looked like my feminine counterpart. She even carried the same mole marks as I did. From the first meeting onwards, I began to address her as my mother, and as strange as it may sound, we continued to treat each other as mother and son, even though she was only just over a year older than me.

I immediately went to my guru and gave him all the pieces of the unsolved jigsaw puzzle that I was unable to fit together in my mind. He listened carefully, and with a sigh, replied, "It happened exactly as I feared."

He then asked me to get my notebook and pen.

When I returned, he gave me the address of a place

somewhere in the northern Andhra Pradesh region of India. He also spelled out a few names and said, "These are the names of the people whose voices you have been hearing during your practices. And this is the place where you can go to meet some of them." He then said, "In your childhood, your parents called you by the name Manu, isn't it?"

"Yes."

"Do you know who Manu is?"

I could not understand which Manu he was talking about.

He explained, "Manu was the first-ever teacher of mankind. It was he who formulated the rules and conduct of behavior of man. He was not born to any ordinary parents. He was created directly out of *Brahman* or the Supreme Self. The Sun is regarded as his father."

After telling me this, my guru asked me again, "Does the mention of the name of the Sun and *Brahman* ring a bell in your head?"

I thought for a moment and replied, "Yes, it does."

He continued, "The person and the place that gave birth to you in your past life also carry names that are very similar to those of your present life."

I instantly realized the woman who I called 'mother' had the name with exactly the same meaning as my father's name in the present life. Finally, the pieces of the jigsaw puzzle were beginning to fall into place. Years later, I actually had the opportunity to visit the village and meet the people whose names were provided to me by my guru. Here the complete picture of my past life was revealed to me.

In my past life, I was born into a poor artisan's family. My mother's name was Suriya. She died a few months after my birth because of post-delivery complications. After my mother's death, my father decided to go to a distant city in search of work and a better livelihood. I was left with my maternal uncle and his family, who shouldered the responsibility of bringing me up. My uncle's name was Jayadev. After arriving at the village, I met Jayadev. He was one of the persons who my guru had mentioned earlier.

Jayadev disclosed that it was because of his own negligence that Suriya's baby ultimately died about a year after his mother. I asked him if he had a photo of Suriya or the baby. Jayadev climbed up onto a chair and pulled down a photo that was hanging from the wall. The picture showed a few women. One of them was carrying a baby. I recognized the woman. I had seen that face so many times before. There was an uncanny resemblance between that face, my face and the face of the woman who I called 'mother'. The face of the baby in the photograph was not clear.

Jayadev was an old man approaching his sixties. He still had a vivid memory of his late sister. As he was speaking about her, his eyes moistened. He blamed himself bitterly for not taking care of her baby, who could have been a support to him in his old age. With difficulty, I suppressed the raging urge to tell him, 'I am the baby of Suriya in his next life!'

Instead, I sympathized with his condition. I didn't forget to give him some money before I left, towards the support that he expected from his late nephew.

∞∞∞∞

The effects of *Pranayama* can be far reaching. The complete cleansing of the impurities that surround the discriminative intelligence not only reveals the depths of our memory, it also gives us the suitable conditions and ability to concentrate. The ability to hold the mind together at one point is difficult. Until now, the outcomes of my practice had been overwhelming, but I was nowhere closer to my objective. I had begun to undertake this long and arduous journey with the one objective of immersing myself in the 'voice of silence'.

From the first day of my quest, I had undergone some very rigorous processes. Firstly, I purified myself, absolutely and thoroughly. Secondly, I steadied my body and detached my thoughts from the physical limits. Thirdly, I achieved the seemingly impossible task of unraveling the depths of my memory and intelligence. Yet, I felt nowhere closer to my objective. I realized the futility of nagging my teachers as I already knew there were no short cuts, and there cannot be any short cuts to substantial truth. I patiently waited for the next step of my practice.

I asked Nirupanand, "Is the clarity of intelligence that one achieves as a result of the successful accomplishment of *Pranayama* to be treated as an achievement? Or, is it only one of the intermediary processes for further development?"

He replied, "The answer is both," and went on to explain. "Every step you take towards your objective is, in fact, an achievement in itself, but that is not your final step. Being an achievement in itself, every step is also a process to reach the next one. After standing on any of these steps, you can pause only for a moment to relish the sense of achievement, but never stop there forever. You can go higher up only when you are prepared to step away from it."

Maharshi Patanjali, in his sutra, *'Dharanasu ca yogyatamanasah'* (2:53), has denoted the achievement of the effects of *Pranayama* as 'a condition that provides the eligibility to achieve the concentration of the mind'. This was good news for me. I went to Nirupanand to enquire when I could start my next practice. He answered in his usual straight face, "I am not going to give your next practice."

Incredulously, I asked, "Why? What did I do that you won't teach me anymore?"

He replied, "Because from now on, all your practices will be given to you by Guru Angadanand himself. Soon you will be given initiation into the lineage of yogis. You will have to take the vows of this lineage, and then Guru Angadanand will start giving you your further lessons."

There was nothing elaborate about my initiation ceremony. It consisted of the process of obtaining the *diksha*, or initiation. I repeated the lines after my guru and vowed to abide by the rules of the yogic life. I vowed not to disclose anything about my teachers or ashram that might disturb the peace and privacy of the ashram. I also vowed not to demonstrate any spiritual or psychic powers in public or before anyone. After all the vows were taken, I had to pronounce my resolve to continue my practices until I achieved the final objective. As I have realized today, this process of preparing me was very much necessary. I was set upon the path of achieving the absolute control of my mind. The phrase 'absolute control of the mind' was by far the most high-sounding *kriya* I had ever heard. As soon as I was told that I was about to practise the *kriyas* of subjugation of mind, I was a little unsure how that could happen. How can one control the mind whilst they 'change their mind' several times in one day?

We don't actually change our minds as such. The expression 'change of mind' can only be attributed to the uses, or abuses, of the English language. This expression usually denotes an 'after-thought', or a 'change of intention'. A change of mind does not actually change the structures of human mind or thought. Let us, in brief, examine how the mind works.

The mind is the function of the brain. The mind has no physical existence, unlike the brain. The brain is the hardware, whereas the mind is the software. As discussed in earlier chapters, the activities of the brain are a result of the electrical discharge rate of the brain cells, and the rate of electrical discharge of the brain cells is closely related to the electro-chemical reactions, which are mostly triggered by external stimuli. What is external stimulation in this case?

The body has five such departments that register external stimulation: the eyes, nose, tongue, ears and skin. The mind itself is considered the sixth department. These organs of our body have the capacity to pick up the finest and most subtle changes in their environment and transmit this information to the brain. The functions of these organs are normally autonomous in nature. Under normal conditions, they cannot choose whether to take or not to take these stimulants from their environment. Let us understand this through some examples.

If you have a working ear, you are bound to hear the sounds around you, or if you have vision, you are bound to glimpse anything that comes before your eyes. Your senses are very closely attached and regulated by the sense organs. But in truth, the senses are not the same thing as the sense organs. Sense organs lie in our body, whereas the senses lie in our mind. Here again, the sense organs are the hardware, and the senses are the software. Let us take an example.

You are holding this book in your hand. Light reflecting from this book enters your eyes through its lenses and creates an inverted image on a screen called the retina, at the back of your eyes. The retina has something called the optic sensory nerves which are the carriers that transmit the sensory data to the brain. The software of the brain analyzes this data and comes to the conclusion that you are looking at a book. Hence the 'seeing' of the book was a function of your mind and not a function of the eye.

In simple terms, your eye is like a closed circuit camera through which your mind sees. Here, one thing becomes clear. The sense of vision does not lie in the eye; rather it lies in the mind. It is the decision of our mind that concludes what is before our eyes. The same example can be repeated to explain the relationship of the other sense organs with the mind. We will come to know that the senses of taste, sound, smell and touch also lie in the mind, and these external organs are employed for the collection of the data.

In a normal person's life, these sense organs play a very important role. Whenever stimulation is given to these organs, there is always an outcome. There is always a sense of pain or pleasure. Every person in the modern world would like to provide the finest sensory stimulations to all their organs. Our love for good food, good music, good aroma or fragrance, or good sex is only an expression of our desire for the enjoyment of senses, and everyone knows how difficult it is to satisfy the perpetual demands of the senses. The common man constantly modifies his life and yearnings in pursuit of the satisfaction of the senses. In the case of a yogi it is different. He is not regulated by his senses; rather he regulates the senses, for it is he who knows all the senses lie in his mind.

A yogi enjoys all the sensory outcomes, but for that, he does not depend on his sense organs. His sensory bliss originates right in his mind and not from any part of his body. This is a condition where the yogi becomes free from the dependency upon his sense organs. A yogi is a master of his senses, whereas the common man is the slave of his senses. This is accomplished by a yogi who practises to gradually withdraw his senses from the sense objects and makes the senses move in the direction of the mind in such a way that the mind comes to regulate the entire functions of the senses.

Maharshi Patanjali, in his sutra 2:54, states, *'Svavisayaasamprayoge chittasya svarupaanukara ive indriyanam Pratyaharah.'* This broadly means 'When the senses are detached or disassociated from the sense objects and made to follow the common course of mind habitually, it becomes *Pratyahara'*. In simple terms, *Pratyahara* is the withdrawal of the senses from the sense objects and the subjection to the regulations of the mind.

A highly intellectualized discussion on *Pratyahara* never yields any results. *Pratyahara* is not something to be understood; rather it stands for an experience. *Pratyahara* is the ultimate subjugation of senses. Contrary to widespread belief, subjugation of senses is not achieved through a combination of half-baked psycho-physical manoeuvres.

We have understood that the senses and the sense objects are different. Our senses depend upon the sense objects, and our enjoyment depends upon the capacity of the sense objects. The extent of our enjoyment is always limited because of the limits of the sensory organs. However, as we have seen, the capacity of the mind is not as limited as that of the sense organs. When we begin to experience our senses right in the mind, we will naturally come to know that the limits of our senses and enjoyments are unlimited. That means, what we see without the help of our eyes is much more than what our eyes can see. What we hear, taste, smell, or feel will be much more than the limits of our physical senses. The experience of *Pratyahara* thus spans far beyond the world that we have so far experienced.

The practice of *pratyahara* is a matter of extreme technicality. The base requirements for this practice are the successful accomplishment of Asana, and to a certain extent, the correct practice of *pranayama*. A few days after the completion of my six-month long solitary practice, I was certified eligible for the practice of *pratyahara*. It only took about three weeks to begin to experience the withdrawal of the senses. The practice of *pratyahara* is accomplished by a series of concentration practices, accompanied by the resonance of sound vibrations.

One afternoon, my guru came to the cave where I was practising. He stood very close to me and held my right hand in his hands.

He made a small change in my incantations and asked me to continue until I hear his voice. I did exactly as I was instructed. I don't know exactly how long I continued the practice before I heard his voice. His voice sounded very funny and unnatural. It was not actually a voice; it had a deeper impact on me than spoken words. He was asking me to open my eyes. I opened my eyes and could not see anything, as it was kind of dark and cloudy. I tried to open my eyes wider and struggled to see what was around me. I still could not see anything. The cave, the mountains, the bright sunlight, my guru - everything that was around me had disappeared. I looked around to find my guru, but I couldn't see him.

Before I began to panic, I heard my guru's voice, "Don't worry, my boy. I am right next to you. I know you cannot see the things that are usually around you, but have patience."

Upon hearing my guru's voice, I relaxed. The darkness before my eyes was slowly changing into a greyish-violet. It gradually became clearer, but I still struggled to see what was around me. I heard some kind of voices from a distance. They were not exactly human voices, but appeared to be some meaningful sounds. They had a very strange tone in them. As some of the sounds came even closer to me, I recoiled in panic. I felt my guru's grip tightening on my hand. My whole body shook in a violent fit and the gloomy darkness exploded into bright light.

After my eyes adjusted to the light, I became aware of my surroundings. I was there, sitting in a cave with my guru next to me in the bright light of the afternoon.

My guru smiled down at me and asked, "Were you frightened?"

"Yes, I was frightened. What happened to me?"

"For a short while you had visited a world of a different dimension."

I asked in earnest, "Was I dead?"

My guru laughed as he replied, "No, you were not dead. You

were all the time sitting right here in this cave with me next to you. All that happened was just a little experience beyond the limits of your natural senses. Tomorrow we will do this again. You don't have to panic because I will be with you in that world."

I spent the rest of the day in high excitement and anticipation. My brief but vivid experience was far beyond the comprehension of my limited understanding. The next day my guru asked me to do the practices again. Within a short while I again drifted into the greyish-violet semi-darkness. After being in this darkness for a short time I asked, "Gurudev, are you sure that I am not dead? Why can't I see things around me?"

No sound came out of my mouth, but I knew that my whole question came out in a non-verbal way. In a similar manner I perceived my guru's answer.

"Look carefully, you can see me in front of you."

Within a few moments, I began to experience the vision of a bright halo in front of me. It had no exact description. It roughly resembled a human shadow, but it was different from the darkness of a shadow as it was bright and illuminated. I wanted to touch his feet, but I could not feel the sensations or movements of any of my limbs. I felt my guru saying, "Come, and let us move around a little."

I felt as if I was being pulled forward by some magnetic force. I tried to look at myself, but I could not see any part of my body. The only thing I could perceive at that dimension was the illuminated halo of my guru.

There were voices and other bright shadows that seemed to be moving in the distance. Some of the shadows went past me. I could not say that I was not panicking, but I constantly experienced a very peculiar and strange sense of apprehension. However I slowly began to relax, as I thought to myself, 'Why am I confused and nervous when my teacher is right next to me?'

Gradually, I began to take stock of the situation. My guru was saying, "My son, at this moment you are experiencing such a state where there is no physical presence or existence at all. All the common thoughts, feelings and emotions exist in the plane of physical matter only. Your human thoughts are only an impediment to your entry into this state. No matter what your thoughts look like, they don't have any space here because your thoughts are not you. The more you are free from your thoughts, the more you will experience and enjoy this state."

A short while later, I once again experienced the violent shake-up and opened my eyes to my usual surroundings. My guru explained to me the only reason I had experienced the greyish-purple night-like surrounding was because of my human inhibitions, and the human notions still present deep inside my beliefs. He advised me to practise the *kriyas* of *pratyahara* more sincerely and rigorously. It was not until a few weeks later that I was to attempt this journey again. Gradually the night-like situation faded away, and I began to notice that the less tense I was, the brighter and more peaceful became my experience.

It was not long before I nearly got addicted to the blissful experiences of this state of withdrawal. The more I relished *Pratyahara*, the more I became disinterested in the pleasures of daily life. As a result of my practices, I had acquired some strange capabilities. I discovered this when I was humming the tune of a song, a favorite since my childhood. Suddenly it appeared as if the tune had come to life. I was not exactly humming it; I was hearing the tune very clearly, as if it were being played somewhere nearby. I stopped to look around, but it did not appear to be coming from any particular direction. There was definitely no possibility of a musical instrument being played within fifty kilometers from any direction. I thought for a moment and went back to my humming, and there again! The tune came back to me clearly and vividly. I stopped humming the tune and changed to a different one, and within no time this tune also became clearly audible to me.

That evening I asked my teacher about this strange experience. He explained to me, "Since the memory of the tune is in your mind, you no longer need a musical instrument to hear it. The moment you think of it, it is brought to the surface of memory, and you experience it as clearly as listening to an instrument. The greater control you have on your senses, the better you can apply this phenomenon to other senses. The pleasures and experiences, which a common man attempts to purchase by paying great amounts of money, can be experienced by a yogi without actually buying them. With the power to control his senses, a yogi, by a simple wish, can acquire all the pleasures of life."

At this point, my guru told me several tricks by which I could test my prowess of experiencing anything and everything that I wanted. I was delighted at the prospect of enjoying almost anything that I wished or desired. But at this point of my life, I barely retained any of my childhood fantasies or desires.

I was overwhelmed with my experiences of *Pratyahara*. As I looked forward to the complete subjugation of my mind, I stopped indulging in the pleasures of these capacities.

One day my guru explained to me, "The purpose of *Pratyahara* is not to experience the beautiful benefits of the withdrawal of senses, as these benefits are only side-effects. In the evolutionary order, a species not only enjoys a unique position, but also suffers the corresponding advantages and disadvantages of that position. Human beings enjoy the most benefits in correspondence to their position in the evolutionary order. Yogis are but a more evolved human species. As the capacities of man are far beyond the comprehension of animals, similarly the capacities of a yogi lie far beyond the comprehension of the common man. As a superior animal, man has higher responsibilities in nature, and in the same way, yogis have a superior purpose of existence in comparison to anyone else. That is why the capabilities of a yogi are seldom directed towards enjoyment, unlike common human beings; a yogi takes these capacities as merely incidental to his position and never allows these powers to distract him from his aim."

All these superhuman stages are to be treated only as insignificant milestones in the process of spiritual practice. The only purpose for which they exist is to indicate your location on the path. They need to be approached with respect and left behind with indifference. A yogi who has approached this point, and has experienced the unraveling of endless opportunities of sensual indulgence, needs a strong guideline and direction to retain his attention. Without a powerful direction to move through, one is likely to be affected and absorbed by these overwhelming opportunities. At this stage, the supremely capable and unaffected mind should be harnessed to concentrate. The ultimate outcome of *Pratyahara* is the 'highest subjugation of mind' (Yoga Sutras 2:55), but the one and only purpose for the subjugation of mind is for its further concentration and one-pointedness.

One day my guru asked me to go for a walk. I happily accompanied him. After a long walk, both of us sat down and drifted into silence. It was a perfectly beautiful and blissful silence. As I was slowly beginning to close my eyes, my guru said to me, "You should begin to concentrate and try to hear something that you have always wanted to hear - the voice of silence."

Until this moment, the idea of using my power to listen to the voice of silence had not occurred to me; whereas in the meantime, I had actually acquired the capacity to accomplish this. I felt utterly thankful to my guru for reminding me about the true use of my *siddhis*.

Very happily I closed my eyes and began to concentrate. It did not take long before I began to experience what I had already experienced in the past. But soon I came to realize that today the silence was much deeper and much more profound. After a long time I opened my eyes. I had experienced the realm of silence as a soft and fluid ocean of bliss. Even after opening my eyes, I continued to feel as though I was floating in this endless, fluid realm of bliss. A little while later, my guru also opened his eyes and joined me back in this world. He asked me almost in a whisper, "How was the experience with silence?"

Without a thought, I answered in a single word which could best describe my experience, "Divine."

This experience, which can be described by the one and only term 'divine', is Meditation. Meditation is an experience which lies far beyond the impurities of the body, the stability of the posture, the duality of the opposites, the austerity of *tapah* and the subjugation of the mind. At the threshold of silence all these efforts cease to exist, and all the desires culminate into only one. It is no more an effort, no more a struggle, and no more a desire. Meditation is perfectly fluid and absolutely spontaneous.

CHAPTER SIX

The Final Stage of Evolution

Meditation is divine. A glimpse of its experience was enough to convince me about the values of a spiritual practice. I had taken to its regular practice. It gave me immense pleasure, and it was gradually spiraling into an obsession. One evening after my usual round of meditation, I was in conversation with my guru. He said, "Manmoyanand, I wonder when you will stop behaving like a five year old. On the achievement of even the smallest of things, you are completely taken away by excitement. If a yogi becomes content with the experience of *siddhis*, how will he achieve the final purpose of Yoga? During every little step of your practice you have displayed this childishness. So many times in the past I have reminded you that this is not yet it. This is not yet it."

I listened silently as he told me about my stupid and super-ficial satisfactions. I knew he was right, but I couldn't help them. I spent many years of my life as a desperate seeker, and never before had I dreamt about the success I had that day. Before coming to the ashram, I had no idea what a *siddhi* could be. Just a glimpse of these powers would have convinced me about God. Like everybody else, I would have ended up worshipping anyone who could explain to me or display the powers of Yoga. Coming from such a background, I had every reason to be content with what I had now.

I asked my guru, "If desire is the cause of all sufferings and contentment is a virtue, don't you think I should be content with what I have got so far?"

My guru explained, "Contentment is a virtue when it is applied to material greed. The niyama of contentment does not actually apply to the spiritual desires of the aspirant. To ascend in the realms of spirituality, contentment is only a hindrance. A yogi should always remind himself *'neti-neti'* (this is not yet it, this is not yet it).

Yoga is not about experiencing the Divine; it is about realizing the Divine. It is not about knowing the cosmos; it is about being the cosmos. The bliss of Meditation is not an end in itself; it is a necessary tool to practise the higher *kriyas* of concentration. At this stage, your mind has only learned to remain unaffected by mundane provocations. If you stop going any further, this will become another addiction. In order to experience the permanence of the meditative bliss, you will have to continue its practice for a long time. Only then it becomes spontaneous. Without this element of spontaneity, the practice is only another psychological gyration. You must take this opportunity and begin to learn the techniques of concentration."

I was beginning to ask myself, 'What could possibly lie beyond such a perfectly blissful state?'

My guru explained. "The state of mind that one acquires after the achievement of *Pratyahara* needs to be concentrated at a particular space and for a particular length of time. The first sutra of chapter three in the Yoga Sutras states: *'Desabandhascittasya Dharana,'* which means 'If the mind is confined to one space or object it is Concentration'. In other words, Concentration is the one-pointedness of the supremely pure mind into one space. On achieving the one-pointedness of the mind, it is prolonged sufficiently to achieve the next step.

The second sutra of chapter three states *'Tatra Pratyayekatanata Dhyanam'* which means,

'If the mind is continued to be held or confined to that space for a prolonged length of time, and oneness is acquired, it is called Meditation'. The term *'Ekatanata'* can be dissected as *'eka – one'*, *'tana – rhythm or vibration'*, *'ta – ness'*. Therefore *'Ekatanata'* would broadly mean 'oneness with the vibration'. Meditation is the effect of Concentration. It is a state where oneness is realized with the object of meditation. As mentioned earlier, Concentration is only a tool to take the yogi beyond the limits of the *vijnanamaya* and *anandamaya koshas*."

After the yogi is established in the absolute state of bliss, there is still a necessity to move beyond the final layer of *anandamaya kosha*. The *kriya* to achieve further transcendence from the *anandamaya kosha* is *Samyama*. *Samyama* is the conscious and simultaneous application of Concentration, its extension and oneness.

I remembered the onion-like example of the five sheaths of the supreme consciousness: how they extend from subtle to gross as they move outwards, with the external body being the grossest manifestation of the internal subtle elements. My attention went back to my guru's elucidation.

"Bliss, no matter how beautiful it is, is only a sheath that surrounds the supreme consciousness. Only the tools of prolonged and powerful concentration can take the yogi beyond the alluring realm of bliss."

Here I interrupted as I was unable to comprehend the process beyond Meditation. "How does one become the universe? Does anything change for him? Does he look the same again? What happens to his body, mind, behavior or capacities? I somehow cannot fathom the meaning of this statement."

"The experience of being the universe is difficult to explain. At this stage I can only give you a small glimpse about the process of becoming the universe. Let me give you an example.

As you have studied earlier, the physical universe is made up of five great elements. The microcosmic body and the macro-cosmic universe are made up of the same elements, same atoms or particles. But the elements do not behave in the same manner in the body as they behave in the external universe. Take the example of a glass of water. Water inside a glass and water inside the ocean are the same matter. But the glass is not the ocean. The only difference between the water in the glass and the ocean is that the water inside the glass is confined whereas the ocean is not confined. The physical limits of the body and the ego that is attached to it greatly reduce our notion of the universe. The moment you remove the ego and come to realize your own cosmic self, the glass of water will actually behave like the ocean. Touching your body you can feel some warmth, but in truth, you are the great *agni* (the fire element) yourself. The difference in becoming the universe is you can experience the unlimited and universal dimensions of *agni* in your body."

As he was talking, my guru picked up a small piece of wood kept aside for the fires. He held it tightly in his hand, closed his eyes for a moment, and then continued, "In the language of the universe, I do not merely have some warmth in my body; I am fire myself."

As he was speaking, smoke began to drift from his closed fist. As I looked on, the piece of wood slowly caught fire. As he continued to hold it, the wood burnt completely in his hand and soon dropped away as a handful of ash.

That was not the end of the demonstration. My guru further stated, "I do not merely hold some water in my body. I am the ultimate source of water. I am water."

He cupped his hand, and from it poured fresh, clean water. The hand that burnt a piece of wood a moment ago was dripping water the next.

I collected water in my palm and tasted it. There was no doubt it was real. These experiences were better than any magic show I had seen. With reverence, yet in a light tone, I asked, "How are you going to prove you are earth yourself?"

He held out his palm and asked me to sit, or stand on it. As I was attempting to get onto his hand, he said, "Billions of people and objects have been standing on this earth for ages without hurting it. You, or a billion like yourself, can come and stand on me."

With a little difficulty, I stood on the rock-steady platform of his hand.

My smiling guru prompted me, if I was not satisfied, I could go ahead and stone his hand if I wished. I picked up rocks of various sizes, and whilst he kept his palm on a rock, I hammered it for some time. Even after considerable effort, I could not dent that hand. Seeing my childlike frustration, my guru was only mildly amused.

"Particles in the universe behave in a very funny way. It is unbelievable, but true, that a single particle can be present at more than one place at the same time. It never travels through a well-defined path or orbit, but it can make itself available at a different space without traveling through the intervening space. That is why a particle is to be treated as a 'tendency' instead of a 'thing'. This is what your quantum physics has already proved. But they have yet to show you the presence of the particle at more than one place at the same time. When you become the universe yourself, very much like the particle, you can be found at all the places of the universe in just the same way you see me in front of you, behind you, and all around you."

I jumped to my feet and ran around like crazy to witness this phenomenon. Well, he was everywhere! I walked into different caves and found him there sitting, continuing what he was talking. I ran up to the ridge and found him there waiting for me. After a while, I thought to go back to the point where we had originally been sitting, and here my guru corrected me.

"There is no place in the universe to where we originally belong. We never came from any particular place, nor are we going to any particular place. The particles that have formed your body today have lived and experienced every part of this universe before you. At this moment we are sitting here, and that is the truth of this moment. Just like the particle, the next moment will see us everywhere. Until then, let us continue to sit here."

I do not know what I understood about becoming a universe, but one thing was beyond all doubt: Meditation was definitely not the last step. In my understanding, the spontaneous stage of Meditation was synonymous with the ultimate human achievement. My notions were not clear as to what actually happens in the state of Meditation. I had understood that the 'state of bliss' explained in Meditation was the answer to all human suffering, and after the achievement of this stage, one need not do anything else but sit back and enjoy the fruits of this bliss. Then somehow in this process, maybe due to some automatic deepening of the Meditation or by prolonged practice, the practitioner was said to achieve *Samadhi*. I admit that at this stage I had no idea of what *Samadhi* could be. My imagination had comprehended some kind of ultimate, blissful state and nothing more than that. After the experience of merging with the silence, I concluded I had nothing more to do. I was hoping that my practice would gradually and automatically deepen to give me visions of absolute knowledge or the Divine.

All these notions were wrong. I tried to hide behind my justification that this present state of bliss was much more than what I ever could have hoped for, and therefore I was quite content as ultimately it was my happiness that counted.

My guru responded, "Spontaneous Meditation is not a stage to stop at, it is just the threshold through which you enter into *Samadhi*. The entire process of hard work is already over. What is waiting is the realization of the purest self and the experience of being the universe."

He explained the term '*Samadhi*' in a very simple way: '*Sama*' and '*Dhi*' - '*Sama*' stands for 'equilibrium' and '*Dhi*' stands for 'mind' or 'intellect'. Hence, *Samadhi* is a state where there is no difference between the individual mind and the cosmic mind.

"At *Samadhi*, you strike the perfect balance and equilibrium with the cosmic nature of yourself. In other words, you become the cosmos."

Slowly I was becoming starry-eyed. The possibility of getting anywhere closer to *Samadhi* was too much to resist. Suppressing my excitement, all I could say to my guru was, "Please take me to the point of self-realization. I am here to complete the journey. You won't ever find me complaining about the time or process that I have to go through. You have my obedience, and you have my resolve."

The right time arrived seven months later. During all this time, I had never once asked my teacher about my next phase. I practised my meditations very sincerely and religiously. I usually spent about half a day in my meditation and the other half in silence. I cannot say if there was at all a beginning or intermediary stage to my meditation, as I was perpetually floating in the blissful state of Meditation. This condition prevailed throughout the days, weeks and months. In every activity I did, everything I spoke, in my wake and in my sleep, I experienced a permanent and perpetual 'high'. I enjoyed a gradually increasing sense of indifference and dispassion throughout every moment of this period.

One evening, my teacher took me for a walk towards one of the highest ridges in the area. This place was a few kilometers away from my ashram. From the highest point of this ridge there was a great view of the surrounding peaks. The northern side was, as usual, very clear and open. My guru stopped and asked me to sit beside him. As I sat down, he began to speak.

"The success in a spiritual *sadhana* depends upon so many things. The first and foremost factor is your level of spiritual unfoldment. The more evolved you are, the more support you have to embark upon a spiritual journey. Without the right degree of evolutionary maturity, you would not even feel the least amount of spiritual urge. You would rather be happy enjoying and indulging in all manner of sensual pleasures. The second factor is the correct effort. The third is the correct knowledge. The fourth and most important factor for the success of your *sadhana* is your karmic balance.

The effects of your karma always follow you everywhere. All 'good' karma results in support of your practice, and all 'bad' karma manifests itself as your obstacles. Over hundreds of lifetimes you gradually incur the huge accumulated effects of your karma. The rigorous *tapah* that you have undertaken so far has cleansed a lot of your bad karma, but not all. Any further movement from this point necessitates a perfectly balanced karma on the part of the yogi. Without a favorable and positive karmic balance, it will be difficult to move any further from this point. The more you practise meditation, the more indifferent you shall become. This indifference is not exactly synonymous with *vairagya*.

Vairagya is a blissful state of 'non-possession'. The indifference of *vairagya* results in the outcome of a steady reminder of bad karma. Somewhere deep inside, everyone has a very real question: 'How much do I owe in terms of my karma?' As long as this question persists in the mind, it will stand as an obstacle to your future practice. Spiritual absorption will not be possible without the complete eradication of this sense of karmic debt.

Karmic debt can be resolved in two stages: in the first, you repay for all that you owe, and in the second, you pay for all that mankind expects from you. *Samadhi* is experienced in two phases. These two processes of payment will be accomplished at two different phases of entering into *Samadhi*. The first is *Sabeeja Samadhi*, and the second is *Nirbeeja Samadhi*. *Sabeeja Samadhi* is achieved when the meditator is completely absorbed in the subject and object of his meditation. This phase of spiritual absorption is only the external limit of *Nirbeeja Samadhi*. The yogi continues to experience *Sabeeja Samadhi* in the form of numerous *siddhis*, or superhuman accomplishments.

During *Sabeeja Samadhi*, a yogi continues to hold the option of regaining physical consciousness, but in *Nirbeeja Samadhi*, this option is not available. *Nirbeeja Samadhi* is the complete fusion of the yogi with the cosmos. For this reason, these two stages of *Samadhi* are also denoted as *Savikalpa* and *Nirvikalpa Samadhi*.

In my opinion, you are standing at a stage which is ripe enough to experience the *siddhis* of *Savikalpa Samadhi*. For this purpose you have to go through the gradual phases of the *siddhis*. Your first and foremost duty is to achieve a favorable balance of karma by paying off the karmic debts before the beginning of this phase of *Samadhi*."

My guru clearly explained the process by which I could pay off all my karmic debts. It is to be accomplished with a practice called *dhriv sadhana*. This is a practice whereby a yogi has to undergo several weeks of rigorous practice involving the concentration upon the pole star.

My guru gave me a mantra and explained in detail the process of this *sadhana*. He then pointed to a flat piece of rock and asked me to start my practice. Only now did I come to realize the reason he had brought me all the way up to this point. I touched my guru's feet and proceeded towards the flat piece of rock.

It was yet to be dark, so I walked leisurely towards the very top of the ridge to reach the seat of my practice. Upon reaching my seat, I was surprised to find a handful of flowers that were carefully kept in a small heap. Initially I didn't pay any attention to the flowers, even though the sight of them gave me a nice feeling. After a while I began to wonder, 'How did such fresh flowers come to arrive at such a snowy height of the Himalayas?' The mystery in my mind deepened, as I noticed that these flowers only grew in the plains of India and not in the Himalayas. I continued to wonder upon this mystery until it became dark and I was able to locate the pole star.

I sat down facing the pole star and began to invoke the support and blessings of the cosmos, my Guru, and mankind in general, for the success of my *sadhana*. My guru had explained that the invocation ends with the offering of a handful of flowers to the pole star. Only after I reached the end of the invocation did the mystery about the flowers become clear. With deep respect and reverence to my guru, I picked up the flowers and let them drift away through my fingers.

After three hours of chanting the mantra, I finished the *sadhana* for the day and walked back to my ashram. The next day at exactly the same time, I was back at the flat piece of rock to begin my *sadhana*. As the *sadhana* continued day by day, I gradually developed a strange sense of melancholy. Many times during the *sadhana*, tears would roll uncontrollably from my eyes. As the *sadhana* advanced, I plunged into deeper and deeper depths of melancholy and depression. I decided to ask my guru about my state. I went to him, but on my arrival I found it difficult to express anything. My guru ran his hand over mine in deep sympathy and understanding, but he too didn't say a thing - although without uttering a word, he let me understand that I was to go through the entire *sadhana*, no matter how difficult or impossible it became.

The effect of the *sadhana* was extremely overwhelming. All the practices and *tapahs* that I had experienced until then had given me a very tough and robust sense of body and mind, but in the practice of *dhriv sadhana*, every part of my being appeared to be melting under some sheer pressure. Gradually, I identified these deepening feelings to be the overwhelming sense of remorse and repentance, but I was still unable to make out the exact relationship of these feelings with any of my past deeds. Many a time I contemplated breaking the practice, and on numerous occasions, I thought about going against my resolve. The more I struggled to get out of this condition, the more my agony increased.

One day, my suffering reached its ultimate limit and rendered me completely incapable of pursuing my *sadhana* any further. I sat down looking at the pole star, but could not bring myself to chant the mantras. I just began to cry very bitterly. After a long time, I somehow walked back to my ashram, went straight back to my cave and continued to cry. Without taking any food or speaking to anyone, I went to sleep. Throughout the next day I remained in a similar state of mind and didn't speak to anyone or show interest in doing anything else. This condition remained with me for more than a week, until one day my guru came to me and hugged me. Back in his arms, it felt as if I was entering a new life. Something inside me had permanently died. I was craving my guru's support and strength, and coming into contact with his infinite love and kindness, I began to regain my usual self.

Dhriv sadhana is an ancient *vedic* practice. Several lineages of yogis and sages have practised it for thousands of generations. According to the scriptures, *dhriv sadhana* was originally performed by kings and rulers to ascertain impartiality and truth-fulness. The kings and monarchs of the old times used to perform certain sacrificial rites called *yajnas* from the *Vedas*. The *Sukla Yajurveda Samhita* provides the details of such rituals. *Dhriv sadhana* was provided as a primary condition to ascertain the eligibility of the performer for the rituals. Prior to this *sadhana*, the priest or the guru initiates the aspirant with the *sadhana* mantra. The initiate is then required to perform this austere practice until he experiences the overwhelming outcomes of the *sadhana*. Depending upon one's karmic balance, the effects of the *sadhana* could vary; whatever the outcome, the effects are always respected as just and deserving.

In fact, the practice can be performed by anyone with a fairly good quality of concentration. Anybody can achieve the effects of the *sadhana*, and it generally takes only a few weeks for its completion. However, what is important to note is that this practice should not be given and performed by anyone just for the fun of it. Only after the thorough and rigorous *tapahs* of the yogic practices, and armored with sufficient courage, detachment and determination, should a spiritual aspirant practise it. Its practice should always be conducted with the presence and guidance of a guru. The outcomes of the practices are not generally discussed in public, as the practitioners are always advised to keep them secret. However, it is not uncommon to find mention of these practices in some modern books on yoga or spirituality. Let me narrate the effects of this practice when it was conducted by somebody without the correct conditioning or guidance.

I had a friend in Delhi who was a self-proclaimed spiritual master. He had the habit of going to different discourses and events only to form his own opinions, which he would then apply to create an impression on others. My friend was one of the most foul-mouthed people you could ever meet in your life. He was highly clever, witty, shrewd, smug, and vile in nature. He always projected his spiritual pretence and never forgot to give others a list of do's and don'ts whenever the opportunity presented itself.

On one occasion, I accidentally met this gentleman in Delhi, and within a few minutes, I came to know of his latest 'profession' of spirituality. After a while he began to ask about the truth or genuine nature of several spiritual practices. He was a skeptic, but on this occasion he seemed hard-pressed to know the details of dhriv sadhana. Upon hearing about this practice from some spiritual discourse, he decided to practise it on his own. Somehow he managed to collect the practice procedures from some source or other. The moment he knew that this practice in reality existed, he was hell-bent on performing it. I tried my best to discourage him from doing so, but after all such attempts failed, I eventually agreed to give him the corrections for his practice. I wished him luck and hoped that the poor fellow found the right balance of his karma.

For this act of transgression, I later had to do a penance in my ashram.

Many years later I came to know about the effects of his practice. This time, my friend was in Rishikesh. The moment I saw him, I went over to him to ask about this practice, but to my surprise I found that he had lost his power of speech. One of his acquaintances narrated the tale of his practice to me. He had followed the directions and guidelines of the practice correctly. After about two weeks of doing the practice, suddenly one day his dog came up and started to talk to him in a human voice. My friend never disclosed to anyone what the dog had actually spoken. The moment the dog stopped talking, my friend discovered that he had lost his own power of speech. His family members took him to several doctors and specialists, but he never got his speech back. He lives in Rishikesh until this day and is known as the 'Silent Baba'.

In my personal experience of *dhriv sadhana*, nothing disastrous happened. After a few strong weeks of suffering, I was able to regain my composure. My masters in the ashram were happy to see me reconstruct myself. It was a matter of immense satisfaction for everybody to see that I had emerged from my practice without much harm. I was also happy that I had overcome one of the toughest tests of the settlement of karmic debt.

∞∞∞∞

My guru designated an auspicious day to begin the performance of my *Samadhi*. Until the arrival day, I was asked to perform the *shaktichalana kriya*, which is akin to the perfection of the lotus pose. Before going into the narration of *Samadhi*, let me take the opportunity to explain the perfection of the lotus pose.

The lotus pose, contrary to popular belief, is not merely a sitting posture. It is a posture wherein the ultimate experience of Asana is realized. It is named after the *padma* or the lotus for a very specific and definite reason. Have you ever seen the flower of lotus? If not, take a lotus or a picture of it and observe it carefully. You will see that the little boat-shaped petals of the lotus are like perfect hyperbolic reflectors. They act like concave mirrors that reflect light or energy into one point. The petals of the lotus are naturally arranged in such a way that the focal point of all the petals lie on one straight vertical line. This invisible line extends from the tip of the lotus cone to the zenith in the sky. The opening and closing of the lotus depends upon sunrise and sunset. With the rising of the sun, the lotus opens, as it opens, the common focal point of the petals begins to ascend. With the gradual spreading of the petals, by midday, the focal point reaches the zenith. In the afternoon as the sun begins to set, the lotus gradually closes up. With this gradual closing of the petals, the focal point, by the polarized effect of the petals, descends and gradually reaches the tip of the lotus cone by the time the lotus is closed. A full cycle of this natural phenomenon takes place with one revolution of the Earth.

The lotus pose is the most desired position for the performance of *Samadhi*. However, there are no hard and fast rules that make *padmasana* an absolute necessity. Due to the natural qualities of the lotus, *padmasana* is by far the most practised *Samadhi* posture. There are a few technicalities of the lotus pose. One must make sure that the hips, thighs and most importantly the knees, rest evenly on the floor in this asana. Any tightness or stiffness will only lead to the restriction of blood supply to the lower limbs, and soon it will become impossible to continue the asana any further. One must use a non-conductive mat to sit upon. The *mooladhara* chakra must stay as close to the floor as possible. The position of the spine should be perfectly perpendicular to the floor (apart from its natural curves) as viewed from all angles.

After conforming to this 'stable and pleasurable' posture, one has to start with the *shaktichalana kriya*. This practice owes its origin to the tantric tradition. With conscious psychic direction, the controlled and regulated *prana* is made to travel complete cycles between the *mooladhara* and *sahasrara* chakras. A few days of this practice is necessary to arrive at a comfortable rhythm for the introduction of *Samadhi*. *Samadhi* is practised by the rhythmic introduction of *Pranav*, or 'cosmic resonance'.

On the appointed day, I began my practice of *Samadhi*. I was determined to perform this practice consistently. Specifically in this practice, my teacher warned me to observe as much patience as possible. He told me the slightest impurity of intention or the smallest attempt to quicken the process would result in the fluctuation of the rhythm and resonance.

This is the most delicate of all yogic practices. Its correct practice results in the achievement of powerful *siddhis*, but repeated failure can result in permanent psychic damage. There are many instances of yogis who, when unsuccessful at this final point, had decided to give up their body with the only objective of taking a re-birth for the sake of the completion of *Samadhi*. After listening carefully to the delicate nature of the practice, I told my guru that I was not feeling confident enough to practise *Samadhi*. Without any further persuasion, he welcomed my idea and instructed me to suspend the practice. However I was to continue the preliminary *kriyas* until I gained full confidence.

Confidence didn't come just like that. For the next few months I cautiously practised to achieve a subtle balance. Every time I sat down for practice, I made it a point to be present with my guru. He never interfered with my process or struggle. However, one day he simply pointed out, "The longer you take to gain your desired balance, the more impossible it will become to achieve it." Hence my notion that by acquiring more patience I would someday be able to achieve the necessary confidence was incorrect.

One day my guru carefully calculated an auspicious date and time and declared, "If you cannot achieve your *Samadhi* under these astrophysical conditions, then I will have to teach you the secret yogic method of giving up the body." (Yogis know many strange and amazing *kriyas*. They can give up their body at any moment they like. It usually takes about four minutes to pass away from life into death. At a later period, I was successful in acquiring the secret of this practice.)

My reaction to this was a strange mixture of emotions. A chill ran through my body, but without giving rise to apprehension, it only resulted in a strong determination. My guru again pointed out, "Determination is a good quality, but it should always be coupled with respect for the cosmic will. Over-determination can lead to a clash with your own destiny. You know that you can never fight with yourself. The idea of outdoing yourself is futile, and in this case, it might just prove dangerous."

I suddenly got up from my practice and said, "I am suspending my practice for the time being. I don't think I will practise until the final day of the designated period. Instead, let me use this time only to relax, as there is no point in getting overcharged with anticipation whilst conducting such a fine and delicate experiment."

In my days as a student, I always behaved in this way. I used to pay full attention in class and never actually studied at home. Prior to the examination, I would discover the books and lessons and made it a point never to study on the day before the examination. Instead, I would go and play cricket or watch a movie. These relaxing activities gave me confidence. Incessant study, with the pressure of examination, always gave me the jitters. Therefore, I had devised this method to deal with such situations, and this is precisely what I did in my ashram on this day.

I told my guru, "This is how I prepare myself for examinations. If my method fails, I am ready to give up my body the next moment."

The next few days I did everything to relax. I spent long hours in a meditative silence and did the things that made me happy. One of the things that gave me immense pleasure, where I would squeal like a child, was to argue persistently with my guru. Strange as it may sound to others, these were my most sought-after moments. On such occasions I always felt like a small child who incessantly nagged the elders for his favorite sweets. In the presence of my guru, I was forever hungry for the sweets of his wisdom, and my guru never disappointed me.

Eventually I was prepared for the big day. On this day I was either to pass over my human limits, or I was to pass away. I took the blessings of my guru and all the seniors of the ashram and sat down in the lotus pose facing the rising sun. I chanted the invocations and gradually drifted into the depths of my concentration. I passed beyond all the senses, all the thoughts and into the ocean of bliss. Once I was completely immersed in silence, I thought I was hearing some kind of rhythmic and vibrating sound. Soon I realized this was not my imagination. I hurriedly brushed away my thoughts and got back into concentration. This time I was chanting the *Pranav* with the same natural rhythm, which was rising and falling like a wave somewhere in the background. I cannot describe what happened after that. The experience was very real. I was definitely not in a trance-like condition. Instead, I was extremely aware. The mind was perfectly still and at rest. Never before had I experienced such a state of mind. My brain seemed to have melted into an ultra-fluid tranquility. There were no choices, no ideas, no thoughts and no experienced description of consciousness.

As I was later informed, I had successfully passed into *Samadhi*, albeit only for a few minutes. My guru expressed his satisfaction, as I was one of his few disciples who achieved this depth of *Samadhi* on the very first occasion. According to Nirupanand, his first experience of *Samadhi* had only lasted for a few seconds. I was told that it is absolutely futile and stupid to attempt to quantify the experience of *Samadhi*. It is not the length of time of the *Samadhi* that counts; it is the quality of absorption that makes it a *Samadhi*. Over the next few days I practised *Samadhi* a few more times under the direct guidance of my guru. Soon after, I was allowed to continue the practice on my own.

For the curiosity of the common man, the state of *Samadhi* can be described as 'ultra-fluid-spiritual-absorption'. This is a state where the practitioner, with his psycho-spiritual tendencies, has completely fused with the cosmic resonance. This is just one step before the state where one can merge with the cosmos with their entire tendency. The entire tendency includes the physical and material elements of the practitioner. That ultimate state will be called *Nirbeeja* or *Nirvikalpa Samadhi*. One needs to practise *Savikalpa Samadhi* at least until the point of confirmation. After this point, the practitioner goes through a series of gradual stages towards the achievement of *Nirvikalpa Samadhi*. This is a point of no return. The yogi does not die as such, as far as pathological expressions are concerned. *Samadhi* is not even the renunciation of the body. It is the complete transcendence into the highest realm of existence.

The stages through which the practitioner proceeds to the highest realm of existence are clearly described in the Yoga Sutras. These intermediary processes are accomplished by the practice of *samyama*.

Samyama is the external threshold of *Samadhi*. In *Sabeeja Samadhi*, the cosmic resonance of *Pranav* is the carrier of transcendence; whereas in *samyama*, the mind is made to concentrate at a particular place, subject or object. Let us remember that in sutra 3:1, Maharshi Patanajli has instructed to confine and concentrate the mind at a place or space to accomplish *Dharana*. In the next sutra, 3:2, he has spoken about the extension of this concentration, and in 3:3 he has spoken about the spiritual absorption. The next sutra, 3:4, denotes that the practice of *Dharana*, *Dhyana*, and *Samadhi*, when accomplished simultaneously, amount to *samyama*.

The practice of *samyama* gradually, in successive stages, takes the yogi to *Nirbeeja Samadhi* (3:6). The time, manner and practice of *samyama* should always be obtained from the guru. The first stage of *samyama* is an offering dedicated to the guru and the entire lineage. The yogi pays respect and obeisance to all the gurus, and this constitutes the first stage of practice. Further development of the practice becomes possible only after this dedication. Invariably, every yogi at this point experiences the divine vision of the *siddhas*, the great ancient masters who are the source and inspiration of spiritual knowledge and guidance. The vision of the *siddhas* heralds the successful entry into *samyama*. In the third chapter of the Yoga Sutras, Maharshi Patanjali has enumerated a series of *samyama* practices. The successful accomplishment of *samyama* always results in the accomplishment of a *siddhi* or a superhuman capacity.

Just before my initiation into *samyama*, I asked my guru about the justification of these superhuman achievements. My question was, "Why is it necessary for one to go through these 'superman' skills?"

My guru answered, "These superhuman skills are never the objective for a yogi. No one can achieve them with the expressed intention of achieving them. They are mere side-effects."

As we have already seen, every species, on the basis of its evolutionary position, enjoys the perks of that stage. The more spiritually evolved the species, the higher the amount of perks it enjoys. It does not matter if it actually makes use of those perks, but it is important that it receives them. The perks, in other words, form the eligibility criteria for the further transcendence of the species. Human life is only another stage of evolution. The perks of human life are also limited within the dimensions of this stage. The supremely capable human mind and human body are not only designed for the enjoyment of the perks, but are the necessary tools for a super-conscious transcendence.

A yogi is a more highly evolved species than a normal human being. Physically, a yogi resembles a human being, but in substance, he enjoys a much higher stage of evolution. No matter how much a monkey resembles a man, it is still a monkey. Similarly, the human appearance of a yogi does not make him a mere human. There is a definite length of transition between the human state and the ultimate stage of evolution.

This length of transition that separates human and divine states is described in various scriptures. The *Puranas*, or the mythological accounts of history, describe seven such stages of existence in this intermediary stage. They are described as *lokas*, or spheres of existence. According to the *Puranas*, these different *lokas* are inhabited by different kinds of beings, and these beings are characterized by their various capabilities which they enjoy on the basis of the order of their existence. The Yoga Sutras does not describe any such mythical beings. The scientific explanation of the Yoga Sutras only reveals the existence and the possibility of superhuman life. The stages through which a yogi transcends into the higher stages of evolution are in fact one and the same as the superhuman stages. In the following few paragraphs I will attempt to illustrate the nature and characteristics of these super-human achievements.

Let us begin with the case of human technology. The technology that we have today is the accumulative result of hundreds of years of observation and experimentation. Man is naturally and inher-ently curious. Gifted with supreme intelligence, man did not stop to accept the actions of nature as acts of God; rather he very minutely studied the exact cause and effect relationship of every natural occurrence. Great subjects and theories evolved on the basis of the intricate and mysterious ways of nature.

From the invention of the wheel to modern-day super-computers, every single invention proves only one thing - the way nature works. The thorough understanding of the cause and effect relationship of the natural processes formed the basis of all inventions, and by gradual experience man learned how to manipulate the natural forces. On the basis of the inherent characteristics, he began to create modules and applied the natural principles for new inventions. The entire study of this process is collectively known as the 'science of physics'.

Similarly, all other branches of science were developed. Whichever branch of science one may choose as an example, we see that there is a deep understanding of natural principles behind it. Without the foundation of the natural principles, no technology can exist. However, the magnitude of all the natural principles known and discovered to date does not collate all the natural principles that are to be known. Human knowledge has its own limits. Whatever we know or can explain is termed 'science', and all that we don't know is attributed to 'magic' or 'miracles'. A modern-day scientist would be too jealous and unwilling to accept anything as a miracle, for he knows there is bound to be some yet-to-be discovered law of physics operating behind it.

The *siddhis* of a yogi are not miracles or magic, but simply a set of unexplained, undiscovered, and often misunderstood laws of physics. There is an intricate and amusing relationship between the laws of physics and spiritual truth. Matters of the spiritual realm definitely lie far beyond the limits of physics, yet the principles of spiritual truth are not beyond the principles of physics. Physics is only the little brother of spirituality. Physics constantly follows and endeavors to prove all that spirituality is talking about. Spirituality, on the other hand, relies upon its younger brother to prove the truth of his own claim. As my guru often said, 'Spirituality without science is merely a lie, and science without spirituality has no purpose.'

The *siddhis*, as enumerated by the Yoga Sutras, can hardly be proven with the available knowledge of physics. However, the foundation upon which physics operates can still be applied to test the veracity of the siddhis. The first example that I would cite is the relationship between the navel and the entire physical structure of the body. The navel and the umbilical cord of the foetus play the central role in the process of the formation and arrangement of the human body. As we grow up, the importance of the navel in the body is gradually forgotten. The navel in our body is more than just a scar or birthmark. Even though we are no longer in the process of foetal development, the navel still remains the centre around which the entire physical design revolves. This central importance of the navel, when concentrated upon, can reveal the arrangement of the total body. The sutra 3:28 provides the technique by which *samyama* is performed upon the navel, thus revealing to the yogi the complete arrangement of the body. This technique has been followed in India for a very long time as a part of its medical tradition.

Let us now apply a similar principle by which we can come to know the arrangement of the entire universe. As the navel plays the central role in the arrangement of the human body, astral bodies like the sun, moon or the pole star play a very important role in the astronomical arrangement of the universe. The sutras 25, 26, and 27 of chapter three provide that *samyama* upon the sun, moon or the pole star reveals the entire secret of the position, arrangement and movement of all the astral bodies in outer space.

Life is like a long chain of interrelated events. Every event of this sequence is the effect, as well as the cause, of other individual events. The precise position of a particular event in life depends upon many definitive factors. In this order, we will see that the moment of birth of an individual is also dependent upon some past events. In a very similar way, a series of the present moments will determine the time of the individual's death. Since birth and death are only a never-ending cycle of actions, it cannot remain unknown. The Yoga Sutras provides for the complete knowledge about one's past, present, or future, including the precise time of one's death. It is accomplished by the performance of *samyama* upon the fruitive nature of one's action (3:21). Similarly, a yogi acquires the complete knowledge of his previous lives from the direct observation and *samyama* upon the factors of conditioning in his current life (3:18).

From the *samyama* over the body, a yogi can regulate the inward and outward movement of energy and light. The yogi, if he so wishes, can achieve the complete stoppage of the incidence and reflection of light from his body. Consequently, regulating the reflection of light, a yogi can attain the capacity to become invisible.

The *siddhis* arise not only from yogic practices, but also from any other practice of a spiritual nature. Yoga is but one of the paths available for spiritual development. The Yoga Sutras of Maharshi Patanjali provides the indication of other modes of practices from which these *siddhis* can arise. According to the first sutra of chapter four, there are five proven methodologies through which one can achieve higher stages of evolution and the corresponding superhuman powers. The sutra reads, '*Janmausadhimantratapah smadihijah siddhayah,*' which means 'The *siddhis* are obtained by means of birth, medicinal herbs, incantations, mortification and practice of *Samadhi*'.

The number of *siddhis* is eight in total. These eight *siddhis* in Sanskrit are *anima, laghima, garima, mahima, praptih, prakamyam, ishitwam* and *vasitvam*. With the help of these *siddhis*, the practitioner can accomplish almost everything that he wishes. He can become invisible or change his body into any size or shape - extremely large or microscopically small, heavy or light - as he wishes. A *sadhak* can obtain any object or material, out of thin air, merely by a wish. He can travel any distance, to any place, with the blink of an eye and make himself available at several places simultaneously.

Let me cite an amusing instance that took place a few years ago.

Once I had gone on a pilgrimage to Amarnath. This place is famous for its never-melting phallic symbol of Shiva, which is completely made of ice. After spending a few days around Amarnath, I was returning while Nirupanand was also available in that area. A few kilometers away from the small town of Anantnag, he was living in a cave. As per previous arrangements, I had decided to visit him as soon as I had completed my trek to Amarnath.

While I was walking through the town of Anantnag, I suddenly came upon an old friend who used to study with me in school. He was now serving in the Indian army. During our conversation I discovered that he was traveling to South India in the next few days. But as soon as he came to know I was going to meet a yogi in a cave, he insisted on accompanying me. My friend, in his complete army gear, started marching beside me to Nirupanand's cave. When I think about it today, I wonder what a surprising and amusing spectacle we must have presented - a frail looking half-clad ascetic accompanied by a majestically dressed army man with his automatic weapons, walking side by side! We continued until we reached the cave of Nirupanand.

In order to prevent any unwanted situation, I briefed my friend on how he should behave in a yogi's presence. Nirupanand was happy to see me, and we discussed the possibility of going to the Kumbh Mela together. All the while, my friend was gaping in wonder. At one point during the talk, Nirupanand included my friend in our conversation. As soon as my friend became comfortable and felt safe, he started poking the usual layman's questions. Whilst I was witnessing Nirupanand's limits of patience, I had to nudge my friend a few times to stop being so silly, but he would not listen to me. I found that Nirupanand was not irritated, but somewhat amused at my friend's curiosity.

However my friend soon turned argumentative, as he challenged, "I see absolutely no reason why anyone would choose the life of an ascetic. If you had the right amount of money and connections, you would not have been sitting in a cave in such a miserable condition."

Nirupanand calmly replied, "I have money and connections, but I like being in a cave."

My friend sarcastically replied, "When I say money, I don't mean the few coins that you could be carrying, that you may have earned through begging. If you possessed anything like a hundred thousand rupees, you would not be sitting here. Probably, you would have been there in Bombay, enjoying the company of a couple of hookers."

Nirupanand, still in his calm, undisturbed composure, replied, "I have one hundred thousand rupees with me, but I still prefer to be in a cave meditating than being in Bombay. One hundred thousand rupees makes no difference in my attitude, and I have no use for it. If you think you have good use for that amount of money, then I am willing to give the money to you."

My friend burst out laughing and exclaimed, "You have one hundred thousand rupees, and you say you will actually give it to me? Come on! Show me your hundred thousand rupees! I think I have some good use for it! I wish to repair my old house and buy a new motor bike!"

Remaining completely unperturbed, Nirupanand lifted the corner of the folded blanket on which he was sitting, and from underneath he pulled out two bundles of crisp, new five hundred rupee notes. He tossed the bundles in front of my friend and said, "Here is your money. You can take it and use it as you like."

Startled, my friend jumped up and shouted, "Bloody hell! Is that real money?!"

I asked him to pick up the money and see if it was real or not. With trembling hands, he picked up one of the bundles, took it close to his face and began to examine the notes. His shock was mounting. Nirupanand prompted him to count the money to be satisfied that it was nothing less than what he had asked for. My friend seemed to have lost his words. With a dropped jaw, he gaped alternately at the money, Nirupanand, and me. It took quite some time for him to regain composure and return to his argumentative mode. He was not at all ready to believe that the money could be real as alleged. "You people are doing some kind of magic! I won't believe your magic until I see and feel some real effect of it."

A highly amused Nirupanand began to instigate him. "If you want, I can give you something else that can convince you that this is not magic."

After a little thought, my friend gathered the courage and said, "What about something to eat or drink?"

Nirupanand guaranteed, "You name it, and you will have it."

Again after a few moments of consideration, my friend placed his order. "I will have a bottle of Jack Daniels and some hot french fries."

Without hesitation Nirupanand produced these items out of thin air and placed them before my friend. My friend's reaction made Nirupanand and I laugh our heads off. He was in a perfectly confused and bewildered state, calling out the names of all kinds of gods and goddesses, including his mother and grandmother. After he calmed down, Nirupanand prompted him to open the bottle and have a drink. I also joined in the process of coaxing my friend to taste the whisky and french fries.

Reluctantly, he picked up a fry and exclaimed, "It's hot!" He put it in his mouth and restarted his chanting of names.

For the rest of the day, he carried a dazed and confused expression on his face. I was happy that this was to be the end of his arguments with Nirupanand. As evening approached we took leave from Nirupanand's cave and walked back to Anantnag. My bewildered friend was carrying the money and the liquor with him. Time and again he was dipping his hand in and out of his bag to check if the money was still there. Five days later, while parting from me at the Waltir railway station, he asked me in a very humble voice, "I want to be a yogi. Tell me what I have to do to be that."

I tried my best to discourage him, but he was too carried away by the powers of a yogi to be dissuaded. At last I suggested that after his service in the army was over, and if his family and parents allow him, he should then come to me, and I would be happy to teach him all the 'tricks' of a yogi.

As far as the powers of the *siddhis* go, everybody in the world would be highly interested in becoming a yogi. Everybody thinks that they could make good use of the *siddhis*, but not many people would be prepared to go through the entire length of practice and hardship to achieve this stage. Absolute detachment, renunciation and humility are all very necessary conditions to possess these superhuman powers.

∞∞∞∞

It had already been more than six years since I first arrived at the ashram. During my stay, I witnessed the arrival of many seekers and the departure of many accomplished yogis. There were at least one hundred practitioners present at the ashram at any given time. Before the end of this particular winter, I noticed a substantial increase in the number of visitors. Many senior and old students of the ashram had chosen to visit at the same time. Slowly the ashram became full. At one point, I counted one hundred thirty-two yogis living together, many of whom I had never met, and only some had I heard of before. This was a great opportunity to know the senior and accomplished products of the ashram; it was like an unofficial alumni. The gathering was slightly surprising for me. I did not pay much attention to what was going on, but I noticed that a group of senior yogis were constantly engaged in discussions with my guru and other masters of my ashram.

One day my guru called me to his cave. Nirupanand was also present when I arrived. Nirupanand invited me to sit next to him and then put his arm around my shoulder. I was a little surprised to be treated this way. In my view, only friends, those who treated each other as equals, behaved in this manner. I had not expected Nirupanand to display this kind of behavior.

My guru had sensed my surprise. "Soon you are going to be standing at the same platform as Nirupanand. So let Nirupanand invite you to his position. I wish to appoint you and Nirupanand to take upon the responsibilities of teaching. After my departure, it will be the two of you who will carry forward the invaluable and secret knowledge of Yoga on behalf of the entire lineage of gurus. I have reached the end of my journey. Before the end of *uttarayan* (northward movement of the sun), I will take *Samadhi*. Before I give up this mortal body, I wish to assign you both your respective responsibilities."

I suddenly interrupted, "You can't just choose to die like this and leave me and so many others midway. What do you think will happen to our practices? What are we all going to do without you? You just can't choose to go, as and when you like! You are not that old and you are still in perfect health. Think about us! You too have some responsibilities for others."

My guru was silent, but Nirupanand was beginning to smile. Affectionately my guru replied, "Manmoyanand, when will you grow up? The one and only purpose for which a yogi lives is to complete his own journey of spiritual evolution, and when that time comes, he has to go and merge with the cosmos. Do you know how old this body is? I have been carrying it everywhere for the past ninety-four years. My time has come, and soon I will achieve the ultimate purpose of my existence. One day the same opportunity will come for you. On that day, will you allow anything or anybody to stand between you and your *Nirvikalpa Samadhi*? I think not."

After a moment's reflective silence, my guru continued, "All of us have been going through uncountable cycles of births and deaths, uncountable *tapahs* and hardships, only to be able to arrive at this point where nothing stops one from his *Samadhi*. You, like Nirupanand, are standing between *Savikalpa* and *Nirvikalpa Samadhi*. In the journey, Nirupanand is much further ahead than you; therefore his time will arrive before yours. You know that the knowledge of Yoga has been preserved undiluted in the hands of only a few yogis. It is a difficult task to preserve this priceless treasure. Someone has to take upon the responsibility of preserving this knowledge from being diluted or distorted, and protect it from falling into the wrong hands.

You will find so many people in the world bent upon distorting and destroying the truth of Yoga. This knowledge cannot be allowed to die. Somebody from the younger generation must carry it forward. You are the youngest accomplished yogi in the history of this ashram, and I am extremely pleased to put you out as an *acharya* (teacher) of the great *Naga-Saraswati* lineage. In my opinion you have the right age, the right experience, the right training and *siddhis*, and the right attitude to be a convincing spiritual teacher. Nirupanand does not need any more training to take up this responsibility. Over the next six months, I will teach you the qualities and ethics of a spiritual teacher which you should always keep in mind whilst dealing with any student. After these six months of training, you will go out into the midst of the common man to teach, while Nirupanand will continue teaching in the ashram."

Each word of my guru hit me with a strong impact, but my mind was in no condition to contemplate upon them. My heart was slowly sinking into despair. I was not quite prepared to leave the company of my guru. The thought of living without him was dreadful, and what tormented me most was the thought of going back to wretched human civilization as just another one of the many thousands of yoga teachers.

I began to protest. I announced his decision to be cruel and unfair. I exclaimed, "Why me?! Don't you think I am too young and inexperienced to deal with such a mad world? I think it would be a better idea to send Nirupanand out there. Surely he has the right kind of strength and experience for such a task. I will stay in the ashram until I become somebody like him. Then I promise I will go back amongst the world, and Nirupanand can come back to the ashram and take *Samadhi*, if he likes."

Both of my masters were smiling, obviously amused at my childish arguments. Before I fell into tears, I concluded, "It is not going to be an easy task for me to be out there."

My guru replied, "It was not an easy task for any of us here to teach you, Manmoyanand. You have proven to be the most difficult student any teacher could ever wish for. If you can give us such a task, you should be prepared to accept such a task for yourself. Remember all the endless questions and arguments that you have hurled at your teachers in this ashram. You should be willing to face at least that many questions and hardships in your own teaching career."

I responded, "Oh, I see. So you are throwing me out of the ashram as punishment for all those honest and innocent questions?" That was surely a lie, for all my questions had not been that innocent in nature. In my early days, I had inflicted an uncountable number of arguments upon my guru, only in an attempt to disprove and discredit him. At this particular moment he was generous enough not to bring up that issue and remind me of what a brat I have been.

Instead, he calmly replied, "None of us could ever think of punishing you, my child. All of us have enjoyed and relished the wonderful experience of witnessing your evolution as a yogi. There are some very specific reasons why you have been chosen to go out of the ashram.

Firstly, you know the language spoken by the common man - by language, I mean to say your ability to relate to their queries and questions on the basis of their previous conditionings. It will be difficult for any university-educated man to relate to the ashram style of teaching. You have a university background. Therefore you will be better suited to deal with modern people, rather than someone who never went to school. The second important reason is that you are too young to take *sannyasa* (renunciation). There are some nice surprises waiting for you in life. One day you will get married, have children and run an occupation to go through the *sadhana* of the householder to acquire the necessary completion of your life."

At the mention of marriage and occupation, I got up in a frenzy and made a scene as I screamed, "Before I even agreed to go out, you have imposed a marriage and the job of a house-holder on top of me?! I am not going to marry or go out of the ashram!"

I sat down with a decisive thud and refused to listen to anything else on this topic.

My guru continued in a soft, but firm tone, "I am not finished yet. The third important reason why you should go and live the life of a householder is that this is the means by which you are going to pay off your karmic debt, which is very much necessary if you want to open your path towards *Nirvikalpa Samadhi*.

For hundreds of lifetimes a lineage of forefathers, a lineage of gurus, and of course the Creator, has supported us to come to this final phase of life. Hundreds of lives have been employed to support your growth physically, mentally and spiritually. In this process, your life also contains the purpose and intention to become a support for the perpetuation of nature. Without repaying nature and mankind for its support, you cannot escape and achieve the freedom to enter *Nirvikalpa Samadhi*. In your life, you have needed the support of parents, teachers, neighbors, friends and enemies to develop yourself into this position. Now, this is your opportunity to pay back every element of the universe in a very similar manner by becoming a parent, teacher, neighbor, friend or even an enemy.

The last condition for why you should go out as a teacher is that you owe something to me, the teachers of the ashram and the entire lineage of yogis. You can never make use of your learning until you pay the *guru-dakshina* (tuition fees) to your teachers. Your teachers gave you everything you wanted to learn; therefore you must not hesitate to pay the fees they want. As a fee to us, we want you to become a teacher of all the subjects that you have learned in this ashram and not to discontinue your teaching until you have created at least one teacher who is as knowledgeable and realized as you. After which you have the option to do whatever you like. You will then be free to take *Samadhi*."

The third and fourth responsibilities placed by my guru completely nailed me. There was no way to escape from these responsibilities. After some time in thought and contemplation, I got up to touch the feet of my guru and submitted to his wishes.

The seventh of June was chosen as the most auspicious moment for my guru to take *Samadhi*. Nearly six months away. The last months of his mortal life were quite busy and hectic. He was constantly engaged in giving the final teachings to his students. He assigned each and every one of his students their respective responsibilities. Nirupanand was constantly at his side to take the cue from my guru's final activities. Everyone seemed to be at ease. I felt as if I was the only one growing miserable inside. Kripanand was designated to succeed my guru as the chief organizer of the ashram. His responsibility would be more towards looking after the ashram affairs than active teaching. Kripanand was first in line to take *Samadhi* after my guru, Nirupanand was second, and I stood at seventh position to take up the responsibility of the ashram before taking *Samadhi*.

∞∞∞∞

My 'teacher training' started. Teaching is synonymous with touching a soul forever and is not merely a means of transmitting information. There is a vast difference between these two. The transmission of information can take place through various modes, such as giving a lecture, writing an article or book, or even publishing a web page. The modern use of electronic media has obviously achieved revolutionary development in the process of information transmission. In the case of information technology, it is always the receiver who decides how much to take. Depending upon his hunger for information, he will accept or reject the learning in accordance to his own desire. It is very much like eating in a restaurant.

In a restaurant we come to see an array of food offered for sale. We pick and choose our food on the basis of our taste, habit or preferences. We pay for the food, and the food arrives appetizingly garnished. We eat the food to our satisfaction and leave the rest. If we like the taste of the food and its after-effects, we sometimes come back for more. However, this is not the case when your mother is feeding you.

Your mother knows when you are hungry. Your mother knows everything about your taste, habit and preferences. Your mother also knows which food is best for you, whereas the restaurant has no idea. You get the best food at home without having to pay for it. Your mother also knows how much you enjoy the food. The taste and after-effects of food are guaranteed at home. Your mother waits for you to come back for your next meal. When you were a baby, your mother was the unlimited source of your nourishment. Your mother knows how to put you to play and make you hungry. Your mother lets you suckle her as much as you want. Her satisfaction lies in your growth.

A teacher is like your mother. The teacher is an embodiment of the ultimate and unlimited knowledge. He precisely knows what you are looking for. He knows your capacity to digest, and he also knows how to give you the hunger. A teacher is not just the supplier of knowledge. He is the one that invokes your hunger for it. Teaching is a non-verbal form of communication. Anything that is verbally or literally transmitted can only constitute information. The most and correct teaching takes place when the teacher and student are locked into one another in a non-verbal mode of communication. It is much easier for the teacher to be part of this, but it is not always so easy for the student. After the initial resistance and with support from the teacher, the student gradually learns to connect with him. Once this connection is established, they become one and inseparable.

No matter how good or bad, wise or dumb the teacher may be, he always remains respectable in the eyes of the student.

A teacher never makes the student; it is always the student who makes a teacher.

A teacher is only a teacher for the purpose of a student.

A teacher does not claim himself as such; rather it is the student who recognizes him as a teacher.

The answers from a student only reflect his recollection capacity, while his questions reveal the way he thinks, and this is precisely what the teacher is looking for.

The mode of questioning of a student always helps the teacher to modify his teaching, and thus allows the teacher to remain completely aware of the student's questioning pulse.

A teacher is never satisfied with the correct answers provided by the student; rather he looks for the correct questions from the student.

The teacher should never be jealous and protective about his teachings and should never attempt to give his teachings a concrete shape in the mind of the student.

The teaching has to be perfectly fluid and flexible. Creating a rigid and concrete block in the mind of a student causes more damage than any long-term benefit. Such kind of teaching is less teaching, more brainwashing. Hence, all attempts to create a solid 'belief' in the mind of a student must be avoided.

The teacher should bear in mind that he is only a passing phase in the student's life, and any attempt to hold onto that phase will only prove disastrous for the student.

A teacher has no right over the future of his student.

The teacher should be willing to pass away from the memory of the student.

The teaching is never judged on the basis of how much knowledge was imparted, but on the basis of how much knowledge was demanded.

A teacher can expect nothing from his students, though he deserves and is entitled to a 'tuition fee' from his students, which he can ask for only at the end of the teaching - not on the basis of how much he has given, but on the basis of how much the student has taken.

Greed and expectation always spoil and dilute the teacher-student relationship.

As long as a teacher has not embodied the correct mindset of teaching, he should not commence teaching.

No one can own Knowledge. A person can only acquire a certain amount of information in a lifetime. There is a subtle difference between information and knowledge. Knowledge belongs to every particle of the universe in equal measure. Every single individual is born with the complete knowledge of the universe engraved in every cell of their body.

Like all the senses, knowledge is always triggered by a catalyst. Books do not actually contain knowledge; they only act as triggers to invoke knowledge. By looking at the black and white lines of this page, every person does not understand the same. Each line you read triggers a greater realm of knowledge to illuminate and surface in the mind. Knowledge has to be treated not as one's personal belonging, but as a privilege the Creator has bestowed upon us.

Sometimes teachers subconsciously project their pride of ownership of knowledge onto their students. This tends to happen when the speaker identifies himself with the 'information' he 'knows'. No matter how subtle these projections may be, they are always perceived by the audience. Along with the teaching, the audience comes to acquire and integrate these projections, and subsequently everyone in the lineage continues to project and propagate the pride and arrogance from generation to generation. In this process, over a short period of time the entire substance of the teaching is lost, and only arrogance and pride remain. Hence it is important for every teacher not to identify himself with his knowledge or teaching.

The knowledge that I have received from my gurus has been preserved for ages, without dilution or distortion. The secret reason for this successful preservation of knowledge over millennia is due to the fact that no teacher in the process identified himself with what he was teaching. Every true teacher most humbly dedicates the entire credit of his teaching to his guru. As long as this is done, there is no place for his pride to determine the teaching. The teacher not only owes the knowledge to his guru, but also owes it to his students. He should humbly relay the entire knowledge to his students without any conditions, reservations or attachments. By the purest manner of transmission of knowledge, the substance of the teaching becomes more and more luminous in the process, and is never lost.

I had come across many teachers in my life, but after having met my guru, my whole image of a teacher changed. In my opinion, as a teacher he was the most perfect living specimen. Whilst he was explaining to me the beautiful role of a teacher in the life of a student, I interrupted by saying, "Gurudev, I don't know how long I will remember these profound principles of teaching, but I can guarantee one thing. Every time I will teach, your face will remain visible to me in my memory. I will just repeat the words which I will make out from the movement of your lips. With your face before my eyes, I hope not to err even once in my life."

At this moment, not only my notions of a teacher, but also my notions of teaching had changed forever. For the first time in life, it was here in my ashram that I came to hear about teaching on the basis of the past-life experiences of the student.

Before the commencement of teaching, it is necessary for any teacher to know the exact academic background of the student. For example, when someone applies for admission into a school or college, it is compulsory to provide all the relevant information about the subjects previously studied.

Previous training always plays a very important role in ascertaining the present condition and compatibility of the student. These previous trainings are of two types, *samskara* and *prabajya*. *Samskara* is the sum total of the person's training and conditioning of the present life; *prabajya* denotes the sum total of spiritual and karmic virtue that is accumulated during the previous lives. If it is necessary to know the academic background of a student, even for the purpose of teaching arithmetic, one can only imagine how important it is to know the spiritual background and compatibility of a student prior to commencing his spiritual teaching.

Yoga is primarily and essentially a spiritual training, hence it is imperative to know the spiritual past of a student before even giving the basic practices. Some people have high compatibility for asanas whilst others find them difficult to perform. While one's *samskara* comes in the way of achieving purification, his *prabajya* might be highly supportive for *pranayama*. It is always important to find out these subtle elements about one's spiritual nature. On some occasions, students show extreme resistance to a certain mode of spiritual practice. In such cases, it is important to find out if he had followed or practised any specific path in his past life, or if he has vowed his obedience to any guru or lineage, as one could have a surviving guru. Without finding this information about a student's past, it is impossible to support their spiritual development.

The student is never in a position to know or remember his past. It is always the duty of the teacher to find out the spiritual background of every student prior to taking responsibility for his spiritual growth. Knowing the past-life spiritual qualities of a student also reveals the entire series of events that has shaped the student into the present condition. Every difficulty, resistance and conflict of the student can thus be easily resolved. The exact nature of the practice of every single student should always be based upon their *prabajya* and *samskara*.

Since I was to become a teacher, my guru had decided to teach me the fine skills of calculating both the *samskara* and *prabajya* of a person. This calculation is accomplished by the use of *vedic* astrology and the application of certain *siddhis*. Astrology reveals bits and pieces of information about the student's past, but the pieces of this jigsaw puzzle are mostly insufficient to form a clear picture. Taking this information into a deep state of Meditation, the entire picture of a student's past becomes clear and complete. At that state of contemplation, there is no scope for doubt, reason or confusion. The teacher actually comes to 'see' the past lives of a student. This information gradually and automatically comes to be revealed to the student with the subsequent development and advancement of their practice.

It is a complex procedure. It took weeks for me to come up with a satisfactory result of my first-ever calculation. I asked other members of the ashram for information about their birth date, place, and time along with the names of their parents, and I would sit down for days to calculate and reveal the incidents and where-abouts of their past lives. After every calculation, I sought confir-mation from my guru to check its correctness. Gradually my skills improved, and I was able to do the calculations at a much faster pace. I also acquired the ability to go much deeper into one's past-life background.

I calculated and discovered the complete information of my own last four lifetimes. When I realized my present existence as a culmination of past events that stretched over a hundred years, I came to understand why my guru had forbidden me to discover such information. Without the intervention of my teacher, my curiosities would have landed me in the midst of grave and serious trauma.

With my guru, I very carefully studied the process of how to relate these findings to the process of training a student. As he was explaining these fine details, a curious question popped into my mind. I asked, "What if I find somebody who has a much higher *prabajya* than my present level?"

My guru answered, "Before you gain sufficient experience in teaching, such a case should be referred to Nirupanand. But after you have gained enough experience and confidence, you will have to handle that student on your own. You don't have to worry and compare his state to yours. Firstly because you are two separate entities, there is nothing to be compared between you. Secondly, he is a lion with the notions of a lamb, and he is depending upon you to give him his true identity."

The concept of teaching on the basis of *samskara* and *prabajya* was never previously known to me. I never heard of such a sensible way to initiate a spiritual training. The more I thought about it, the more I began to feel the weight of my responsibilities as a teacher. I knew for certain that I was not going to be yet another 'yoga shopkeeper' that I had found in abundance in the modern world.

Out of curiosity I asked my teacher, "How many people do you think are living today who know the process of calculation of *samskara* and *prabajya*?"

"Very few," my guru answered. "This fine art of teaching is gradually on the decline. After me, there will be at least two such teachers available in the world. One is Nirupanand, and the second is you."

In the course of my teacher training, I was gradually exposed to the finer skills of teaching. My masters explained the essential indications of a student's practice. When the student sits down for practice, he becomes transparent in the eyes of the teacher. A skilled teacher actually 'sees' and reads every symptom that is revealed within the body and mind of the student. In front of such a teacher, it is impossible for a student to fake his practice. On the other hand, a student's apparently strong resistance may actually reveal itself to be no resistance at all. A teacher does not go by what the student projects about himself; he goes by what his 'x-ray' vision reveals.

I asked my guru, "Don't you think it will result in a bit of discomfort on the part of the student to be flipped inside out?"

My guru laughed as he replied, "Generally the student doesn't know what the teacher is looking at. Secondly, the teacher doesn't look at any uncomfortable elements, and thirdly, one becomes a true student only when he submits himself to the maximum exposure of his shortcomings!"

I had learned how to see the concentration levels of a student during the practices of asana, *pranayama*, meditation and such other *kriyas* of spiritual practice. According to my guru, through experience a teacher develops the very fine skills of perceiving even the slightest psychic change of a student.

As the days passed by I became more and more confident about my soon-to-be acquired 'profession'.

I was spending a few hours everyday in the company of my teacher. One day he said, "Manmoyanand, I owe you something."

I could not understand what he was referring to. How did he come to owe me anything? Rather, it was I who owed my lifetime's achievements to him.

He continued, "You have been such a good student. I am really happy to set you out into the human world. I would love to see how you contribute to change the face of spiritual belief in the modern world. This task may at times appear very hard. But never worry, as the force of the entire lineage of yogis will be behind you.

Do you remember - I had always dodged your requests to experience the powers of your *siddhis*? Before I go, I wish to give you the secret keys to the enjoyment of all these powers. I am very confident that you will never abuse them."

I was overwhelmed with happiness and gratitude, yet as my guru's final day came closer, I could think of nothing else. I was constantly trying to suppress a rising sense of despair in my heart. The thought of this instantly brought tears to my eyes.

With folded hands, I begged my guru, "I don't want the *siddhis*. What will I do with them? After all, I have never experienced them; therefore I will not miss them. But you surely know what I am going to miss. If you are pleased with me in any way, then please let me see you whenever I need you. I am sure you can manifest before me if you so wish, even after your *Samadhi*. If you think that I was a good student for you, please bless me with this privilege."

My guru came up to me and gave me a big hug. Very affectionately he said, "That goes without saying, Manmoyanand. I will remain forever present in your life. Every time you teach and every time you speak about us, I will always drop in to listen to this young yogi. Nevertheless, I am going to give you your *siddhis* as they are the result of your *tapah*. You rightly earned them. I kept the performances away from you in order to prevent you from using them prematurely. You should accept them because they are rightfully yours. Besides, how do you think I can go without returning your achievements to you?"

The last words of my guru hurt me very much. I knew very well that in a few days he was going to sever all his connections to this mortal world forever. His last words gave me the feeling of being severed at that very moment. I could not control myself anymore and began to cry in his lap.

True to his words, my guru began to teach me the methods by which I could demonstrate and experience my superhuman capacities. One by one, he taught me every single technique, as he encouraged and supervised my practice and performances. I felt like a small child being taught by his father how to ride a bicycle. At the end of the practice, he would always congratulate me by saying I was doing very well and give me suggestions on how to improve my skills. Those were some of the finest days of my life. I was living my childhood fantasies of being a superman. These days presented me with the best of everything. I received the finest of my guru's teachings, the sweetest of his attention, and his closest and most affectionate company.

As the day of my guru's *Samadhi* drew closer, he began to maintain more silence. For long periods of time he would sit in Meditation, and none of us wished to disturb him. He never once forbid me to disturb him, but something told me to just leave him with himself during the last days of his mortal life. At ninety-four he was in perfect health. His body radiated the same metallic glow as ever. There was no sign of fatigue, stress or old age in his absolutely relaxed face and composure. I was wondering if it was at all possible for him to become melancholic in these days. Did he ever wish for anything in life? Could he be nostalgic about some unknown part of his past?

My child-like curiosity always haunted me. I talked to Kripanand about my feelings for my guru. Kripanand explained to me, "Such things happen to people when they know they are going to die, but Angadanand is not going to die. He is taking the last and ultimate step into the final stage of evolution. Standing at this point, there is absolutely nothing in the whole universe he has not acquired or experienced. *Nirvikalpa Samadhi* is the complete fusion of every particle of the individual with the cosmos. How can he die when he is going to be present in every single particle of the universe?"

The day of my guru's *Samadhi* arrived. Until that day, I kept a very close watch on the developments of his health and was keenly observing every aspect of his behavior. I could not see anything negative or disturbing about his appearance or behavior. On the day of his *Samadhi*, he went to have a nice thorough bath and changed into fresh clothes. We all gathered outside the ashram to attend his last discourse. My guru spoke for some time and reminded each of us our roles and purposes in life. Then he remained silent. We were all waiting for him to speak, but no words came out of his mouth. He continued to sit there, looking at us in his usual benevolent expression.

There was a gentle breeze blowing in from the north. In that blissful silence we could hear the cascading water of river Saraswati in the distance. The eastern horizon was gradually becoming brighter. The unending snowy tops of the surrounding mountains began to reflect the golden hue of the early morning sun. The moment was more than perfect. All of us were carried away with some unknown resonance that was passing between ourselves and our guru. He was sitting there before us without speaking, but each one of us realized that he was not silent. In that short span of time, without uttering a word, he had success-fully communicated to us our finest lessons in life. My guru was speaking in my most cherished language, the voice of silence. Slowly, he got up from his seat and said it was time for him to go.

Each of us, one by one, went to him to touch his feet and take his blessings. As I approached to touch his feet, I was very surprised that I was not crying. At last the most profound reality of existence had dawned upon me. After touching his feet, I asked him in a whisper, "Gurudev, what does it feel like?"

He answered in a sweet child-like voice, "I am very excited. It feels as if I am going home and back to my parents."

After the last of us detached ourselves from him, my guru walked to the flat piece of rock on which he had given me my first lessons of meditation. He sat there facing the sun. His face reflected its golden aura. He folded his hands and whispered a prayer. A brief moment after the prayer, he audibly uttered a clear and prolonged '*Aum*'. As the resonance of the *Aum* drew closer to its end, I noticed a very faint shiver that ran like a wave through his entire body, and with the end of the sound it became still. Right before my very eyes, my master, whom I revered as the living God, left the mortal limits of his human body.

CHAPTER SEVEN

Crucifixion and Resurrection of Yoga

For a long time I continued to sit there. I was witnessing the most incredible and profound event of my life. Everybody else from the ashram was also watching this phenomenon. Some of them joined their palms together as a mark of absolute respect towards my guru as he was sitting in *Samadhi*. Was he actually sitting? After passing into this phase of existence, it would be very improper to say that he was sitting. I should correct myself to say that the mortal body of my guru remained, before our eyes, in a sitting position. Visibly there was no difference in his body before or after taking *Samadhi*. It still had the usual youthful glow which my guru always radiated. It didn't turn pale or discolored, even after a long time, and to my surprise it didn't fall down like you see in the movies. For a very long time I just continued to sit there. Maybe I was reluctant to leave the company of my teacher so soon.

After a while I looked around to find no one else was around me. I was the only one who remained sitting there, gaping at the body of my teacher. I felt a little stupid, as I thought to myself that I perhaps needed a few more lessons on detachment, whereas the rest of the people of the ashram appeared to be in perfect control of themselves. I decided to talk about my feelings with Nirupanand. Finally, I got up and went to join the others.

Most of the people had assembled in the cave in which my guru usually practised. A few days earlier my guru himself had supervised the making of a large pit in that cave. There the body of my teacher would be placed. After making all the arrangements in the cave, all of us went to take a bath.

On my return I found Nirupanand sitting in front of the body of my guru. From a distance I could see his lips moving; he was reciting certain mantras and incantations. After a while, a few of us gathered to carry the body to the pit. We lifted the body very carefully to retain its lotus position. Gingerly, we carried it to the cave and lowered it into the pit. The body was placed facing east in its lotus position. It was not like a usual burial whereby the grave is filled with soil. In this case, large pieces of rock were carefully arranged to form a complete covering over the pit. The body of my guru would remain in that state until eternity.

The next morning I went back to the cave to pay my respects to my teacher. I knelt down beside the pit and kissed the stones that covered it. As I did, I experienced a faint fragrance which appeared to be coming from the pit below. I bent down to smell it once more, just to be sure that it was a fragrance. It certainly was. Over the next few days the fragrance filled the entire cave. The beautiful fragrance is still available in that cave until this day. Over the years the cave has become my most sought-after pilgrimage.

One evening I sat amongst a small group in the ashram discussing the future course of our activities. Acharya Kripanand was assigning each of us our practice schedules. During the course of the discussion, I found that I was the only one designated to be going outside of the ashram to enter into a different phase of yogic life. On realizing this, I quietly moved closer to Nirupanand and asked if I could stay a little longer, as in my belief I had yet to learn the absolute sense of detachment. I went on to explain how I was still a 'cry-baby' when it came to my teacher. "Do you not think that it is a little immature for a yogi to be crying like this? Do you not think that it is a little 'un-yogic' to miss somebody?"

In his usual bold and graceful voice he replied, "You are not the only one missing Angadanand. Your tears for Angadanand

yogi manmoyanand paying obeisance near his guru's Samadhi place - his favorite pilgrimage.

cannot be compared with another man's lament for wealth, possession or prosperity. The term 'attachment' is only used to denote love for material possession. The desire for divinity or the love for a guru can barely equal the desire for wealth or a woman. Had it been so then Buddha's incessant desire for truth or nirvana would have been taken as the worst example of attachment. You are not the only one who has shed tears for your teacher. Everybody who knew Angadanand will miss him forever, and that includes me. Shedding tears for Angadanand is only a mark of the utmost respect and reverence. If you prefer to call it crying, then tell me - don't you think a guru like Angadanand is worth crying for?"

I stayed in my ashram for about a month after my guru took *Samadhi*. Most of this time was spent in deep contemplation. Sometimes I would meditate for days on end. This helped me to brace myself and face the frightening prospect of my future life. Many times I had vivid visions of my guru standing before me and comforting me. He would always remind me that if the ordinary man can continue to survive in a society full of greed, avarice and conflict, then why did I believe that it would be so difficult for me? A yogi who has ended the conflicts of dualities forever is surely immune to the provocations of human society. If there is anyone who is most suited to live in a society of constant provocation, he has to be a yogi. A yogi is like a fish that lives in water but never gets wet. A society does not change a yogi; a yogi changes the society he dwells in.

The kind and encouraging words of my guru gradually gave me enough confidence to enter into 'normal' human society.

On the day of my departure I paid my respects to everybody in the ashram and began my long walk to the foothills of the mountains to start my new life. I knew I would have to pick up some kind of job or occupation to support my survival. I was beginning to wonder about the kind of job I should look for that would conform to my understanding of ethics. I promised myself that whatever job or occupation I would take, my first income would go towards my *guru dakshina*. The thought of *guru dakshina* made me think that the job and its earnings should reflect my utmost love, respect and gratitude for my teacher. It would be absolutely useless to pay for the knowledge which I had earned with money that was not equally hard earned. After a little thought, I decided to become a rickshaw puller. I went to Dehra Dun and enquired about getting a cycle rickshaw. Without much difficulty, I managed to find a man who owned many rickshaws, and he agreed to let me hire one for a fixed fee of fifty rupees a day. I gladly accepted the offer, and with my rickshaw I went out to explore the lanes and by-lanes of the city. Within an hour of wandering, I was in business.

I continued this occupation for a month. In the beginning I faced some difficulty in pulling and maneuvering the rickshaw amidst the crowded streets, but soon I improved my skills. I was barely forty kilograms when I left my ashram. The month of grueling work reduced my frame to next to nothing. However, within a month I had managed to save nearly three thousand rupees which I decided to spend towards the payment of my *guru dakshina*. I went to the military cantonment in Delhi and bought some good quality heavy-duty blankets and ground sheets. I then further purchased many articles that a sadhu would need whilst practising in the remote caves of the Himalayas. I carried all the items back to the mountains and distributed them amongst the sadhus and ascetics. After completing this task I went to my ashram for a short stay. Kripanand was happy to see me and expressed immense pleasure at the manner in which I had chosen to pay my *guru dakshina*.

Once back in Delhi I bought some second-hand jeans and cheap t-shirts. Then after nearly seven years of not seeing my face, I went to the barbers and got a shave and a haircut. Whilst the barber was going about his work, I looked into the mirror and witnessed the physical transformation of a Himalayan ascetic into a city dude.

∞∞∞∞

During my days of seeking I had come across many kinds of ashrams and quasi-ashrams that purported to teach yoga. I visited quite a few of them, especially the ones that were established or run by some kind of yogi or sadhu trust. Most of them had some kind of religious or political affiliation. Presently, as I entered the spiritual supermarket not as a shopper, but as a seller, I decided to keep my distance from them. I knew for a fact I was not going to attract a huge number of spiritual seekers amidst the present-day conditions, but neither was I looking for such a thing to happen. I remembered what my Guru had told me: all I needed to do is find just one true seeker who is spiritually ripe, and teach him all that I know. As soon as I had done so, I would be free from my obligation and be able to go back to the ashram and take *Samadhi*.

The task at hand appeared quite simple, but how was I to find that one person who would give me my salvation? I took a piece of paper and a pen and began to make a list of such places that were frequented by spiritually disturbed people. I took the help of magazines, newspapers, gyms, health clubs, spas and occasionally religious institutions. Places like Rishikesh, Haridwar and Varanasi provided ample opportunity to interact with potential seekers.

After a fair amount of running around, I thought that joining some yoga institution would give me constant exposure to seekers and allow me to pursue my agenda. This would not only give me the opportunity to impart correct teaching, but also give me the chance to peep into people's past lives to single out the true student. I began to apply for the job of a 'yoga teacher' in various yoga institutes, studios and spas. In my applications, I carefully presented my experience and proficiency in Yoga. In spite of my extraordinary qualifications, most of my applications were rejected. At only two places was I given the chance of an interview. The first was at a 'holistic' spa.

Before commencing with the interview, the lady at the front desk told me to have a good look at the spa, to which I obliged. The spa was no smaller than an indoor stadium. The entire spa was air-conditioned. It was surrounded by beautifully manicured and maintained gardens and lawns. Incense, fragrances and Tibetan music were drifting from hidden sources. I was shown tennis court-sized massage parlors and phone booth-sized meditation cubicles. As I was returning to the reception, I saw a group of not-so-small women attempting to do yogasanas on the lawn. I paused for a brief moment and in my mind praised their commendable efforts to bend and twist.

I was interviewed by two women. One of them was short, stocky and displayed several colors on her face. The other, who had just walked in still dripping with sweat, was dressed in tight-fitting gym clothing. It was she who was more polite to me in the interview. After introducing herself as the present yoga teacher who was soon to leave, she went on to ask about my experiences. I carefully framed my lines and gave her a brief account. She then asked, "Can I see your certificate, please?"

"What certificate?"

She clarified the question, "We would like to see the certificate that shows you are a qualified yoga instructor."

"I have no such certificates."

Regretfully, she emphasized that it was necessary to have a proper and formal education in yoga instruction along with a certificate from a recognized institution before one plans to teach yoga. Without the support of such necessary evidence, it would be difficult for them to entrust the precious health of their clients in the inexperienced hands of another.

The long-forgotten reality of yoga suddenly dawned upon me. Until this point, I had entirely forgotten that I was talking yoga in the fitness supermarket. I very politely tried to explain the reason for which I had applied for the job. Since they were a 'holistic' spa, I presumed they were something more than a regular gym. The mention of the term 'holistic' had given me the notion that this establishment would purport 'holistic yoga' rather than 'gymnastic yoga'. I noticed my interviewers were becoming amused. The painted one reclined back in her chair. The other brought her face forward and asked with a twinkle in her eye, "What is the difference between 'holistic yoga' and 'gymnastic yoga'?"

Very much like an obedient child, I answered, "Yoga for spiritual development is holistic yoga, and asana-lookalike exercises for fitness and flexibility is gymnastic yoga."

She burst back, "That is your opinion! And in our opinion, you are not suitable for this job."

She then came round from the table and opened the door for me.

The experience left a bad taste in my mouth. When I was summoned for another interview a few days later, I made a promise to myself that I would blast them back if they demanded certificates from a yogi.

On this occasion, the interview was in a sports complex. The company had undertaken the responsibility of providing 'yoga training' to boost the concentration and relaxation levels of the athletes. They had arranged an entire panel of health experts ranging from body builders to laughter therapists to evaluate and choose a yoga trainer. As soon as I appeared before this panel, taking a good look at me one of them commented, "You look too young and immature, and it seems it is you that could do with some proper exercise."

Then directing me to a yoga mat, they impromptu asked me to demonstrate a series of asanas. As I removed my shoes I wondered how long I was to hold the asana. I suppressed the urge to ask them how they were going to 'see' the asana only from its physical presentation, as I didn't think any of them had the capacity of Kripanand to actually evaluate an asana. However, I took my time in performing the asanas, holding each one of them for about a minute. After having completed them, I folded my hands with a silent prayer for my teacher. A few of the inter-viewers got to their feet and returned my namaste. They seemed obviously pleased with my demonstration. I was beginning to feel hopeful, until one of them held out his hand and asked me for my resume. After briefly glancing at my resume, he wanted to see my certificates.

I tried my best to conceal my disappointment as I said, "See. I am a yogi and not a fitness instructor. In my experience, I know that the correct practice of yogasanas can result in extraordinary standards of physical tolerance along with a high degree of relaxation. I learnt the finer skills of yogic practice from yogis and sages of the Himalayas. I don't think the capacity of a yogi can be evaluated by someone who is not a yogi themselves. Thus, a yogi is less likely to possess a certificate."

My asana demonstration definitely had a great impact on their judgement. Had this not been the case, I was quite sure they would have thrown me out. As soon as I finished, all of them started to speak simultaneously. Eventually one of them asked, "Do you mean to say that you cannot give us a single certificate, or even a single paper in support of your claim of authenticity?"

I politely replied, "What you just saw was a reflection of my authenticity and competence, but I am sorry I cannot prove it otherwise."

Even though all of them agreed with me on this, they still refused to relax on the requirement for papers. One of them nearly pleaded, "There is no doubt of your competence, but without an authentic certificate - who will believe you?"

I prepared myself for my last move. I stood up, took a sweeping look at everybody and said, "How did you believe Swami Vivekandanda, Yogi Aurobindo, Ramakrishna, Dayanand Saraswati, Yogananda and the likes? What kind of certificates did they produce for millions of people to believe in their authenticity?"

Leaving them with a blank look on their faces, I walked out.

My experiences taught me that as far as the profession of a yoga teacher is concerned, a certificate from some kind of institution is more sought-after than the competence of a yogi. This was a shock, yet not the worst of its kind. I later discovered that most of the 'proper' yoga teachers possessed a thirty or sixty-day crash course yoga certificate. Most of the certificates came from ashrams or institutions located in Rishikesh, Varanasi or Kerala. All these thirty day 'yogis' who possessed such certificates appeared to be very proud of them. However when I asked them who certified their institution, none of them could give an answer.

After being turned down a few more times, I was gathering more insight into this profession. One day I was talking to a gentleman who was a regular to a certain yoga class. During our conversation, he told me he stopped going to the yoga studio because he picked up an injury during his asana practice. Medical opinion suggested that the injury was of no ordinary nature and he must take at least six months of bed rest. This injury not only severely affected his business, but also gave him a huge medical bill. The combined effects of both the physical and financial distress created a fury in him, and he was contemplating legal action against the yoga studio.

This was important news to me. I asked him why he thought the yoga instructor was at fault. The exercises the instructor taught were not meant for an injury. What causes an injury is not the instruction, but its incorrect practice. If you do anything incorrectly, you are likely to incur an injury. Besides, I could not see in which way the instructor was at fault. The instructions, as well as the good faith behind his intentions, have to be taken with respect. He was only trying to help.

The gentleman disagreed. His distress was far too much to pay attention to my reasoning. He contemptuously declared, "You don't know these people! These guys are very incompetent, unqualified, and have no idea what they are doing to people's health! I was such a fool to have trusted them. Nothing is going to stop me from bringing a lawsuit against them and closing that bloody place down! It doesn't matter if I don't get damages - it will at least teach them a lesson, and their closure shall save many people from being injured."

In my mind, I thought this must be the reason behind the mandatory requirement of certificates. The business of a yoga teacher is definitely no smooth sailing. The idea of looking for a job in the yoga faculty lost its hold on me. Instead I decided to pursue freelance yoga teaching.

For this purpose I left Delhi and moved to Varanasi. I knew for certain that it would not be easy to earn my livelihood from this profession. Besides, the idea of earning money from Yoga didn't appeal to me. Arriving in Varanasi I picked up a job as a waiter in a small restaurant. This provided me with a livelihood as well as a place to sleep. In the morning and evening, I conducted yoga classes in the corner of a field not far from the *ghats*. Within a few weeks I managed to collect a handful of students from the immediate locality, though I can't say that I was very happy teaching Yoga to this group.

Between the students and myself, I was beginning to notice that a very apparent difference of expectation was growing day by day. The intentions behind my teaching were to genuinely help people modify their present lifestyle and beliefs. The outcomes of my practice were of a lasting nature, and it required sincere and patient practice. I had unlimited patience to explain the complex intricacies of Yoga and its psycho-physical benefits. However, my students held entirely different objectives. Most of them were suffering from some kind of ailment or other, and most of those sufferings came from their lifestyles. None of them was prepared to introduce positive modifications into their lives.

No matter how useful the modifications promised to be, none of them was ready to accept the discomforts of change. It was gradually becoming obvious to me that they were looking for some shortcut or quick-fix remedy to their problems. All my explanations of psychosomatic relations of diseases and their deep roots in their lifestyle fell upon deaf ears. I did not know why all of them harbored a strong belief that Yoga was some kind of short-cut miracle cure to all their problems. The more I explained that Yoga needs patient and persistent practice, the more inadvertently I displayed my incompetence in their eyes. They cited some examples of Swamis and Babas and argued that the asanas of 'so-and-so' Baba or the *pranayamas* of 'so-and-so' Swami had successfully cured people they knew of diabetes, cancer, even AIDS.

I could not cope with the ever-increasing demands of my students for miracle cures. I decided to change place, but wherever I went I was presented with the same problem. It was a hard fact for me to digest that the people of the country that gave birth to the ultimate science of Yoga now looked upon it as a mere quack remedy. It was both disheartening and disgusting. This time I chose not to back away from this challenge. After careful contemplation, I decided to launch a crusade against this belief.

I started to openly criticize the system and worked hard to gather supporters in my 'Save Yoga' campaign. I wrote letters to several ashrams and institutions and objected to the practice of yoga teaching for the purpose of curing diseases. Tirelessly, I visited many institutions and teachers in an attempt to convince them of the true values of Yoga and the urgent need to save it from becoming just another alternative cure. Most people could not comprehend what I was talking about, but all of them argued that nothing equals yoga as far as its potential as a cure of diseases. Often these discussions would lead me to the unpleasant task of explaining the superficial effects of the asana lookalike exercises. I always explained at length the strict and sacred conditions of yoga practice. I brought to their attention the hazards of yogic practices for non-yogic purposes. To the more god-fearing and religious teachers, I even pointed out the 'sin' one incurs from practising for inappropriate and insufficient reasons.

I soon became the most disliked person in the Varanasi circle of yoga teachers as a result of my crusade. It gradually became more and more difficult to find someone who had the correct intention to practise yoga. I remembered what my teacher had told me - the lineage would be very happy if I managed to teach at least one person in my lifetime. I was beginning to realize the gravity and impossibility of this task.

The following July, I visited my ashram for a month. This time, much like my first visit, I was full of queries. I bothered Kripanand about the impossibility of the task given to me. However, I made it clear that I had no intentions of giving up. I asked if I could have support of any kind, from anyone, on my mission. Kripanand listened very patiently. At the end he had only one suggestion. He pointed out that I had entered into a war a bit prematurely. In his opinion, I was absolutely crazy to fight a war of this magnitude single-handedly.

I asserted, "Under no condition am I going to run away from the war I have started, and if my ashram is at all concerned, they should provide some help to support me."

Nirupanand gave me a few names. These people were not to be a part of my war, but if I teamed up with them, they might just prove helpful.

After returning from the ashram I went around to collect my team. They were a group of sadhus who traveled from town to town and held small spiritual events, like *satsangs*, yoga workshops and many such activities. I agreed to be a part of their activities, and they were happy to be associated with a yoga teacher from my ashram. Now the appearance of the events began to change as they no longer remained as small gatherings of people chanting and singing *bhajans*. They turned into massive groups pushing a strong agenda.

Over two years we held fourteen yoga camps in various cities of north India. None of the camps had a participation of less than two hundred people. Rapidly, we were growing in popularity. People began to treat us with utmost respect and reverence. After the completion of each event, I usually withdrew myself from all personal visits. Soon this was to prove impossible.

The most horrifying news came to me when I heard that people started to talk about the efficacy of our programs in terms of curing diseases. Never during the yoga camps did I once mention anything about the disease-curing properties of yoga. Many a time I warned people against the incorrect applications of the yogic *kriyas*. Time and again I explained that asanas are meant to take the practitioners beyond the limits of the physical body, and while doing so one endures impeccable health as a side-effect of this practice. Never do an asana to enrich the body and increase your attachment to it, as you will only do the exact opposite of what it is meant for. Without completing the practice of asanas and before achieving the *siddhis*, any attempt to tamper with the breath is dangerous. It is absolutely absurd and foolish to believe that tampering and interference with the breath has any healthy effects.

During the discourses in the yoga camps, my audience seemed to take notice of my instructions. Most of them practised with religious sincerity. There was nothing surprising to find people getting into better shape of body and better frame of mind. But this current development was unexpected. The more people spoke about the wonderful benefits of our yoga events, the more I became concerned about this incorrect propaganda. I called all the organizing sadhus and expressed my concern. From their response it was obvious they were enjoying the attention they received and were relishing their newfound fame. Most of them disagreed with my views as I described the situation as an impediment to each of our spiritual journeys. They had surely overlooked the dangerous prospects of which I was concerned.

A few events later, the propaganda took yet another disturbing turn. Originally it was the events that were glorified by the people, but now the glory came to be attached to our names. Increasingly, people began to refer to us with uncomfortable prefixes like Swami, Shri Shri, Maharaj and so on. Everyday dozens of people visited me to beg for some help or other. They seemed to possess the strong belief that I was personally responsible for all the amazing effects of their practice and well-being, and that my blessings had the capacity to rid them of all their woes. People would fall at my feet and describe their pathetic conditions and pleaded for blessings. But none of them would ever listen to me. I persistently explained that it was not me, but their sincere efforts, that had helped them. Everything they were now asking for was beyond the blessings of anyone. It is not for a sadhu or a yogi to provide blessings for the purpose of obtaining promotions in one's occupation, in arranging suitable marriage partners, or even for the success in elections or lawsuits.

Most of the people who visited me were highly religious in nature, yet none of them appeared to have any practical respect or faith in the ultimate giver. Instead, everyone was interested in getting away with shortcuts through the help of swamis and babas. In my opinion, the greatest misfortune that can happen to a yogi is his followers. Followers invariably raise the status of a yogi to a level that is difficult to resist. The more people praise and raise him, the more he gets carried away with the glory of his own false image.

A yogi is essentially identified with his detachment, indifference and egoless existence. The moment he acquires followers, he begins to lose the absolute purity of his life. The larger the number of followers, the worse his situation. Unless he takes serious measure to extricate himself from his followers, his entrapment becomes too deep. Fame and glory are very short-lived. At the end of his glorious period, a yogi often finds himself to have drifted away from his objective. An aspiring yogi should never forget that he himself is yet to complete his journey. The reason behind my teaching is not only to help others, but also to help myself. In the process of providing spiritual guidance to seekers, I am also contemplating the achievement of my own destination. Teaching is my way of paying for my journey. Followers have no place in my life.

Some of my friends tried to dissuade me as I expressed my desire to quit. After explaining my situation and without even saying goodbye to any of them, I simply disappeared.

I would place all spiritual seekers into two groups: one group follows the teacher, while the other group follows the teaching. I always placed myself in the latter group. After the experiences of the yoga camps I became a little cautious in dealing with my students. I decided to continue my teaching with students, not followers. The decision curtailed the size of my audience, but I was much happier to teach a smaller amount of people who would take the teachings without following the teacher. These smaller groups of students were mostly westerners. My original notion of western students was they were curious, analytical and prepared to learn, but soon I was proven wrong. As the reality of the western notions of yoga was revealed to me, I had the worst shock of my life. It was more outrageous than any of the shocks I had experienced in my teaching career.

One day I was explaining sutra 28 of the second chapter of the Patanjali Yoga Sutras. Whilst explaining the component parts of Yoga and the meaning of the term '*Ashtanga*', suddenly a student from England sprang to her feet and objected, "What you said can't be right!"

According to her, *ashtanga* was a set of powerful and demanding exercises that provided grace, balance and freedom to the body, adding that she had been practising yoga for over thirty years and that her guru from Mysore was the founder of '*ashtanga yoga*'. I cannot describe the impact such ignorance and gullibility had on me. I gently tried to explain that Yoga was presented in the *Ashtanga* form during the 3rd century BC by Maharshi Patanjali and that Yoga is not a creation of the modern man in the current century. I gave her a copy of the Yoga Sutras along with some information about Maharshi Patanjali and his time. I went on to provide all the information about the history of the Yoga Sutras and the commentaries and observations of all those masters who had explained its profundity. After explaining the narrative of the Yoga Sutras, I proved that *Ashtanga Yoga* was not the handiwork of the modern man. Anyone claiming to have founded *Ashtanga Yoga* today, along with all those that believe in such a claim, is only displaying their utter ignorance.

This lady was far from prepared to drop her false notions. After a dismissive wave of her hand, she said, "That is only your opinion."

She was not the only western practitioner of that category. In my teaching career I have come across many similar pseudo-intellectuals. These people, apart from their claims of scholarly wisdom, possessed a very common and distinct characteristic: whenever confronted with compelling and irrefutable logic, they invariably choose to escape by stating 'It's only your opinion'.

There is a fundamental difference between an opinion and a proven scientific fact. Without the application of the appropriate principles of science, every philosophy is but an opinion, and with the correct scientific validation, a philosophy becomes irrefutable. A response in the lines of 'It's only your opinion' is thus a classic display of a poor and lamentable ignorance of science.

In my next few years of teaching I came across many more shocking and outrageous western notions of yoga. These notions were so varied and so numerous that if all their descriptions were put into one book, it would surely become the biggest and most hilarious joke book in the world!

The more I pondered over this deteriorating process of Yoga and its current condition, the more my mind began to be filled with thoughts of revolution. I wanted to single out every individual and every event that had contributed to the crucifixion of Yoga. Who was responsible? And how did they do it?

Once again I turned to my guru to find the answer to this nagging question. The time that was not spent in deep Meditation was devoted towards a thorough historical investigation of the trail of Yoga over the last two centuries. I began spending more and more time in libraries, research circles and with yoga masters, trying to collect every possible bit of information about Indian and western belief systems. The deeper I delved into the painful realities of the process of distortion of Yoga, the more it appeared that it was a certain set of teachers, and not seekers, who were responsible for its demise.

One day while talking to Kripanand, the conclusion of this quest took shape in my mind.

In ancient times, there lived a monkey in the jungles of India. For the purpose of this story, let us name him Sivananda. Like any other monkey, it was very curious and restless in nature. Sivananda, along with his family, was traveling far and wide in search of food and shelter.

On one occasion, Sivananda's family had appeared on the outskirts of a village whilst the other monkeys of his group went raiding the fruit orchards of the villagers. Sivananda was sitting quietly on a tree and was watching the activities of the humans with interest. Unlike the other monkeys, Sivananda had a great fascination with human behavior. He observed that human beings were not much different than monkeys. In his opinion, apart from a tail, the ugly human being was no different than a monkey. Yet he was scared of human beings. He recalled his past encounters with them and wondered, 'What makes them so special? Why should they behave as if they own all the other animals in the world?'

Not far from where Sivananda was sitting, a temple was being built. A lot of humans were working with strange objects in their hands. Sivananda decided to decipher the meanings behind their curious activities. He watched two lumberjacks sawing a log. Sivananda could not understand why these people were holding small pieces of wood in their hands, pulling and pushing them through the log. The more he watched their actions, the more he became intrigued. Human activities did not seem to be very meaningful. He thought to himself that there was nothing about this activity which he could not do.

As evening approached, the lumberjacks gathered their tools and went home. Before leaving, they hammered a small wooden wedge between a half-sawn log. As soon as they were out of sight, Sivananda went down to the log and began to inspect it. As a monkey, Sivananda had a great ability to imitate human behavior. He climbed upon the log.

Sitting astride it, he took hold of the wedge and began to pull and push in the same manner as the lumberjacks.

All the other monkeys watched him with great interest and admiration to see that at least one of them had the potential to act human. In his joy, Sivananda had not noticed that his tail was hanging through the split in the log. As he continued to push and pull with accompanying applause from his clan, the wedge was loosened and suddenly came out. To their great astonishment, all the other monkeys saw Sivananda emerge without his tail. The shrieks of pain of Sivananda were drowned out by the cheers and applause of his clan. Poor Sivananda had lost his tail!

No one noticed the pain and discomfort of Sivananda, as they were all carried away with his heroic human deed and his sudden resemblance to a human being. Instead of sympathy and treatment, Sivananda received respect, reverence, admiration and the glory of a master.

Sivananda did not suffer long from his tail-end pains. His misery was replaced with the pleasures of being treated like a master. Sivananda began to receive more and more visitors who came begging for a few words of wisdom. Initially, Sivananda was ashamed of pretending to be a master, but gradually he began to believe in his own publicity. He concluded that if so many of his clan had chosen to worship him, surely all of them could not be wrong! Undoubtedly, he had to be an enlightened master, guru or even a messiah for the rest of the world.

For the rest of his life Sivananda took maximum advantage of being a 'guru'. He plotted and schemed to maintain his position – preaching and propagating his monkey wisdom all over the world.*

Mr Sivananda lives on today. He is found everywhere in his numerous manifestations. He is the single embodiment and representative image of the entire genre of yoga and spiritual

---

* This story has been adapted from the Panchatantra, which is a collection of teachings in story form written by Pandit Vishnusharma in the 2nd century BC. In the original story, the monkey had lost his testicles and not his tail.

masters who have contributed to the demise of Yoga. His followers have spread all over the world along with his 'wisdom'. He has never revealed to anyone how he came to lose his tail, at the same time never failing to preach his tail-less wisdom.

In the course of time Mr Sivananda continued to create and modify his schemes to suit the needs of the contemporary spiritual world. Over centuries Mr Sivananda has systematically crucified Yoga. In order to understand and expose the schemes of Mr Sivananda, one needs to be a rebel. Everyone may not find it to be their cup of tea, to raise voice against the age-old norms of spiritual correctness. A few may even find it dangerous to do so. In order to resurrect Yoga, somebody has to step forward and rebel.

Listening to my frame of mind, Kripanand was not amused. Very thoughtfully he advised, "You have the blessings of the lineage if you choose to become that rebel and contribute to the resurrection of Yoga. But make sure you do not end up becoming another Mr Sivananda."

∞∞∞

The last few pages of this chapter will contain the sad and unfortunate process by which the teachings of Yoga have deteriorated. While writing about the degeneration of Yoga from a spiritual science to a fitness regime, I experienced a storm within myself. It was hard and painful to bring myself to narrate something that may sound like the gunshots of a spiritual Taliban. In the world of spiritual correctness and pretense and religious hypocrisy, I do not know how my readers will receive this sudden change of tone.

Here we live in a world that is experiencing a tremendous change in social order, world economic chaos and nuclear madness. Under the weight of these compelling conditions, people are slowly beginning to seek the solace of their spiritual roots. At such a time of need, Yoga, which holds the answers to every spiritual question, is found to be reduced to a system of gymnastic fitness!

Our hunger for spiritual awareness is natural, but our gullibility cannot be excused. Solely for the benefit of all those seekers who have an unquenchable thirst for spiritual awareness and decline to compromise with anything less, allow me to reveal and expose the ploys and tricks of the so-called masters of yoga and spirituality. The only purpose behind an action that stands the chance of being dismissed as outrageous is to enable a true seeker to identify an authentic master and a genuine path.

For clarification, the term 'Mr Sivananda' is used as a metaphor for a pseudo or pretending master of yoga or spirituality.

Mr Sivananda's greatest strength lies in the ignorance of the seeker. He survives only as long as his pretence is not identified. Let us recall the story of the monkey.

The story reveals there is a fundamental difference between the rational actions of man and the imitation of human activity. The activities of the lumberjacks were based upon a definite purpose and a clear understanding of its implications. Plainly speaking, they knew what they were doing. But that was not the case with the monkey. The monkey had no understanding about the implications of what he had observed. The monkey's activity cannot be compared with the actions of man. All that can be said about the monkey's activity is that it was a foolish imitation. Action and its imitation have very different implications. The monkey got into the act of imitation, not because it had applied any sense of rationality, but because it was only a reflection of its monkey-ness.

The meanings and implications of a yogic practice are far too profound to be understood through mere observation. Though certain practices of asana apparently look like gymnastics, they are not. To invoke, experience and achieve the correct outcomes of an asana, it is necessary to study and prepare oneself beforehand. In the story, Mr Sivananda had only lost its tail. But the imitation of yogic asanas without an absolute and clear understanding of the process and its implications has far reaching and disastrous effects.

A yogic asana when practised for the sole purpose of promoting physical well-being has terrible psychological side-effects. The forceful manipulation of the body can temporarily provide physical flexibility, but as long as there is no corresponding psychosomatic fluidity, the body cannot retain its suppleness. Thus the practice of asanas becomes a never-ending grappling with the psycho-physical stiffness. As one continues to subdue the body, he is only constantly engaged in a war against himself at a deeper psychic level.

Without the correct psycho-spiritual participation, the asana only promotes further resistances of the body. Once a practitioner is caught in this vicious cycle, he is left with only one option, a sustained and perpetual war with his body. Such a practice can have flexibility of the body, but never provides a blooming fluidity of the spirit. There is movement but there is no opening.

Physical flexibility from this kind of practice does not show a corresponding development of awareness. From my own experience, most of the modern yoga teachers and practitioners have achieved a certain degree of physical flexibility of the body, but inadvertently have acquired an extremely high psycho-spiritual density. Contrary to their claims, they are in fact the most stressed people you will find in the field of yoga.

Mr Sivananda never knew this delicate difference between a true asana and an imitation asana, but always maintained his secret about how he came to lose his tail. He never allowed anyone to question the so-called implications of an imitation asana. Every seeker treading the path of Yoga needs to understand the correct implications of the practice before they actually get into it. Never allow Mr Sivananda to impose his ignorance upon you. The moment you begin to question, you are likely to be termed 'arrogant and disrespectful'. But I'm sure you don't mind being branded as arrogant or disrespectful, rather than remain ignorant forever.

As expected, our tail-less Mr Sivananda began to encounter questions and faced a strong resistance from a growing number of disciples. As he began to suffer the pressure of true seekers, his exposure became imminent. Perceiving the seekers as potential threats to his own position, he devised techniques to escape his demise. What could be a better solution to improve his weakening position than turning the investigators into teachers!

Mr Sivananda very well knew most modern-day seekers suffer from a certain degree of frustration and identity crisis. He carefully cast a net to catch hold of this particular group of seekers and turned them into teachers. He taught and trained them about the tricks of the game, which had nothing to do with the psycho-physical, let alone spiritual practices of Yoga. The training would last a few weeks or sometimes a month or two. What depth of Yoga can one possibly achieve with such a limited time frame? Hence, the emphasis was not put upon the responsibility of a yoga teacher, but upon the survival of a yoga teacher. Mr Sivananda churned out batch after batch of 'yoga teachers' with nil to laughable understanding of Yoga.

This technique served Mr Sivananda on two critical fronts. On one hand, he diverted the questioning minds of his disciples by making them teachers, and on the other hand, he added numbers to his side to confront his critics. There emerged a generation of green 'yoga teachers' elated with their new found identity. Mr Sivananda's ploy paid off solely because he took advantage of the sense of futility and frustration of the seeker. He only failed when a seeker remained robustly honest in his seeking. A seeker who remains unshakeably honest in his path and refuses to yield to the temptations of a pseudo-spiritual profession definitely comes to realize the fruit of his quest, whereas those who amuse themselves in the midst of an inexperienced teaching career only stall their further progress. Basically a seeker is one who is willing to be a student and remains distant from the temptations of becoming a teacher.

Mr Sivananda not only offered his garb to the frustrated seekers, but also extended his invitation to celebrities. In his logic he thought that if celebrities can make chemical cosmetics and unhealthy drinks glamorous and sellable, then why not use a few to add weight to his own credibility and status.

Celebrities have a certain grip on the minds of a modern consumer. At a time when Yoga has been reduced to a mere commodity, the use of celebrity promotion has become inevitable. Rock stars, musicians, politicians and renowned faces of show business adorned Mr Sivananda's living quarters, which he calls his ashram. People who failed to identify themselves with the monkey could now associate themselves with their desired celebrity. Mr Sivananda wrote books, and his celebrities wrote the forewords. No one wondered how a violinist, who has no relevant background, could write a foreword to shed light on Yoga!

The ultimate challenge to the pseudo-yoga masters came from science. Time and again he confronted a group of skeptics who refused to buy anything that didn't carry scientific validation. The increasing demand for scientific explanations drove his business into rough weather. Mr Sivananda had little to nil understanding about science and its relationship to spirituality. But nothing stopped the master of pretence to devise ways and means to bypass this crisis. As a ploy to add 'scientific' color to his claim, he hired out a few television channels and began a campaign. Mr Sivananda could never provide a single scientific explanation of

Yoga, nor could he show the ingredient of science in his teaching. All he did was a lot of ranting like an orange parrot - 'yog is science, yog is science, yog is science'.

Armed with a band of political heavyweights, he proceeded to trample every objection raised from the scientific quarters. He defied all available laws of medicine, physiology and physics. He persuaded scores of people to vouch for his claim, at the same time making them sign several documents of disclaimers to absolve him from all legal disputes. His celebrity list extended to include top government heads, industrialists, doctors and even a former chairman of an atomic commission. Now none of his critics can touch him with a ten foot pole as far as his claims of 'yog-science' are concerned.

Under the patronage of political god-fathers, Mr Sivananda did away with all the spiritual ingredients of Yoga, claiming that all the notions of yogasanas and *pranayamas* are old, outdated and impractical. He made no bones about dumping the practices of *rechaka*, *kumbhaka* and *puraka* from the system of Yoga by terming them as useless and unhealthy. He declared that health is everybody's birthright, and a few gymnastic exercises coupled with his trademark set of '*pranayamas*' would cure any disease on earth. Let us in brief examine the effects of these so-called *pranayamas*.

Breath, in its common understanding, is an involuntary physical function that supplies oxygen to the body. Every organ of the body needs oxygen for its functions. Breath draws air into the body from the atmosphere, and after using the oxygen, the body releases the rest of the air. The lungs work like the bellows of a blacksmith, to feed the fire of life in the body. Wherever there is a shortage of oxygen in the body, the breathing rhythm automatically undergoes a change called reflex-action and modifies itself to meet the increased requirement of oxygen.

Inside water or in crowded, dusty environments people often gasp for breath. This signifies that there is a higher and urgent need of oxygen. In the modern world people live under highly polluted conditions. Pollutants from air, water and food clog and affect the functions of one's body. Over a slow and gradual process, this develops some form of sickness. It is not to be forgotten that each of such sicknesses has a deep mental connection. People who suffer from such symptoms need an induced gasping (or hyperventilation, as it is called in medical terminology). Small, measured doses of this artificial gasping does help to remove clogging and aids the decarbonization of the blood. It is also possible to treat a small number of superficial diseases with such breathing practices. However, one has to keep in mind that such practices should only be adopted with competent medical advice. Human beings, like every animal, have a specific breathing rhythm unique to their species. Prolonged practice of this hyperventilation stands the risk of serious interference with one's natural rhythm of breathing, which is definitely not a healthy option.

Many *pranayama* 'gurus' have come up with numerous ideas and creations regarding this artificial gasping. All of them claim there is always an instant feeling of relaxation that results from this practice. Recently, a study conducted on the psychological outcomes of hyperventilation suggested that during the practices of these so-called *pranayamas*, the hormone that triggers this feeling of relaxation is the same as that which is activated during sexual intercourse.

The innocent villagers, rustic farmers and the stressed, gullible modern man barely have the resource or inclination to find and understand the scientific truth behind these practices of hyperventilation. This claim of Mr Sivananda is nothing but outrageous. It not only defies all notions of science, but goes a long way in destroying the science of Yoga.

With a growing number of followers, Mr Sivananda tried to elevate his position to match the luminosity of the greatest of scientists and philosophers. He secretly relished being referred to as the new age Einstein of consciousness. Mr Sivananda was a very sick monkey and was unable to relate his sickness to his consciousness. His believers never understood why the condition of his health did not reflect his 'levels' of consciousness. If a healthy body is a reflection of a pure mind, then what kind of mind did he carry around in his sick body? This so-called Einstein apparently had no understanding or experience about the relationship between the physical and ethereal dimensions of the body.

Body is a manifestation of consciousness. Hence, one's physical conditions are always a reflection of one's state of mind. Fifteen years ago the World Health Organization (WHO) expanded its definition of 'health' as that of 'complete physical, mental, emotional and spiritual well-being'. Over the past decade there has been a corresponding change in the medical attitude of the world. Age-old systems of medicine that provided psychosomatic explanations of diseases have come to prominence once again. An increasing amount of specialists and intellectuals are beginning to make use of the deep and profound connections of body and mind.

Now, modern-day intelligence can never comprehend physical health without the support of a healthy mind. Every attitude has a neuro-chemical manifestation in the body. When a negative attitude is harbored for a long time, the cumulative effect of this neuro-chemical shift manifests itself as a sickness in the body. The roots of all of our diseases can in fact be traced into the depths of our mind, which holds the answers to our apparent suffering. This also goes a long way to prove why the human body suffers from a much wider range of disease than our animal counterparts. Every intelligent healer and scientist of the modern world is aware of this simple truth.

The only one who is ignorant of the psycho-physical correlation is our beloved monkey, Sivananda. Mr Sivananda teaches people techniques to get rid of all their diseases without the slightest change in their attitudes. People usually earn their diseases over a long period of unhealthy lifestyle and inappropriate behavior. Every person would like to have a remedy for their problems, but not many can actually change their lifestyles and attitudes. This is where Mr Sivananda comes in. He deceptively created a scheme to enslave the innocent and the gullible. He could never explain as he never knew the psychosomatic relationship of health, but went on to claim he could cure people's diseases without a corresponding change in their lifestyle.

Thousands of people flocked to his classes. The promise was too difficult to resist. Who doesn't want to have an easy and quick-fix means to health? There cannot be a more convenient idea of health which does not require any change in the corruption, exploitation, abuse, violence, greed, accumulation, treachery and similar activities one commits in everyday life. Millions of people have become addicted to this 'yoga', but no one is ready to accept that this claim can never be true. In the meantime, Mr Sivananda continues to hammer in nail after nail to crucify Yoga.

Let us now look at the fallacies of Mr Sivananda with a simple analogy. How does one put an elephant inside a cupboard? You must be thinking what a silly question: no elephant can fit inside a cupboard! Let me answer – if it is possible to fit Yoga into a modern lifestyle, then why is it not possible to fit an elephant inside a cupboard? In both these cases, it is only a matter of space. If you think carefully, we can actually fit an elephant into a cupboard. To accomplish this, one needs to modify the cupboard, not the elephant, since the elephant cannot be modified. Similarly, in order to fit Yoga into our lives, it is our lives that need modification, not Yoga. An elephant in its original form is quite big. So is Yoga. As it does not make any sense to cut an elephant into pieces and place one of the pieces into a cupboard, similarly it makes no sense to place a small part of Yoga or a yoga-lookalike activity into our life.

One of the most destructive contributions of Mr Sivananda is 'Yoganomics' - that is the economics of yoga. The unfortunate blending of ignorance and greed can be demonstrated in the following story.

A priest went to a mental asylum. With good intentions, he visited the inmates individually, blessing and praying for them and their fast recovery. He talked with them, played with them and extended his sympathy and support to them. As he was moving from person to person he came across a young man sitting in a chair facing the backrest. Taking hold of the backrest, the man was pretending to be driving a car. He was even making the sounds of a car. As the priest approached him, the man 'honked' a few times and ultimately came to a screeching halt. In a perfectly normal voice, the man told the priest, "Now you can cross the road, father. It's not always a good idea to come in front of a fast moving Ferrari. My dad gave it to me a few days ago, and I really enjoy driving it around the town. Do you know how many people envy me because of my Ferrari?"

The priest instantly understood the situation. Very kindly he sat down next to him and began to explain,

"My son, you are sitting on a chair and that too, facing the wrong way. I can understand your desire and aspiration that may have got you into this asylum, but what you need to know is the reality. This chair is not a Ferrari, and you are not driving it around the town."

The young man was amused by the priest. He argued, "If you want me to believe that this is not a Ferrari, I want you to believe that you are not a priest."

The priest began to explain to the young man from several angles and tried to prove that the chair was not a Ferrari. As the debate was continuing, the attendant of the young man suddenly came running to them and took the priest aside.

"What are you doing father?" she asked.

The priest replied that he was only trying to explain the reality to the young man.

The attendant requested, "Please do not do that father. None of us knows what the reality is. The chair is his Ferrari, and that is his reality. I am paid a few rupees everyday to wash his car, and that's how I make a living. This is my reality. He is happy to drive his car, and as long as he thinks his chair is a car, I will earn my livelihood. Why are you trying to puncture his reality as well as mine?"

There are millions of people around the world who spend considerable amounts of time, resources and sincere effort in practising what they believe to be yoga. This attracts and invites an equal number of manifestations of Mr Sivananda.

Mr Sivananda knows there is money to be made, and as long as people continue to believe in his yoga, he will be able sell them anything and everything in the name of yoga. He has created an enormous industry of yoga products and accessories. Mr Sivananda didn't bother to know that the practice of yoga does not require any fashionable accessories like straps, shoes, chains, blocks, bars or Om painted bikinis, and that the desire for them is more a hindrance than a support for the practice of yoga. To keep his yoganomics going, Mr Sivananda gave it a fashionable and glamorous twist.

Originally not many people were interested in the quiet, renounced and simple life of a yoga practitioner, but its marriage to show business quickly yielded attention. Following the path of spirituality is not everyone's cup of tea. It takes several lifetimes of spiritual evolution to experience even the first pang of hunger for it. The path of spiritual development is far from glamorous. It is very easy to comprehend the sense of frustration experienced by seekers who are not yet ready to give up their attachment to glamour and a comfortable life. But this frustration should not be remedied by the glamorization of yoga. If the path of Yoga was strewn with rose petals, everyone would have walked it. But ultimately, the blessed ones who tread upon it are the ones who see no difference between flowers and thorns.

Within a decade of fashion and glamour, the yoga industry reached sky-high, and under its weight, the humble and simple tradition of Yoga got buried.

Mr Sivananda did not stop there. As he continued to twist and turn and distort Yoga to meet each of his crooked intentions, he came to face a new problem. Time and again this pretending monkey encountered real human beings. He was getting away with his human-like pretence with the monkeys, but in the presence of real humans, he found it difficult to hide his true identity. He knew for certain real human beings would never accept him as one of them, and at the same time he had to prove to his fellow monkeys that he was a master. The only answer he could devise is - 'This yoga is of a different style'.

Let me tell you a story from my college days which will, to some extent, help readers understand the birth of different styles of yoga.

In my college hostel there used to live a unique cook who prepared food for the hostel inhabitants. He was not a good cook by any means, and when complained against, he would always give some excuse or other and promise to correct his mistake the next time. Undoubtedly, he knew very little about cooking, but he always got away with it through his beautiful explanations.

His one unique explanation warrants a special mention. Whenever he was confronted about the poor quality of the food, he would answer that he had cooked the dish in a different style. He even gave names to his mistakes. Sometimes he would call his inedible dishes 'French' or 'American'. Every time he damaged a dish he would give it a new name. And so he went on to create dozens of different styles of dahl, hundreds of different styles of curries, and an even greater number of pulaos and chapattis. None of his food was acceptable, and for years we craved the simple and most basic rice, dahl and vegetables, which we never received.

We were becoming increasingly frustrated with this cook. One particular day, after a long succession of lectures, hungry and tired, a few of us hurried to the hostel mess hall. Most of us were in a bad state of mind. The moment we saw the horrid food, one of my friends rose with fury. He called the cook and exclaimed, "What the hell do you think you have cooked?!"

With his nice smile and quintessential explanation, he replied, "This cooking is of a different style!"

Like the cook, Mr Sivananda never admitted the fact that he knew nothing about Yoga. Every time he was confronted, he got away with the same quintessential explanation, 'This yoga is of a different style'. In this process Mr Sivananda incidentally or intentionally ended up creating dozens of different styles of yoga. He not only created different styles of yoga, but even had the audacity to copyright them!

Creating a style of yoga is like re-inventing the wheel. Since the day of its invention, a wheel has been round. The round shape of the wheel has served the purpose of the inventor and everybody else that used it subsequently. It worked for them, it worked for me, and it will also work for anyone who is willing to use it. In order to be a wheel, it has to be round. There are no two ways about it. Yoga in its traditional and original form is more than complete and perfect. Its exact principles and correct applications have worked for thousands of practitioners. Sages and yogis of different lineages have followed the definite equations of this science and have time and again proven the truth behind the sutras. Any change and modification of the true principles of Yoga can only render it useless and ineffective, in very much the same way as any change in the shape of a wheel defeats its purpose.

Mr Sivananda took pride in his long years of teaching. His followers began to revere him as a living master with the ultimate experience. After all, he himself practised 'yogasanas' for no less than sixty-five years. While taking great pleasure and enormous pride in his sixty-five years of asana practice, he never failed to emphasize its depth.

Yogasanas are not like any other exercise. The effects and outcomes of the asanas are permanent and irreversible in nature. If the scriptures of Yoga have clearly described the permanent effects of asanas and take it only as an intermediary stage, then why did Mr Sivananda do asanas for such a long time?

Let us say one of my friends remained in elementary school for twenty years. Would you take him as the dumbest person on earth, or regard him as a master of elementary school lessons? When you see Mr Sivananda doing asanas for sixty-five years, would you still think he could be a master of asanas, let alone Yoga? If his practices were correct in any way, shape or form, he would not have been doing the asanas for sixty-five years. Very much like my elementary school friend, he surely cannot be regarded as a master of his discipline.

Mr Sivananda made fifty million people spiritually hungry without actually offering any substance to satisfy their cravings. Alluring his readers into the mystical and fantastical realms of his autobiography, he kept the seeker at arm's length by presenting an untouchable account of the life of a yogi. Mr Sivananda, on many occasions, described the state of ignorance or 'un-enlightenment' and on innumerable occasions, gives his description of the state of enlightenment. However, he always failed to describe the practice or path that lies between these two states, leaving the even hungrier and even more desperate seeker at the mercy of the next Mr Sivananda.

It is for every spiritual seeker to be prepared to face the most arduous of journeys. It is not even the devil's job to reduce Yoga to a lazy man's pastime. Mr Sivananda, in one of his latest tricks to allure even more people, did just that. He explained the practices of yoga and spirituality as a set of 'do-nothing' notions. Let us examine and expose this latest scheme of Mr Sivananda.

In this context, as usual, I will illustrate this tragedy with an example. I believe in the use of a lot of illustrations because they tend to give a lighter tone to an otherwise painful reality. Secondly, of course, this was how I was taught myself.

Let us compare the spiritual journey of an individual with a marathon race. Whether we like it or not, we have to go through the entire length of the marathon in order to reach the other end. Some people find it difficult and often fantasize about having a much shorter and easier marathon. If anybody would show them a shorter or easier marathon, they are bound to change tracks. This is precisely what Mr Sivananda did. Time and again Mr Sivananda claimed that the race for spiritual realization is very much shorter than our notions of it. Once in a while he would drop into the race and misguide everybody by giving false and incorrect descriptions about the finishing line. He would then disappear, with a good number of runners following him.

Over the past two centuries, Mr Sivananda has appeared on innumerable occasions in front of the runners and has diverted them from their objectives. As Mr Sivananda's activities continued unabated, his courage escalated, and ultimately he dared to appear right next to the starting line of the marathon. Taking a good look at the long line of runners, he declared, 'What are you running for? The ultimate purpose of the marathon is accomplished the moment you step onto the track. You don't have to run anywhere because the ultimate truth is - the starting line of the marathon is in itself the finishing line!'

The first time I came to hear of this claim by Mr Sivananda, I was amazed by its apparent profundity. I did my best to decipher and understand the scientific principle behind it. At the same time, I peeped into the background of his personal practice. Both the investigations gave me two entirely different findings. His background did not reveal any practice, spiritual or otherwise, to which his claim of 'I AM THAT' can be attributed. Secondly, I found that his idea of 'being' did not carry any experiential validity.

In science I have studied that if a line is extended in one direction infinitely, it will almost certainly arrive at its beginning point; this phenomenon explains the hypothesis regarding the shape and nature of the universe. Even though the starting line and the finishing line exist on the same plane, the entire universe lies between the two. The journey suggested by any genuine spiritual path is usually a complete process or realization of the entire full circle, and everything that lies in between. A statement that claims the starting line to be the finishing line without explaining the universe in between is indeed, empty and absurd. Mr Sivananda clearly has no idea of the Universe or its realities, but that does not stop him from chanting, 'I am that, You are that, Everyone is that!' This mantra of self-help affirmation is the worst-ever tragedy to befall the seekers of truth. Not only does it bring the seeker to a dead-end, it also gives an escape route to the perpetrator of the merry-go-round.

The series of events that ultimately led the seeker to this dead-end can be illustrated with the help of the following story.

A politician visited his constituency. Like every other politician, he was also pretending to be concerned about the needs of his voters whilst, in reality, he was searching for avenues to launder some money. He indicated to the people that it was so unfortunate for them to live in such a large village which did not even have a small lake. A lake would not only give the villagers clean water and swimming facilities, but would also give a lot more benefits ranging from irrigation to entertainment. The villagers happily accepted the prospect of a lake within their village.

The politician collected the 'demands' of the people in paper and submitted it to the government.

After the usual amount of bargaining, he managed to obtain a grant of one hundred million rupees to carry out the work of the lake. A few years passed. In the meantime, hundreds of people, including bureaucratic personnel, excavators, engineers and laborers working together created an excellent and beautiful lake on paper. The entire grant was successfully spent to fill the pockets of all these people in appropriate proportions. Five years passed, and the term of this politician came to an end.

The next politician elected from the constituency came to visit this village after hearing about its beautiful lake. As he could not find any lake, he began to enquire about what had happened to it. From the villagers he learnt the entire story of the lake and how it was never built. Being determined to unearth the mystery of the lake, he went on to investigate all the people who had received payments for the work. His findings were both interesting and encouraging.

It didn't take much time for this genius to place his own scheme on top of the invisible lake. He went to the government with the demand that the villagers desperately needed to introduce fish in this lake to maintain its cleanliness and biosphere balance. He argued that without the timely implementation of this scheme, the lake water stood the chance of becoming polluted and unhealthy. He too managed to obtain a grant, and the entire amount was spent in the previous manner. As a result, invisible fish were introduced into an invisible lake. The story doesn't end there.

Term after term, many more politicians came and reaped the benefits of the invisible lake and its invisible developments. As the reputation of the lake was spreading far and wide, the government became worried as the truth of the lake slowly began to leak out. The latest politician of this area came out with the ultimate plan that not only saved the skin of his predecessors, but could also make him the richest of all.

He drafted an urgent demand and went to the government. He lamented that the lake made in the village many years ago had become polluted, and it had become a danger for the people in the locality. He cited that many people and livestock of the area had died because of its polluted waters. The most urgent and necessary step the government needed to take was to fill it up!

Pursuing the government at a war-footing, this genius of a minister obtained the biggest-ever grant of the budget. Needless to say, he simply pocketed the entire grant, collected all the available papers and documents about the lake and set fire to them. The potential threat to the health of the villagers was successfully averted, and everyone was given a reason to celebrate and rejoice!

Since the day yoga was displayed in the spiritual supermarkets across the world, Mr Sivananda in his numerous manifestations has reaped every possible benefit from it. He has morally, psychologically and financially exploited every single spiritual seeker, and this exploitation has continued for centuries. But no one can be fooled forever. In the course of time, as people came to think about the logic and reasoning behind his theories, they became increasingly skeptical. Mr Sivananda was not consistent; at different stages, at different places, he had stated his theory in different ways. As a result, people began to question the truth behind his teaching. It became increasingly difficult for him to maintain his original lie, as he had to tell many more lies to cover the first. As the twentieth century drew to a close, Mr Sivananda perceived his imminent exposure. After having dipped his fingers into the resources of innocent seekers for nearly two centuries, very much like the corrupt politicians, he then slashed the ultimate quest of mankind by declaring, 'You are that!'

The list of Mr Sivananda's ploys and tricks are endless. It won't be possible to provide a complete list and description of all his schemes within the scope of this book. I have only attempted to bring forth a few of his most deceptive and dangerous schemes with the humble intention of helping a seeker. Every genuine seeker who follows a spiritual path deserves to know the myths and untruths that have been tossed around for centuries. Many extremely incorrect notions have been given the status of tradition, and the so-called masters of these traditions have meticulously kept the seekers away from the reality.

Mr Sivananda is the embodiment of spiritual corruption and the representative image of all those people who consciously committed the worst-ever crime against mankind. I, myself, suffered as a victim of this crime and witnessed innumerable instances of Mr Sivananda's criminal activities. I attended to his injured victims and shared their heart-rending accounts. I followed Mr Sivananda constantly, and I have taken first hand notice of his transgressions.

I hold Mr Sivananda guilty on two accounts: one, he is guilty of crucifying and burying the ancient, pure and scientific tradition of Yoga; two, he has taken undue advantage of the innocent and genuine quest of a seeker. As seekers, all of us have been the victim of one Sivananda or another. I refuse to support or ignore Mr Sivananda's presence in the life of any genuine seeker. The uncompromising and unquenchable thirst for knowledge and truth should not be dismissed as insignificant, irrelevant or mere discontentment. Here in this book, I have attempted to present an honest and genuine account of my findings. It is for every seeker to re-evaluate the role of Mr Sivananda in their own life – for each and every seeker has a right to know the truth and not a lie.

BOOKS

O books

O is a symbol of the world, of oneness and unity. In different cultures it also means the "eye", symbolizing knowledge and insight, and in Old English it means "place of love or home". O books explores the many paths of understanding which different traditions have developed down the ages, particularly those today that express respect for the planet and all of life.

For more information on the full list of over 300 titles please visit our website
www.O-books.net

SOME RECENT O BOOKS

The House of Wisdom
Yoga of the East and West
Swami Dharmananda Saraswati and Santoshan
Swamiji has shared her wisdom with her students for many years. Now her profound and enlightening writings, and those of Santoshan, are made available to a wider audience in this excellent book. The House of Wisdom is a real treasure-house of spiritual knowledge. **Priya Shakti** (Julie Friedeberger), author of *The Healing Power of Yoga*
1846940249 224pp **£11.99 $22.95**

The 9 Dimensions of the Soul
Essence and the Enneagram
David Hey
David Hey has taken the psychological elements of the Enneagram & added them to the study of Essence, which are the qualities of being. It makes for an in-depth and enlightening analysis. He even delves into how countries and hierarchies function under the rules of the Enneagram. For those wanting to learn more about themselves from the core levels to the displayed traits, this is the book for you! **Rev Dr Sandra Gaskin**, www. spirit-works.net
1846940028 160pp **£10.99 $19.95**

How to Meet Yourself
...and find true happiness
Dennis Waite
An insightful overview of the great questions of life itself: a compelling inner tapestry that encourages the reader to willingly embrace life being exactly as it is. Readable, relevant and recommended. **Chuck Hillig,** author of *Enlightenment for Beginners*
1846940419 360pp **£11.99 $24.95**